The Times Reports
The American Civil War

The Times Reports

The American Civil War

Extracts from *The Times* 1860–1865

Hugh Brogan

**Introduced and edited by
Hugh Brogan**

Preface by Colin Bell
Series Editor

TIMES BOOKS

First published in Great Britain in 1975 by Times Books, the book publishing division of Times Newspapers Limited, New Printing House Square, London WC1X 8EZ

ISBN   0 7230 0127 8 (cased)
ISBN   0 7230 0130 8 (paper)

Designed by John Lucioni

Map drawn by K.C. Jordan FRGS

Copies of original material from The Times *contained in this book were supplied by Newspaper Archive Development Limited, Reading*

Printed in Great Britain by Tinling (1973) Ltd. Prescot, Merseyside (a member of the Oxley Printing Group Ltd.)

*Dedicated to
the Washington Brogans*

CONTENTS

PREFACE

The Times is perhaps the best-known newspaper in the world, and only 'perhaps' because one must allow for those great nations which no longer permit their citizens to know of any newspapers but their own. It is not the oldest — not yet quite 200 years old — nor the thickest, the richest or, at least beyond all argument, the best; but it is, and has been for the greater part of its history, among the best, and among the most influential. Foreign governments have frequently suspected that it spoke for the British government; British governments, that it spoke for the most important section of the British people. It is an institution, to be ranked in the social history of Britain alongside the Civil Service, the Church and the Monarchy, rather than among the rest of the Press.

This unique standing gives a special status to its files. They contain, of course, the news stories of the past, and those stories were rarely covered more extensively in any other paper, although on occasion more perceptively. But the full significance of *The Times*'s coverage of any great event is not that it is a newspaper of record, supplying the historian and the student with contemporary raw material; it is that *The Times* is itself an important actor in the drama.

Sometimes this importance lay, as we have seen, in the tendency of foreigners to take *The Times*'s views as official, and there have certainly been periods when Westminster and Whitehall helped shape what was said in Printing House Square. Whether this was the result of straight corruption, as with Pitt's subsidy to the paper in the 1790s, or natural identity of view, as with the close consultations Dawson had with Baldwin or Halifax in the 1930s, it must be said that there have been times when those foreigners have been right. Sometimes, too, the view of *The Times* has reflected what the British Government might want to do, or want to be thought to want. There is no better place for any politician to float a 'trial balloon', and however scrupulously a newspaper resists such attempts, it cannot always tell in time that this is what is happening. So to look at history through *The Times* is on occasion to see what other countries believed, or were led to believe, was Britain's policy.

This very authority, this dominating position among the

Press, has meant that British governments have been just as sensitive themselves to what *The Times* has said, since others might think that some particular stand represented Whitehall's orders to *The Times*. Whitehall has always been aware that it might as easily represent middle-class England's orders to Whitehall. The paper rapidly established, in the era of Barnes and of Delane, a solid command of circulation among the civil servants, academics, leading industrialists and financiers, among the Justices of the Peace and Lords Lieutenant, country parsons and army officers, among that class which constituted for so long 'political England'. It was the newspaper in which they told each other of their births, marriages and deaths, in which they advertised their needs and wants — frequently bizarre — and in which they addressed themselves to their peers on any subject which seemed to them important. They drew their information about the world from *The Times*; and when they had any views about the world, they sent a letter to the Editor. Politicians know all about 'constituency opinion', and they know therefore that a newspaper too has got its own constituency; in the case of *The Times*, a very powerful one, whose opinions matter. So to look at history through *The Times* can also be to see what political England believed, or what the British government thought that they believed.

Not all leaders in *The Times* echoed Whitehall, or the readers' known or suspected views; most probably the majority of those which evoked that special tone which has led to the paper's nickname of 'The Thunderer', sprang from the Editor and his little group of leader-writers, informed and advised by the paper's specialist reporters and correspondents. Arguably because it has so often spoken for other powers in the State, *The Times* has long been a power in its own right, a leader of opinion as well as the channel for opinions. What is printed about a dynamic situation becomes itself part of that situation; if *The Times* takes a line hitherto ignored, then it can be ignored no longer. Rejected, opposed, amended, but not ignored, so that it is frequently impossible to look at history without *The Times*.

All these points made with particular reference to the leaders and the letters, can equally be applied to the news reports. A report in *The Times* may, and very often does, tell posterity what actually happened; but even when posterity has discovered that *The Times* got it wrong, it remains true that what was reported was what was necessarily believed at the time to be the case. Believed not only by the English educated public, but by Government, whose own sources of information were by no means always as good as, let alone better than, those of the paper, and believed by much of the rest of the world. Once more, if what the paper said was not in fact right, but was the information on which a decision was taken, a political stance adopted, it is of historical significance. It may not clinch many arguments to say 'but I read it in the papers', but in the absence of compelling proof, to cite *The Times* carries special weight.

That weight derives, quite properly, from the reputation of the paper's staff, and from the unimpeachable accuracy of much of what it carries. In this series matter easily obtainable elsewhere, such as Parliamentary Debates, Law Reports, texts of Treaties, major speeches, White Papers and Royal Commission Reports, has had to be excluded, but the fact that *The Times* carries such material, recognises the responsibilities of a newspaper of record, necessarily reflects not only on the reader's acceptance of what else he reads, but on the reporter's and sub-editor's approach to every other story. *Times* men may be misled, misinformed, may make mistakes of judgement, but with rare exceptions they can be assumed to be reporting rather than propagandising or entertaining. Their copy may prove of propaganda use, and may indeed be. entertaining, but the first consideration, *The Times* angle, is usually to relay what happened.

This series has been conceived, then, with two aims in mind: the first is to give the general reader a view of great historical events as they were seen at the time by a great newspaper, a view which is often just as accurate as, and far more vigorous and enthralling than, that offered by a modern textbook. The second aim is to give the more serious student, and the specialist, a time-saving tool, which, although it cannot free him entirely from the labour of ploughing through bound volumes or microfilm in search of his subject, makes *The Times* as accessible as it is indispensable.

On every subject there has had to be extensive editing. Important topics have usually been recognised as such at the time, and *The Times* covers important topics thoroughly. Every editor in this series makes his first priority the telling of the story — using the news reports to make clear the development of events. Thereafter, he chooses leaders which show what the state opinion was, or which are now known to have carried great influence, letters which illustrate public reaction, or which had repercussions of significance, news stories, right or wrong, which demonstrate what was then thought to be happening, and 'unmissables': the unmissables are those items which are too good to miss — the report of a minor battle by Russell, a letter from Keynes with the first glimmerings of Keynesianism, a speech by the young Churchill which takes the modern reader by surprise, a leader which proclaims the imminent victory of the Confederacy.

The editors themselves are drawn from scholarship and from journalism, not separately and distinctly, but from those with experience of both, since this series is about history, but history as seen by, and influenced by, a newspaper. It is of some importance whether a particular story is carried across the main news page, or relegated to the bottom of a column on some remote page near the classified advertisements, and of importance, too, to know what the effect of deadlines can be on the accuracy of a story.

The notes which the editors have contributed are designed to make such points, as well as to supply such information as non-specialists may need, and which the original readers knew already, and to put each excerpt in its context. Unless specifically marked, they have made no cuts *within* any excerpt, nor any alterations, save to typographical errors and, occasionally, punctuation.

COLIN BELL

INTRODUCTION

I

When the Special Correspondent of *The Times*, William Howard Russell, reached Washington in late March, 1861, he was warmly welcomed in official circles. The Secretary of State, W. H. Seward, took him to call on the President who, Russell tells us, was most affable —

[he] put out his hand in a very friendly manner, and said, 'Mr Russell, I am very glad to make your acquaintance, and to see you in this country. The London *Times* is one of the greatest powers in the world, — in fact, I don't know anything which has more power, — except perhaps the Mississippi. I am glad to know you as its minister.' . . .

Lincoln's flattering hyperbole will have struck no-one who heard it as ridiculous — certainly not Dr. Russell. His paper, 'The Thunderer', was then at the height of its earned fame. It had made it its business to be the voice of English public opinion, and was recognized as such at home as well as abroad. Governments courted its favour even when they deplored its influence. There were scoffers, but they could have no effect in face of *The Times*'s various triumphs, based as they were on the tradition established by the Walter family and two great editors, Thomas Barnes and John Thadeus Delane; a tradition of full, solid and accurate reporting, a tradition embodying the great Victorian virtue of 'character'. *The Times*, Barnes had taught the world to believe, was independent, honest, thorough, intelligent; uniquely well-informed; read by everyone in England who mattered. Delane devoted himself heroically to strengthening the paper's reputation; and it was in the first fifteen years or so of his editorship that it rose to the summit of its glory.

Of that glory Russell's reporting was the chief symbol. First and greatest of Special Correspondents, he had enjoyed the unflinching support of his chief when he began to send back his scarifying reports from the Crimean War. In an age which had not yet conceded — scarcely conceived of — the right of journalists to accompany an army and report its operations at first-hand,[1] *The Times*'s representative set out to expose the atrocious mismanagement of the British Army which led to the horrors of Scutari and the winter trenches before Sebastopol. English opinion rushed to support the journalist's crusade. Florence Nightingale and the troops she tended were the chief beneficiaries, but Lord Palmerston profited too. The storm of indignation carried him to the Premiership, where he soon made a pact with *The Times*, which thus had its reward. Still, it had taken courage to launch the attack on Lord Raglan and the Aberdeen Government, and this was still more true of Russell's next assignment, the Indian Mutiny and its aftermath. The Special Correspondent told his tale as well as ever, but he also exposed the horrors of British vengeance at a time when opinion was rabidly hostile to the mutineers. Nevertheless, *The Times* once again triumphed, and the British stopped firing sepoys from the mouths of cannon.

So when the Southern states seceded, and a civil war in America seemed likely, it was not only in *The Times*'s interest, but almost its public duty, to send Russell to this new arena. He was the man for the hour; his paper would speak the verdict of the world. The assumption was reasonable and universal; no wonder Lincoln was polite.

And then it all went wrong. Within a few months *The Times* was despised and detested by Americans north and south. A year after his landing, Russell was driven from the country. Within England itself a murmur of criticism arose, which by the end of the war was, if not a shout, at any rate a loud and unrelenting chorus. The paper itself, twisting and turning with the fortunes of war, eventually admitted its fault by changing its thunders to whimpers; and the epitaph on this chapter in its history was written by the young Leslie Stephen in a searing pamphlet which no-one could ever contradict, a pamphlet whose indictment was substantially accepted by the official history of *The Times*, seventy years later.[2] *The Times* made a fool of itself over the American Civil War; it toppled from its pinnacle; it became, in

---

[1] The right was not entirely conceded during the American Civil War, either. Sherman, for example, refused to have reporters with him during his epic march from Chattanooga to the sea.

[2] '*The Times*' on the American War: a Historical Study, by L.S., London, 1865.

xiv

certain quarters, a standing joke. The nemesis of *hubris* involved, in this case, an alienation from much that was most vital in English life.

Russell partly caused, but was not at all to blame for this collapse. His voluminous chronicle, as it appeared every few days in *The Times*, wholly justified his reputation, and still constitutes a first-rate historical source. He succeeded in conveying American actuality and his views thereon, while leaving his readers free to make up their own minds about the matter. He was intelligent, diligent, truthful. In the first disastrous year of the war this last trait was enough in itself to annoy the North, and had it alone led to his expulsion *The Times* could justly have assumed an air of injured innocence and censured the absurd touchiness of the Yankees. Unhappily Russell's dispatches were unendurable mostly because they appeared in *The Times*. The Special Correspondent was fair-minded and, on the whole, pro-Northern. His paper was neither.

(Here I risk merely echoing Leslie Stephen, who wrote so well on the subject that any successor must feel himself to be a mere plodding plagiarist; it was Stephen who defined a settled conviction of *The Times* as 'an opinion which it does not contradict oftener than three or four times'.[1] The only way to avoid odious comparisons and the repetition of a job superbly done is to avoid, as much as possible, the repetition of Stephen's arguments and quotations. But some duplication is inevitable.)

The Times long shut its eyes to the power and determination of the secessionists, swinging round suddenly soon after Lincoln's inauguration to the view that the North must accept secession as a *fait accompli*, since the South could not and should not be coerced. Thereafter it pontificated endlessly on the imbecility, the wickedness, the fated failure of the United States' attempt to reassert its authority. It stressed the vulgarity, aggressiveness, coarseness of Americans, whether as private citizens or as diplomatists. It repeatedly denounced Seward as a reckless, warmongering demagogue, yet itself led the anti-American pack during the *Trent* affair. Nor did time mend its manners. Misled by the news management, bragging and downright lying that characterized much of the American press during the war, it grew ever more cynical, dismissing all Nor-

[1] Op. cit., page 38.

thern utterances as 'Buncombe'. 'We don't believe one single word that appears in the American journals,' said Mowbray Morris, the paper's manager, who had revealed on an earlier occasion that 'the Northern Government & its policy are an abomination to me & I greatly enjoy to hear them abused.'[1] Above all, it published far too much of this hostile material.[2] Five or six editorials a week, all breathing the same message of contemptuous prejudice, could not be overlooked. It is not to be wondered at that *The Times* became bitterly unpopular in the North. Printing House Square undermined its correspondent. At last Edwin Stanton, the Secretary of War, seized an opportunity, and forbade Russell to go with McClellan's army to the Peninsula. The Secretary thus hoped to silence not so much the journalist as his employer.

It was a bad miscalculation. Russell had hurt many feelings by his candidly fair description of the rout at Bull Run, but not more than had been touched by the first American reports. His successors were neither so capable nor so useful to the Northern cause. The established New York correspondent, an American named Bancroft Davis, had just resigned, largely on grounds of ill-health, but at least in part because of Delane's American views. He was replaced by Charles Mackay, a Scot who shared them. Mackay's chief function was to report from the most important trading city in America, forwarding political and commercial telegrams and sending what other reports he deemed appropriate; he scarcely ever left New York, and when he did it was to confer with Copperheads or with downright rebels, whose cause he championed; worst of all, he never got near a battlefield. During the greater part of the war, then, *The Times* had no regular correspondent with the Northern armies and the Northern government, just as, for the first eighteen months, it had no-one at the South. This last defect was remedied in the autumn of 1862, when the paper sent Francis Lawley to Richmond. He had a far more generous outlook than Mackay, and an eagerness

[1] *History of The Times*, vol. ii (London, 1939), page 384, Mowbray Morris to Antonio Gallenga, 30 July 1863; ibid., page 366, Morris to Charles Mackay, 4 September 1862

[2] *The Times* tended to print too much comment on everything. For instance, it cannot have been necessary to print leading articles on two successive days (5 and 7 April 1862) congratulating the English Government on accepting the lessons to be derived from the battles of the *Merrimac* in Hampton Roads.

to observe, analyse and report military affairs: he was forever moving towards the sound of the loudest guns. Unhappily he became passionately pro-Southern, and there was no pro-Northern voice in the paper regularly balancing his views.

To all this we need only add the continuing bad judgement in London (according to *The Times*, for example, the Emancipation Proclamation was nothing but an incitement to the horrors of bloody servile war) to understand the loathing which *The Times* excited in the souls of many of its former admirers. The only countervailing force was Delane's alliance with Palmerston. The Prime Minister valued the association, but he had no intention of letting it drag him into unwelcome paths. He made sure that the paper held aloof, at least in its editorials, from the clamour to recognize the Confederacy and go to war on its behalf. *The Times* was content to praise Southern valour and stick to the principle of neutrality, thus perhaps deserving slightly more credit for consistency than Leslie Stephen was to grant it.

Still, it *was* inconsistent, perhaps rather in tone than in substance. Delane had a few well-worn principles (or slogans, rather) that seldom varied: the vulgarity of Americans, the inevitability of Southern independence, the desirability of peace. But he never wrote anything in the paper himself if he could help it, and in spite of his clear and firm directions its attitude varied greatly according to who was writing on what topic. Thus there would often appear, alongside a patronizing, if circumspect, diplomatic leading article, or one of the familiar ranting denunciations of American folly, a discussion of the technical side of the war which was businesslike, unimpassioned, soberly pro-Northern. And eventually the paper's general line, after minor wobblings in the springs of 1862 and 1864, again changed decisively. For a long time space had always been found for the gloomiest construction of American news and for any or all apologies for the South. But during the last eight months of the struggle this tendency was replaced by a cautious waiting on which way the successful Northern cat would jump. Not that this did away with the distrust and dislike which *The Times* had incurred, in the North and among the pro-Northern men of England. To malignancy it seemed to have added the vice of meanness, that was all.

It was a fearful *débâcle*. Leslie Stephen explained it by the ignorance and amateurishness of the Printing House Square writers. He gets some support from G. C. Brodrick, one of Delane's stable, who tells us that it is the pride of a journalist to be able to write on subjects of which he knows next to nothing.[1] But it was not just ignorance of America which led *The Times* astray. Delane liked to pass his holidays killing stags and game-birds in the company of dukes. It is not surprising that he acquired the tone of the company he kept, and came to gaze at the Northern Americans as across an abyss, with a cold disdain worthy of Lord John Russell himself. Mowbray Morris had been born in the West Indies, where his family had lost all its money as result of emancipation, or so he believed. He hated abolitionism, and was a strong supporter of the South from the start. With two such men at its head (they were also brothers-in-law) *The Times* fell an easy prey to Confederate propaganda.

Still, men can be mistaken without giving offence. The Americans forgave Gladstone, who indeed became a democratic hero on both sides of the Atlantic, because he at length saw and said that he had been wrong to take up the Southern cause, and made what amends he could. *The Times* was never forgiven, and the work it did in alienating America from England was all the harder to undo. This was partly because *The Times* never apologized, but chiefly because the nature of the offence was different. Year in, year out, while the war lasted, *The Times* had insulted Northern patriotism, belittled Northern victories, gloried in Northern defeats, freely predicted Northern failure. It did all this at great length and at the top of its voice. The North was rightfully resentful, and overlooked *The Times*'s good work in helping to keep England neutral (an enormous advantage to the Unionists). Delane thus did great disservice to his country and his paper. The fault of so clever a man cannot be wholly explained in terms of the personal influences upon him.

At bottom, the blunder arose out of *The Times*'s conception of its role. Leslie Stephen made savage fun of the paper's claim to speak for England; but the matter is too important to be left at that. Honesty requires that the claim, like Palmerston's, or Bright's or (later) Gladstone's, must in a sense be admitted; but it needs interpretation. For what was public opinion? As expressed in *The Times* it was the views of every law-abiding,

[1] G.C. Brodrick, *Memories and Impressions 1831-1900,* London, 1900, pages 139-142.

money-making, church-going, beef-eating *paterfamilias* of middle-class England. Delane might consort with the lordly; but even the country houses had learned to mouth counting-house cant. At any rate, a prolonged exposure to the forty-eight daily columns of *The Times* has left me with an ineradicable sense of the staggering self-conceit of Palmerstonian England. Reality broke through occasionally, above all when it became clear that mighty Britannia could not afford to challenge Prussia's assault on Denmark in 1864; but on the whole the clouds of self-congratulation on English freedom, English wealth, English might and the English Queen fatally obscured the mirror. The mid-Victorians did not ever pray to see themselves as others saw them, so naturally the power to do so was never given them. An orgy of bad manners was the inevitable result. The Americans protested, loudly and often, against the tone of English writing from the time of Dickens and Mrs Trollope onwards; their remonstrances, though made in the common language, were unheeded. And of course the English never suspected that if they had been able to read French or German they would have discovered that the American view of them was nearly universal. The tragedy of *The Times* was that instead of correcting the country's vanity, it expressed it.

For example: *The Times* was, I think, bewildered by the floods of information, misinformation and contradictory comment that poured in upon it during the Civil War. But Delane was psychologically incapable of admitting that any such crisis could be beyond the scope of authoritative interpretation from Printing House Square. Self-doubt, half-tones and hesitancy were not the house style, any more than they were the country's. Complacency of mind concealed from its readers and from *The Times* itself that it did not and could not make sense of the news; as a result it was tendentious and inconsistent, while all middle-class England applauded and Delane revelled in his role of Jupiter Tonans (Mackay's phrase for him). Nor did he fully understand the responsibilities it imposed on him. Precisely because it was universally known that *The Times* was uniquely close to the English government, and universally agreed (except by a few malcontents such as A. W. Kinglake and Leslie Stephen) that it was in some sense the voice of English public opinion, it ought to have occurred to the editor that the perpetual sneer in which, even while professing goodwill to America, his writers alluded to that country, was likely to harm the English national interest, assuming that American friendship was worth having. But the point seems never to have crossed his mind. It certainly did not affect his conduct.

II

The doubts, anxieties and mistakes of the past are as much the matter of history as anything else. Any anthologist dealing with *The Times* and the American Civil War would feel obliged to include documentation establishing some of the foregoing points, but if no more were possible the job would be hardly worth doing, since the story of Delane's waverings is well known and properly treated in all books which have occasion to mention it. Fortunately, this unhappy tale by no means exhausts the interest of the *Times* back-numbers to students of the Civil War in English and American history. On the contrary, it leaves the bulk of the material untouched.

To understand why this is so it is necessary to say something more about the place of *The Times* in mid-Victorian life. In the first place, it was not only the most celebrated newspaper but, still, the one with the largest circulation — between 55,000 and 60,000 — though it was beginning to experience severe competition from the *Standard* and the *Daily Telegraph.*[1] It had gained and kept this position by providing numerous services which had little or nothing to do with its role as a journal of opinion.

Foremost was its ability to be first with the news and the inside story. To the outsider the legendary obsession of newspaper editors with scoops and flashes must always seem excessive if not downright ridiculous; but it cannot be denied (the *History of The Times* documents the point too thoroughly) that one of the management's chief concerns was to maintain the primacy of *The Times* in this respect. Accordingly, many columns were taken up by brief, often garbled, announcements: rather like radio news bulletins today. It was in this form that,

---

[1] See *History of The Times,* vol. ii, pages 294-302. It is unfortunate that this notable work makes no attempt to estimate the size of *The Times's* mid-nineteenth century readership.

for example, the fall of Fort Sumter was first reported to Europe. The page headed Latest Intelligence was a jumble of hot news, made possible by the invention of the electric telegraph and unimprovable for a long time because of the telegraph's limitations. The essence of the news would be snatched from the incoming telegrams in this form, in time for the last editions of the day; the full text could wait until tomorrow.

A letter to *The Times* was already the recognized means of airing a grievance, sharing a joke or a perplexity, and generally addressing the nation (though the letters were not yet gathered all onto one page). Thanks to these communications we can still hear our ancestors talking to each other. Businessmen, civil servants and, especially, statesmen found reprinted in *The Times* the complete texts of innumerable public documents — ambassadors' dispatches, official reports, and of course the complete debates of Parliament — which they needed to know about and which were nowhere else collected so conveniently together. Their wives found everything from governesses to operatic performances advertised in *The Times*. The agony column provided the best means for reclaiming lost sons and daughters ('if you wish to see your mother alive again. . .'). Snippets of entertaining news were used as fillers for the bottom of columns, just as they are today. Curious sidelights on England's involvement with the Civil War can often be discovered in these unpromising materials.

More immediately to our point is the Money Market and City column, which usually appeared on page 5, along with reports on 'Railway, Mining and other Shares', the provincial Stock Exchanges and the state of trade in Lancashire and Yorkshire. Page 5 must have been the prime concern of a great many *Times* readers, and there they could find the vicissitudes of the Civil War reflected in many a delicate barometer — above all in the price of gold on Wall Street. It was not yet true that when the Street sneezed the rest of the world caught cold, but operations in New York were already of vast commercial importance. Accordingly, it is on page 5 that we can best gain a sense of the impact of the war on the business world. On page 5 the Confederate Loan was discussed, and the eccentric finances of the North were repeatedly denounced. Lincoln's Secretaries of the Treasury, Chase and Fessenden, seemed to be impiously blind to the beauties of Gladstonian finance. Free trade, a convertible currency, and the securing of all debt by taxation were shibboleths that the Americans ignored. *The Times* predicted disaster, which strange to say did not occur: the North contrived to finance its war. Still, no accurate assessment of the impact of the war on England can leave out the reasonable doubts about the business which the City entertained from first to last.

On page 8, or thereabouts, would normally be found the leading articles. These bear the same relation to those of today that a Victorian sermon bears to the timid utterance of a twentieth-century cleric. They were frequently very long, and so regularly recapitulated so much of what appeared elsewhere in the paper that it is impossible to avoid the suspicion that many readers of *The Times* were too lazy to read anything but the editorials, and that Delane knew it. As we have seen, *The Times* spoke its mind to the world through its leaders. However, they also served the same purpose as the feature articles that are scattered through today's paper. They could be very specialized, as I have already indicated. Nothing, from a scandal about a Church living to the death of the Russian Czarewich, was beneath their close attention, and so it is from them that we learn what an enormous impact the Civil War had on British naval thinking. The great Moltke is supposed to have dismissed it as a matter of two armed mobs chasing each other round the countryside (a view for which there is somewhat more to be said than is usually allowed); but the leader-writers of *The Times* made no such mistake. To them the Civil War was, among other things, an immensely important testing-ground for theories which had been debated intensely but inconclusively for years. The Civil War also drove them to discuss the defences and political constitution of Canada. We, who know that the long Victorian peace had barely started in these years, may well be startled by the unanimous conviction betrayed by these articles that it would not be long before Great Britain was at war again, either with France or the United States.

The rest of the paper was arranged slightly differently each day, as the availability of material dictated. One recurring characteristic is likely to strike a modern eye: the literalness of the phrase 'newspaper correspondent' in this era. Between the extremes (one of Russell's monster dispatches, say, and a letter complaining about the mismanagement of a railway restaurant) there was contrast enough; but in between only shades of difference. A high proportion of news and comment was cast in letter form. The proportion, so far as the Civil War was concerned, would have been even higher, except that after Russell's return *The Times* relied very heavily on extracts from American papers. One of the New York correspondent's chief jobs appears to have been the filleting of the American press, especially when a big battle had been fought. So some of the most vivid writing about the war came to *The Times* from the *New York Herald*, the *New York Times*, etc., though the London paper always printed its excerpts in peculiarly small and illegible type, as if to proclaim the inferiority of the American product. I have made almost no use of these extracts, since they belong to the history of their own papers rather than to that of *The Times;* still, any assessment of the sufficiency of the information available to *Times* readers must take account of them.[1]

'Our Own Correspondents' always loomed largest. They were a very mixed bag, as we have seen, and present varying problems for the anthologist. W. H. Russell took advantage of the comparatively infrequent and slow transmission of news to Europe to write dispatches of enormous length (his stamina was extraordinary). Collected, they would make a book of great value, and of great bulk. Only the famous Bull Run dispatch could be printed here almost in full, if there was to be room for anything else; and excerpting the others proved extremely difficult, as they are so closely-knit. Accordingly, I have scarcely been able to give them the prominence they deserve.

Second only to Russell in terms of historical importance and intellectual attainments was 'Historicus'. This pseudonym lightly veiled the identity of William Vernon Harcourt (1827-1904), the future Liberal leader. His letters to *The Times* on all the questions of international law raised by the Civil War laid the foundations of a great reputation and were a truly valuable contribution to legal history. Their tone was judicious and moderate, a pleasing contrast to what was appearing elsewhere in the paper, and they still repay study by those trying to understand the temper of the Victorian mind — above all its inveterate legalism. Unfortunately 'Historicus' was as liberal as Russell in taking up space, and so cannot be directly represented in this

---

[1] The same applies to the extracts from English journals that figure in like fashion.

selection. I have tried to make amends by printing the review published in *The Times* when the letters appeared in book form.[1]

The 'Historicus' letters must have been written in some sort of collusion with Delane, if they were not actually commissioned by him. The status of some other important contributions is much less clear. For example, 'J.L.M.' (J. L. Motley, the American historian) contributed two important, long and pro-Northern articles on the causes of the war, which were subsequently published as a pamphlet. Delane must have welcomed such excellent copy, but, his views being what they were, is unlikely to have solicited it. Indeed it seems that Motley was provoked into writing by the tone of *The Times*'s leading articles. The series of letters signed 'S', on the other hand, which put the Southern viewpoint throughout the war, were really commissioned articles, for which 'S' (the Liverpool merchant James Spence) accepted payment in the form of a complete set of the *Encyclopaedia Britannica* (he would take no money). But what are we to make of the huge number of letters from other pseudonymous writers? Most of them must have been unsolicited; but undoubtedly some of them were commissioned, and of course none was printed without the editor's sanction. So they, too, throw light on his methods of informing the public and shaping its opinions (on one occasion he would not print any pro-Southern answer to the arguments of 'Historicus' against intervention).

Mackay and Lawley, the terrible twins, pose contrasting problems. Mackay's identity as the *Times* correspondent came early to be known, his anti-Union bias was resented, and so he was excluded from official circles. He could not even profit from the fairly close friendship he had formerly enjoyed with Seward. Usually void of important news, therefore, his letters to London inevitably make wearisome reading, being largely mere repetitive sermons on such themes as the wickedness of Seward and Stanton and the invincibility of the South. I could only make infrequent use of them. Lawley, on the other hand, is an

[1] There is a valuable discussion of the political importance of 'Historicus' in D. Jordan and E. J. Pratt, *Europe and the American Civil War,* (pp. 117–119). These authors suggest that on at least one occasion the letters were prompted from within the Cabinet, by G. C. Lewis and Lord Clarendon, to influence Palmerston and their other colleagues against schemes for intervening on the side of the South.

agreeable, authentic and voluminous source. The temptation was to over-represent him.

III

The most formidable difficulty in compiling this selection remains to be stated. If this volume were designed merely to illustrate a phase in the history of a great newspaper, it would be hard enough, for reasons already suggested: the material is so abundant. But I have also had to take account of the fact that *The Times* is an important source for the study of the most dramatic and complex crisis in American history: no selection would be remotely adequate which did not try to illustrate the war itself. Finally, the Civil War was an event of great importance to the English. Apart from the repeated danger of fighting between the United States and Great Britain which it brought in its train; apart from the legacy of distrust and dislike which it left behind it, to the great misfortune of both countries; apart from the impact of the American way of war on English military and naval thinking, and of the crisis of American democracy on English politics; there was what is likely to interest a modern reader more than anything, the great cotton famine, which devastated Lancashire. It was most thoroughly reported in *The Times*. Confronted with this terrifying plenty of topic and material, what is an anthologist to do?

To begin with, I had to acknowledge that this book could in no sense be an efficient substitute for a complete run of *The Times* 1860–1865. And one or two practical decisions were easily made. Thus, I have on the whole excluded all texts, such as the Confederate Constitution or Lincoln's Second Inaugural, which are available elsewhere. And I had to abridge material ruthlessly to make a book at all, though its usefulness might thereby be diminished. I soon abandoned any attempt to impose a theme. A tempting one lay ready to hand. England was a spectator of the Civil War, all too likely to become an active participant; a spectator whose vital interests were deeply involved. This involvement is not merely illustrated in the files of *The Times,* it conditioned most of the articles that were printed. It is the chief topic for light on which historians have turned to the paper, and it might well have been the chief topic of this selection. But it could not have been adequately illustrated in the space at my disposal, even if everything else was excluded; and there was much else, as I have shown, which ought not to be excluded. So this volume is best treated as a lucky dip. A reader will be well-advised to have at his elbow a good general history of the war (say Bruce Catton's *American Heritage Book of the Civil War*). He may then find use or pleasure in a book which offers some illustrations of some aspects of the war as it affected England and America. A list of dates, a map, and a few notes are offered as readers' aids. I have introduced only one bias into my choosing, but it is an important one. To my mind, nothing is more tedious than a long run of leading articles. The repetition of editorial opinion does not add to its attractiveness, and its importance, whether to contemporaries or to historians, is easily exaggerated. There must have been many Victorian equivalents of the man who reads only the sports page, the man who reads everything except the editorial, and the man who reads nothing else, but shows by the way in which he apes its rhetoric that he is not only a bore but someone without any true understanding of politics. And so, since Delane was consistently stupid over the Civil War, it seemed better not to waste too much paper on reprinting his views. When in doubt, I have dropped a leader. By way of compensation, I have tried to include a certain amount of material which gives an oblique or low-angle view of the war. Posterity's interest in the subject has proved inexhaustible, and has by no means confined itself to the broad outlines of strategy, tactics, diplomacy and politics. Accordingly I have felt fairly sure of interesting at least some of my readers with everything here included. It has all interested me. Which, I may as well add, considering the hard things I have had to say, seems to me as high a compliment as I could possibly pay to any newspaper at any date. I am happy to be able to pay it to Delane's *Times*.

HUGH BROGAN

PRINCIPAL DATES OF
THE AMERICAN CIVIL WAR

(Events of primary concern to *The Times* or England are printed in italics. Readers should bear in mind that it took at least ten days for news to cross the Atlantic either way.)

1860

6 November	Abraham Lincoln elected President of the United States.
20 December	South Carolina passes an Ordinance of Secession; in the next few months it is followed by Mississippi, Alabama, Georgia, Florida, Louisiana and Texas.

1861

4-9 February	The Confederacy set up at Montgomery, Alabama.
4 March	Abraham Lincoln inaugurated.
16 March	*W. H. Russell arrives in New York.*
12 April	Fort Sumter bombarded.
15 April	Lincoln's War Proclamation.
17 April	Jefferson Davies offers to issue letters of marque; Viginia secedes.
19 April	Lincoln proclaims a blockade.
14 May	*British Proclamation of Neutrality.*
21 July	First Battle of Bull Run (or Manassas).
6 August	*Russell's Bull Run dispatch published.*
8 November	The *Trent* incident.
31 December	Northern banks suspend specie payment.

1862

16 February	Grant takes Fort Donelson.
8-9 March	*Merrimac* and *Monitor.*
4 April	*Russell leaves Washington.* McClellan begins his advance up the Peninsula.
6-7 April	Battle of Shiloh.
24 April	Farragut takes New Orleans.
25 May	Stonewall Jackson defeats Banks at Winchester.
31 May - 1 June	Battle of Fair Oaks.
25 June - 1 July	The Seven Day's Battle.

1862

28 July	*The* Alabama *leaves Liverpool.*
29-30 August	Second Bull Run.
17 September	Antietam or Sharpsburg.
22 September	Preliminary Emancipation Proclamation.
7 October	*Gladstone's Newcastle Speech.*
13 December	Fredericksburg.
31 December	Murfreesboro begins.

1863

1 January	Final Emancipation Proclamation.
3 January	Murfreesboro ends.
29 January	*Emancipation Society meeting in Exeter Hall.*
11 February	*Mason speaks at the Mansion House.*
26 March	*Great Trades Union meeting in London in favour of the North.*
27 March	*The House of Commons debates the* Alabama.
5 April	Dupont defeated at Charleston.
1-3 May	Chancellorsville. Death of Stonewall Jackson.
1-3 July	Gettysburg.
4 July	Fall of Vicksburg.
13-16 July	Draft riots in New York.
9 September	*Laird rams detained.*
19-20 September	Chickamauga.
19 November	Gettysburg Address.
24-25 November	Chattanooga.

1864

9 March	Grant commissioned Lieutenant-General.
5-6 May	Battle of the Wilderness.
12 May	Spotsylvania.
3 June	Cold Harbor.
20 June	Sinking of the *Alabama.*
12 July	Jubal Early's raid on Washington.
20-28 July	The Battles of Atlanta.
5 August	Farragut enters Mobile Bay.
2 September	Sherman enters Atlanta.
19 October	Cedar Creek.

1864

8 November	Lincoln re-elected.
15 December	Battle of Nashville.
21 December	Sherman enters Savannah.

1865

2-3 February	Hampton Roads conference.
17 February	Sherman takes Columbia.
18 February	Fall of Charleston.
22 February	Fall of Wilmington.
2 April	Lee abandons Richmond.
9 April	Lee surrenders at Appomattox Court-House.
12 April	Fall of Mobile.
15 April	Death of Abraham Lincoln.
18 April	Sherman-Johnston armistice.
21 April	*Mowbray Morris dismisses Charles Mackay.*
26 April	Death of J.W. Booth; surrender of Joe Johnston.
26 May	Surrender of Kirby Smith.

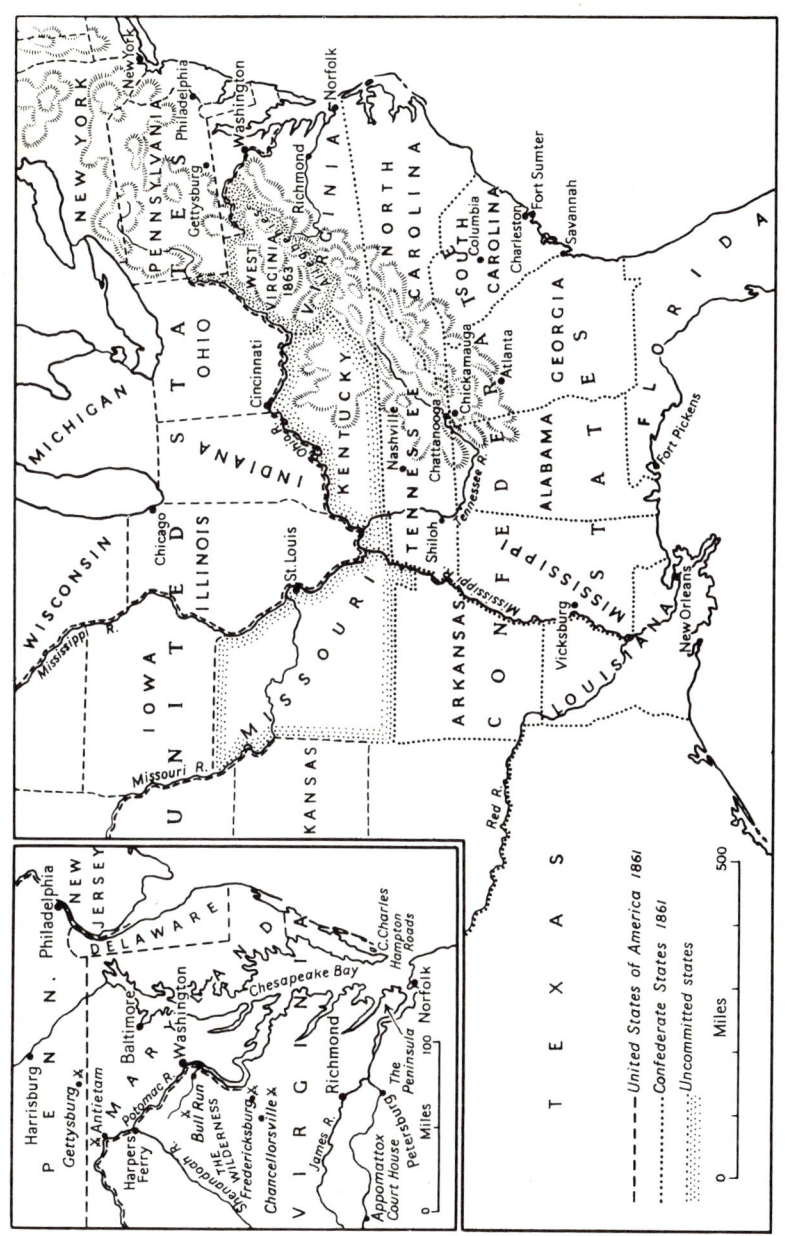

MAP OF THE UNITED STATES DURING THE CIVIL WAR

— — — United States of America 1861
· · · · · · · Confederate States 1861
Uncommitted states

Miles
0   500

Miles
0   100

LINCOLN'S ELECTION AND THE SECESSION MOVEMENT

In electing Mr LINCOLN to the office of President the Northern United States have ventured on a bold experiment. They have determined to test the courage and sincerity of the South, to face unappalled the spectre of secession, and discover whether it be really a terrible spirit potent for evil, or only a bugbear, devised by a clever faction, inflated with the breath of rhodomontading orators, and dressed out with a hideous mask by placemen trembling for their appointments. The next month or two will show how far those are in the right who have calculated on the strength of the American Union and the supremacy of national feeling over all sectional interests. Should South Carolina, Georgia, and the adjacent States separate themselves permanently from the Federation, constituting themselves a new nation, with their own army, navy, Customs, foreign representatives, and all the appanages of independence, then the whole series of American politicians will have been in the wrong, and this journal, which has always declared such an event to be impossible, will have been in the wrong with them. But if, after an outburst of party passion, the Southerners themselves become sensible of the wickedness and folly of their course; if they recognize how far the possessors and expectants of official places are the movers of this agitation; and if, moreover, they are calmed by the reflection that a President, powerful as he is, can do little to alter the policy of the Republic, and nothing at all to subvert the domestic institutions of the several States, then the result will be such as we anticipate, and the United States will continue to combine in one Federation two communities, with widely different politics and systems of social life, but forming essentially and unalterably one and the same people.

For the present, however, the storm is raging throughout the South-Eastern States. South Carolina, of course, takes the lead, and Georgia, throwing off her usual old fashioned quietude, surpasses her hot-tempered sister in revolutionary violence. South Carolina is, however, the first to act. The Federal officials at Charleston have resigned their appointments. The flag of the State is ostentatiously displayed, instead of the stars and stripes. Even a steamer coming into Charleston harbour was obliged to

1

discard the symbol of American unity. Some interference with the Federal fortresses within the State seems also to have been contemplated. In Georgia the Governor, in a special message to the Legislature, is carried by his zeal beyond the bounds of common sense. If we understand him rightly, he proposes not only to separate from Massachusetts, but to carry on a chronic warfare against that offending State. Because the laws of Massachusetts do not protect slave property, or, in other words, "cause plunder from Georgian citizens", Massachusetts must be compelled to make compensation. He recommends the enactment of laws authorizing the seizure of the money or property of any citizen of such offending and faithless State to indemnify the losses of the citizens of Georgia. Hostile tariffs are to be established against the Abolitionists. The population is to be called to arms to support its rights, and money is to be raised to put the State in a posture of defence. This is a specimen of the counsels which are now offered to the Southerners by their magistrates, and at first sight they would seem to portend the immediate disruption of the Republic. But through all this violence we cannot but think that signs of insincerity appear. The Carolinians and Georgians protest too much. The flame is too violent and too sudden to last long. No doubt, much sedition will be talked, and many acts committed which the Federal Government might be justified in treating as treasonable; but when time has been given for reflection the Southerners will be reconciled to their fate—which, after all, is no hard one—and common sense will show them the absurdity of refusing to accept a constitutional election because it has gone against them, and breaking up a great nation through the vain fear that a magistrate of limited powers will do what no despot would be able to effect.

In the meantime, however, South Carolina will make every show of secession. The American papers discuss the prospects of the new Republic, its wealth, material resources, ports, railways, and commercial system. The complications which would ensue on this event are spoken of with much gravity. The effect on the cotton trade especially would be most remarkable, when the produce of Georgia, on its way to Charleston, would have to be bonded, and Tennessee would be divided from the Atlantic and the European world by a "foreign country." So immediate has been the impulse, we hear, that engineers are sent to examine the old scheme of forming a great shipping port at Brunswick,

Georgia, in expectation of this State preferring to remain a member of the old Federation. It is characteristic of the Americans that even the disruption of their beloved Republic should be viewed at once in its mercantile and joint-stock-company light. But, as far as we can see, even South Carolina does not yet propose to make herself a new nation. The first plan is to embarrass the Federal Government by refusing to fulfil Federal duties. South Carolina now has no Federal officials. She meditates withdrawing her Senators and Representatives from Congress, and opposing a passive resistance to the execution of Federal law. The people of the "Palmetto State" will then leave the Government at Washington to take what steps it thinks fit. In short, the scheme of the South Carolinians is not so much secession as "nullification" to use the term current when the same State attempted a similar policy in the time of Mr. CAL-HOUN. South Carolina will not declare her independence of the Federation in the sense in which she declared her independence of England 84 years ago; she will be content with pushing to their extreme limits her rights as a Sovereign State, and, while remaining nominally in communion with New York and Massachusetts, will attempt to limit the constitutional authority of the Federation by her private enactments. There will not be a Carolinian President, with envoys duly accredited at the foreign capitals of Washington and London, but the authority of the Federal Government will be impotent within the limits of the State, and the people, if determined to remain obstinate, will undertake to manage their own Post-office, their own Customs, the lighting of their coasts, and will, perhaps go the length of constructing and arming domestic fortresses. A strong-minded President like JACKSON, whatever his own sympathies, would probably not hesitate to crush the Carolinians by force. It is evident, indeed, on the smallest reflection, that the South, even if united, could never oppose for three months the greatly preponderating strength of the North. A few hundred thousand slaveowners, trembling nightly with visions of murder and pillage, backed by a dissolute population of "poor whites," are no match for the hardy and resolute populations of the Free States. The Northerners have hitherto treated the South like a petulant child, and given in to all its ways; but if ever the day of conflict were to come it would be shown that the South is but a child in its weakness as well as its frowardness.

3

November 26th, 1860

We believe, however, that moderate counsels prevail at Washington. Public opinion is evidently opposed to the use of a military force to quell the agitation. Violence is to be met by calmness, and sedition by a quiet discharge of constitutional duties. The Southerners are not to be coerced, because it is expected that they will shortly be able to restrain themselves. The overthrow of a party so long dominant could hardly be effected without some display of excitement and anger. The extreme section in the Slave States have so long and so vehemently asserted their resolve never to submit to a Republican Executive that they could not without becoming ridiculous quietly acquiesce in their defeat. Everything has been at stake with them—place, power, social position, credit with their fellow-citizens, and now they can hardly bring themselves to believe that they have lost the day. But the South is not united. Whole States are lukewarm in the Democratic cause, and look with horror on anything like a disruption of the Republic. Even in South Carolina there is a moderate party, which, when the first effervescence has subsided, will make its influence felt. To leave the Southerners completely to themselves, to take no notice of the withdrawal of the Senators or Representatives, to avoid as much as possible any conflict between the Federal authorities and the excited populace of Charleston—in short, to oppose a "masterly inactivity" to the excitement of the South, is the policy recommended of the North, and we cannot but think it will be successful. The South will grow accustomed to a Republican President, the movement in South Carolina and Georgia will be confined to only a section of the Slave States, and after some months wiser counsels will prevail even there. President LINCOLN will probably be found by the slaveholders more harmless than they anticipate. Men's acts are never so extreme as their opinions, and, as the Freesoilers have flourished under the dominion of their opponents, so the South may exist in spite of a chief magistrate whose opinions on Slavery are not considered orthodox at Charleston.

J.C. Bancroft Davies (1822–1907) had been 'Our Own Correspondent' at New York (after Russell's arrival he became 'Our New York Correspondent') since 1854. 'A remarkably good specimen of an American,' said Mowbray Morris. He sent in excellent copy until the end of 1861, when he left the United States for a voyage

4

in search of health. When he returned in 1863, he sent two more articles to The Times, *but they were not published because they were thoroughly pro-Northern and by then Delane and Morris were forbidding all such attitudes to appear in the paper. Davis's articles are a first-rate source for Northern hopes, fears and ideas during the preliminaries to the Civil War and the first months of fighting. Delane should have paid more attention to his views; I regret that I could not find space for more than one of his pieces.*

After the Civil War Davis had a distinguished career: three times Assistant Secretary of State, minister to Berlin (1874–1877), judge of the US Court of Claims. His most important appointment was as American agent during the arbitration of the Alabama *claims at Geneva, 1871–2.*

December 4th, 1860   *page 6*

THE UNITED STATES

(FROM OUR OWN CORRESPONDENT.)

NEW YORK, Nov. 21.
The panic and commercial crisis, that had begun to be felt when I last wrote, has since then so overshadowed everything else that men have quite forgotten the political troubles at the South, to which it owed its origin. The days of 1857, those gloomy days when Bank Presidents fainted in their parlours, and merchants cried over their ledgers, have come back again—those days when money, just before plenteously floating about and begging you to bag it, suddenly sinks out of sight and reach. The most unaccountable thing in a New York panic is, where does the money go to? Two weeks ago there was plenty of it. Men would beg you to borrow at the legal rate—7 per cent. Now what a reverse! Without any increase of debt, or decrease in means, New York is filled with produce, and new arrivals are coming every day. She is a creditor of most of the world, and yet suddenly all the avenues of commerce have been choked, and it has been almost impossible to borrow money or pay debts. What has become of the money that was so overflowing ten days since? Where do the bank balances go? Ten days hence money may again be plentiful, and confidence, that slow-growing plant, may be springing up through every chink

5

of the Wall-street pavement. Where is it just now? That is the mystery which I do not feel myself equal to solving.

At the date of my last letter the panic had fairly begun. All before then, however, was a bagatelle to what has since taken place. There was nothing in 1857 worse than the pressure of the day before yesterday. The financial crisis of 1860 may now fairly rank with those of 1837 and 1857 in intensity of suffering. Whether it is destined to be as long enduring, time only can show. It certainly has not as wide-spread a basis of debt to operate upon. On the contrary, fungus-like, it seems to spring out of a rich prosperity, for if the universal testimony of the business world is to be credited, there was never before greater prosperity to this country than now. The great crops are secured and are known to be more valuable than in any former year. The cotton crop, it is true, is not as large as was hoped for, but, on the other hand, the grain crops are larger, and of the specie crops of California this country retains, by reason of non-shipment to Europe, some $20,000,000 more than usual. Less than a month since money was abundant, notwithstanding a steady and healthful curtailment by the banks. The corn crop of the country, owing to the high prices and the European demand, was pouring into New York. From the same cause the autumn railway traffic was increased on all the main lines, and the business of the country was everywhere revived and stimulated in a healthy manner. The new cotton crop also was beginning to move from New Orleans and Mobile, and the cotton sterling bills, in the usual course of trade, to find their way into the New York market. One would fancy that a picture of more complete prosperity could hardly be drawn, a large crop pouring into the seaports for export at high prices, a diminished exportation of specie, and exchange at favourable rates. In an instant this prosperous picture is obscured, from no other cause, as far as I can learn, than political distrust. Business of all kinds was instantly suspended. It became impossible to negotiate sterling exchange. The crops, however, continued to arrive, as well as the sterling cotton bills, against which sight or short time draughts on New York were drawn that must be met. The banks continued to contract money, and, it being impossible to negotiate sterling exchange, except at ruinous rates, the whole business of the country came to a standstill.

The decline in every species of property under the pressure

was great, especially in breadstuffs, of which there is a large amount waiting shipment, and in securities which had to be sacrificed to meet pressing liabilities. When the bank statement for the week came to be made up it appeared that the banks had helped to turn the screw on the business community; for the line of the loans was decreased $2,363,691, while the decrease in specie was $1,661,019, and in deposits $2,835,633. The officers of the various banks—the very inadequate bank capital of New York being distributed among a number of small institutions, each with its own set of officers and its own petty policy—the officers of these several institutions met together to devise some way to relieve the public and move the crop. Of course, there was great diversity of opinion, with nothing done as the result. When they saw, however, that unless they did something with their capital to relieve the public the depositors would withdraw their deposits and compel the banks to suspend, as was done in 1857, they determined to authorize, through a committee, the purchase of sterling bills to the amount of $2,500,000, supposing that this would absorb some of the surplus exchange on the market, and thus set the crops in motion. They came to this determination the day before yesterday. A good part of yesterday was spent in agreeing upon the rate, and upon whose bills should be bought, so that we cannot yet say whether this measure will or will not afford the desired relief. This stoppage of business, taking place in the midst of such extreme prosperity, with such a glut of produce in the market waiting exportation, suggests the necessity of a great financial head, with wisdom in its management to foresee danger, and with power in its coffers to avert it. If New York, instead of 29 or 30 petty banks managed by petty men, without a financial policy, each institution struggling to maintain itself in a rivalry with all the others, unable to expand while any of its associates were contracting—if, instead of such a powerless confederation of capital as this, New York had an institution like the Bank of England, or the Bank of France, or the Old Bank of the United States, I believe that the disasters of the past week might have been prevented. They had no foundation except in political distrust. That cause might easily have been taken care of. As it is, I trust that we have seen the worst here unless the effect on London is more severe than I anticipate. Large orders, have, I understand, gone out for the shipment of gold. These orders need not create any apprehensions, for it is as certain as anything in the future can be, that if the Persia brings back gold here, as much will return with her to England. In the present state of the exchange-market all the California supplies to arrive must remain here. The exchanges at Chicago, New Orleans, and Mobile are such that gold will not go thither from here. The banks of New York have, therefore, only to pursue a liberal policy towards their customers to have trade resume its usual course, and any gold that may be sent here return. What we have more to dread than any feeling created by the shipment of gold is the general dread of American investments that may follow the news of threatened political troubles. Should the alarm be widespread, and should the holders of such securities throw them upon this market in any quantity, the injury might be great both there and here. If I could have the ear of such persons, I would say to them, "Do not be frightened because you see a great decline in Federal, State, and railway securities. That decline has been caused by the necessities of people to have money, and the fortunate purchasers cannot fail to make large gains out of the transaction. These great depreciations do not come from political causes at all. You must not take them as any evidence of the estimate which the people of this country put upon their political institutions, or their property. Your Illinois Centrals, Michigan Centrals, Pennsylvania or New York Centrals, your Eries, your Tennessee or Virginia Sixes, or your Massachusetts or United States' Fives are just as good now as they were a month ago. Do not, therefore, be deluded into sacrificing your property. If you do, some other more fortunate person will be the gainer by it."

W.H. Russell (1820-1907), was in mid-career when he came to America. An Irishman, he began by covering the general election of 1841 in Ireland for The Times. *After his enforced return to England in 1862 he edited the* Army and Navy Gazette *which he had founded in 1860; for though* The Times *gave him an annual pension of £300, Delane would not let him write on American affairs, as he was too pro-Northern (like Bancroft Davis and G.C. Brodrick). He covered the battle of Sadowa and the Franco-Prussian War for* The Times, *and was knighted in 1895. He received an honorary Doctorate from Trinity College, Dublin, in 1855.*

AMERICA

(FROM OUR SPECIAL CORRESPONDENT.)

WASHINGTON. MARCH 29.

... At Washington there is at this moment such a ferment as no other part of the world could exhibit—a spectacle which makes one wonder that any man can be induced to seek for office, or that any Government can be conducted under such a system. The storm which rolled over the capital has, I am told, subsided; but the stranger, unaccustomed to such tempestuous zones, thinks the gale is quite strong enough even in its diminished intensity. All the hotels are full of keen gray-eyed men, who fondly believe their destiny is to fill for four years some pet appointment under Government. The streets are crowded with them; the steamers and the railway carriages, the public departments, the steps of the senators' dwellings, the lobbies of houses, the President's mansion, are crowded with them. From all parts of the vast Union, not even excepting the South, they have come fast as steam or wind and waves could bear them to concentrate in one focus on the devoted head of the President all the myriad influences which, by letter, testimonial, personal application, unceasing canvass, and sleepless solicitation, they can collect together.

Willard's Hotel, a huge caravanserai, is a curious study of character and institutions. Every form of speech and every accent under which the English tongue can be recognized rings through the long corridors in tones of expostulation, anger, or gratification. Crowds of long-limbed, nervous, eager-looking men, in loose black garments, undulating shirt collars, vast conceptions in hatting and booting, angular with documents and pregnant with demand, throng every avenue, in spite of the printed notices directing them "to move on from front of the cigar-stand." They are "senator hunters," and every senator has a *clientele* more numerous than the most popular young Roman noble who ever sauntered down the Via Sacra. If one of them ventures out of cover, the cry is raised, and he is immediately run to earth. The printing-presses are busy with endless copies of testimonials, which are hurled at everybody with reckless profusion.

April 16th, 1861

The writing-room of the hotel is full of people preparing statements or writing for "more testimonials," demanding more places, or submitting "extra certificates." The bar-room is full of people inspiring themselves with fresh confidence, or engaged in plots to surprise some place or find one out; and the ladies who are connected with members of the party in power find themselves the centres of irresistible attraction. "Sir," said a gentleman to whom I had letters of introduction, "I know you must be a stranger because you did not stop me to present these letters in the street."

At the head of the list of persecuted men is the President himself. Every one has a right to walk into the White House, which is the President's private as well as his official residence. Mr Lincoln is actuated by the highest motives in the distribution of office. All the vast patronage of tens of thousands of places, from the highest to the lowest, is his, and, instead of submitting the various claims to the heads of departments, the President seeks to investigate them, and to see all the candidates. Even his iron frame and robust constitution are affected by the process, which lasts all day, and is not over in the night or in the morning. The particular *formula* which he has adopted to show the impossibility of satisfying everybody is by no means accepted by anybody who is disappointed. What is the use of telling a man he can't have a place because 100 others are asking for it, if that man thinks he is only one who has a right to get it?

At the very moment when the President and his Cabinet should be left undisturbed to deal with the tremendous questions which have arisen for their action, the roar of office seekers dims every sense, and almost annihilates them. The Senate, which is now sitting merely to confirm appointments, relieving the monotony of executive reviews with odd skirmishes between old political antagonists now and then, will, it is said, rise this week. Around their Chamber is the ever recurring question heard, "Who has got what?" and the answer is never satisfactory to all. This hunting after office, which destroys self-respect when it is the moving motive of any considerable section of a great party, is an innovation which was introduced by General Jackson; but it is likely to be as permanent as the Republic, inasmuch as no candidate dares declare his intention of reverting to the old system. These "spoils," as they are called, are now being distributed by two Governments—the *de jure* and *de facto*

Government of Washington, and the Government erected by the Southern States at Montgomery. . . .

THE CIVIL WAR IN AMERICA

(FROM OUR SPECIAL CORRESPONDENT.)

CHARLESTON, S.C., APRIL 21.

I find some consolation for the disappointment of not arriving in time to witness the attack upon Fort Sumter in describing the condition of the work soon after Major Anderson surrendered it. Already I have upon my table a pamphlet entitled *"The Battle of Fort Sumter and First Victory of the Southern Troops,"* &c., several "poems," and a variety of versicules, songs, and rhetorical exercitations upon this event, which, however important as a political demonstration, is of small value in a military sense, except in so far as the bloodless occupation of a position commanding Charleston harbour is concerned. It may tend to prevent any false impressions founded on imperfect information to state a few facts connected with the fire in the work, and its effects, which will interest, at least, some military readers.

In the first place, it may be well to admit that the military preparations and positions of the South Carolinians were more formidable than one was prepared to expect on the part of a small State, without any considerable internal organization or resources. This comparative efficiency was due mainly to General Beauregard and his assistant-engineer, Major Whiting, who are both professional engineer officers of the United States' army, and who had capacity and influence enough to direct the energies of the undisciplined masses in the proper direction, instead of allowing them to rush on their fate in the perilous essay of an escalade, as they intended. The State of South Carolina had for a long time past been accumulating arms and munitions of war, and it may be said that ever since the nullification contest she had permitted herself to dwell on the idea of ultimate secession, to be effected by force if necessary. When General Beauregard and Major Whiting came here the works intended to resist the fleet and to crush the fort were in a very imperfect state. Major Anderson and his officers had a true

11

professional contempt for the batteries of the civilians and militiamen, which was in some measure justifiable. One morning, however, as they took their survey of their enemy's labours for the previous night, they perceived a change had come over the design of their works. That "some one who knows his business is over there" was evident. Their strange relationship with those who were preparing to destroy them if possible, however, prevented their recourse to the obvious means which were then in abundance in their hands to avert the coming danger. Had Major Anderson maintained a well-regulated fire on the enemy the moment they began to throw up their batteries and prepare Fort Moultrie against him, he could have made their progress very slow and exceedingly laborious, and have marked it at every step with blood. His command over the ground was very decided, but he had, it is to be supposed, no authority to defend himself in the only way in which it could be done. "Too late,"—that fatal phrase,—was the echo to every order which came from the seat of government at Washington. Meantime the South Carolinians worked at their batteries, and were soon able to obtain cover on the soft sandy plains on which they were planting their guns and mortars. They practised their men at the guns, stacked shot and shell, and furnished their magazines, and drilled their raw levies with inpunity within 1,400 yards of the fort. . . . . .

. . .

At a distance the fort bears some resemblance to Fort Paul at Sebastopol. It is a truncated pentagon, with three faces armed—that which is towards Morris Island being considered safe from attack, as the work was only intended to resist an approach from the sea. It is said to have cost altogether more than 200,000*l.* sterling. The walls are of solid brick and concrete masonry, built close to the edge of the water, 60 feet high, and from eight to 12 feet in thickness, and carry three tiers of guns on the north, east, and west exterior sides. Its weakest point is on the south side, where the masonry is not protected by any flank fire to sweep the wharf. The work is designed for an armament of 140 pieces of ordnance of all calibres. Two tiers are under bomb-proof casemates, and the third or upper tier is *en barbette;* the lower tier is intended for 42-pounder paixhan guns; the second tier for eight and ten-inch columbiads, for throwing solid or hollow shot, and the upper tier for mortars and guns. But only 75 are now mounted. Eleven paixhan guns are among that number, nine of them commanding Fort Moultrie. Some of the columbiads are not mounted. Four of the 32-pounder *barbette* guns are on pivot carriages, and others have a sweep of 180 degrees. The walls are pierced everywhere for musketry. The magazine contains several hundred barrels of gunpowder, and a supply of shot, powder, and shells. The garrison was amply supplied with water from artificial wells. The war garrison of the fort ought to be at least 600 men, but only 79 were within its walls, with the labourers—109, all told—at the time of the attack.

The walls of the fort are dented on all sides by shot marks, but in no instance was any approach made to a breach, and the greatest damage, at one of the angles on the south face, did not extend more than two feet into the masonry, which is of very fine brick. The parapet is, of course damaged, but the casemate embrasures are uninjured. On landing at the wharf we perceived that the granite copings had suffered more than the brickwork, and that the stone had split up and splintered where it was struck. The ingenuity of the defenders was evident even here. They had no mortar with which to fasten up the stone slabs they had adapted as blinds to the windows of the unprotected south side, but Major Anderson, or his subordinate, Captain Foster, had closed the slabs in with lead, which he procured from some water piping, and had rendered them proof against escalade, which he was prepared also to resent by extensive mines laid under the wharf and landing-place, to be fired by friction tubes and lines laid inside the work. He had also prepared a number of shells for the same purpose, to act as hand grenades, with friction tubes and lanyards, when hurled down from the parapet on his assailants. The entrance to the fort was blocked up by masses of masonry, which had been thrown down from the walls of the burnt barracks and officers' quarters along the south side. A number of men were engaged in digging up the mines at the wharf, and others were busied in completing the ruin of the tottering walls, which were still so hot that it was necessary to keep a hose of water playing on part of the brickwork. To an uninitiated eye it would seem as if the fort was untenable, but, in reality, in spite of the destruction done to it, a stout garrison, properly supplied, would have been in no danger from anything, except the explosion of the magazine, of which the copper door was jammed by the heat at the time of the surrender. Exclusive of the burning of the quarters and the intense heat, there was no reason for a properly handled and sufficient force to surrender the place. It is needless to say Major Anderson had neither one nor the other. He was in all respects most miserably equipped. His guns were without screws, scales, or tangents, so that his elevations were managed by rude wedges of deal, and his scales marked in chalk on the breech of the guns, and his distances and bearings scratched in the same way on the side of the embrasures. He had not a single fuse for his shells, and he tried in vain to improvise them by filling pieces of bored-out pine with caked gunpowder. His cartridges were out, and he was compelled to detail some of his few men to make them out of shirts, stockings, and jackets. He had not a single mortar, and he was compelled to the desperate expedient of planting long guns in the ground at an angle of 45 degrees, for which he could find no shell, as he had no fuses which could be fired with safety. He had no sheers to mount his guns, and chance alone enabled him to do so by drifting some large logs down with the tide against Sumter. Finally, he had not even one engine to put out a fire in quarters. I walked carefully over the parade and could detect the marks of only seven shells in the ground, but Major Whiting told me the orders were to burst the shells over the parapet so as to frustrate any attempt to work the barbette guns. Two of these were injured by shot, and one was overturned, apparently by its own recoil, but there was no injury done inside any of the casemates to the guns or works. The shell splinters had all disappeared, carried off, I am told, as "trophies." Had Major Anderson been properly provided, so that he could have at once sent his men to the guns, opened fire from those in barbette, thrown shell and hot shot, kept relays to all his casemates, and put out fires as they arose from red-hot shot or shell, he must, I have no earthly doubt, have driven the troops off Morris Island, burnt out Fort Moultrie, and silenced the enemies' fire. His loss might have been considerable, that of the Confederates must have been very great. As it was, not a life was lost by actual fire on either side. A week hence and it will be impossible for a fleet to do anything, except cover the descent of an army here, and they must lie off, at the least, four miles from the nearest available beach.

THE CIVIL WAR IN AMERICA

THE DEFEAT AT MANASSAS

(FROM OUR SPECIAL CORRESPONDENT.)

WASHINGTON, JULY 22.

... I sit down to give an account—not of the action yesterday, but of what I saw with my own eyes, hitherto not often deceived, and of what I heard with my own ears, which in this country are not so much to be trusted. Let me, however, express an opinion as to the affair of yesterday. In the first place, the repulse of the Federalists, decided as it was, might have had no serious effects whatever beyond the mere failure—which politically was of greater consequence than it was in a military sense—but for the disgraceful conduct of the troops. The retreat on their lines at Centreville seems to have ended in a cowardly route—a miserable, causeless panic. Such scandalous behaviour on the part of soldiers I should have considered impossible, as with some experience of camps and armies I have never even in alarms among camp followers seen the like of it. How far the disorganization of the troop extended I know not; but it was complete in the instance of more than one regiment. Washington this morning is crowded with soldiers without officers, who have fled from Centreville, and with "three months' men," who are going home from the face of the enemy on the expiration of their term of enlistment. The streets, in spite of the rain, are crowded by people with anxious faces, and groups of wavering politicians are assembled at the corners, in the hotel passages, and the bars. If in the present state of the troops the Confederates were to make a march across the Potomac above Washington, turning the works at Arlington, the Capital might fall into their hands. Delay may place that event out of the range of probability.

The North will, no doubt, recover the shock. Hitherto she has only said, "Go and fight for the Union." The South has exclaimed, "Let us fight for our rights." The North must put its best men into the battle, or she will inevitably fail before the energy, the personal hatred, and the superior fighting powers of her antagonist. In my letters, as in my conversation, I have

15

endeavoured to show that the task which the Unionists have set themselves is one of no ordinary difficulty, but in the state of arrogance and supercilious confidence, either real or affected to conceal a sense of weakness, one might as well have preached to the Pyramid of Cheops. Indeed, one may form some notion of the condition of the public mind by observing that journals conducted avowedly by men of disgraceful personal character—the be-whipped and be-kicked and unrecognized pariahs of society in New York—are, nevertheless, in the very midst of repulse and defeat, permitted to indulge in ridiculous rhodomontade towards the nations of Europe, and to move our laughter by impotently malignant attacks on "our rotten old monarchy," while the stones of their bran new republic are tumbling about their ears. It will be amusing to observe the change of tone, for we can afford to observe and to be amused at the same time.

On Saturday night I resolved to proceed to General M'Dowell's army, as it was obvious to me that the repulse at Bull's Run and the orders of the General directed against the excesses of his soldiery indicated serious defects in his army—not more serious, however, than I had reason to believe existed. How to get out was the difficulty. The rumours of great disaster and repulse had spread through the city. The livery-stable keepers, with one exception, refused to send out horses to the scene of action—at least, the exception told me so. Senators and Congress men were going to make a day of it, and all the vehicles and horses that could be procured were in requisition for the scene of action. This curiosity was aroused by the story that M'Dowell had been actually ordered to make an attack on Manassas, and that General Scott had given him till 12 o'clock to be master of Beauregard's lines. If General Scott ordered the attack at all I venture to say he was merely the mouthpiece of the more violent civilians of the Government, who mistake intensity of feeling for military strength. The consequences of the little skirmish at Bull's Run, ending in the repulse of the Federalists, were much exaggerated, and their losses were put down at any figures the fancy of the individual item who was speaking suggested. "I can assure you, Sir, that the troops had 1,500 killed and wounded; I know it." I went off to the head-quarters, and there General Scott's aide informed me General M'Dowell's official report gave 6 killed and 37 wounded.

The livery keepers stuck to the 1,500 or 2,000. The greater the number *hors de combat* the higher the tariff for the hire of quadrupeds. All I could do was to get a kind of cabriolet, with a seat in front for the driver, to which a pole was affixed for two horses, at a Derby-day price, and a strong led-horse, which Indian experiences have induced me always to rely upon in the neighbourhood of uncertain fighting. I had to enter into an agreement with the owner to pay him for horses and buggy if they were "captured or injured by the enemy," and though I smiled at his precautions they proved not quite unreasonable. The master made no provision for indemnity in the case of injury to the driver, or the coloured boy who rode the saddle-horse. When I spoke with officers at General Scott's head-quarters of the expedition, it struck me they were not at all sanguine about the result of the day, and one of them said as much as induced me to think he would advise me to remain in the city if he did not take it for granted it was part of my duty to go to the scene of action. An English gentleman who accompanied me was strongly dissuaded from going by a colonel of cavalry on the staff, because, he said, "the troops are green, and no one can tell what may happen." But my friend got his pass from General Scott, who was taking the whole affair of Bull's Run and the pressure of the morrow's work with perfect calm, and we started on Sunday morning—not so early as we ought, perhaps, which was none of my fault—for Centreville, distant about 25 miles south-west of Washington. I purposed starting in the beautiful moonlight, so as to arrive at M'Dowell's camp in the early dawn, but the aides could not or would not give us the countersign over the Long-bridge, and without it no one could get across till after 5 o'clock in the morning. When M'Dowell moved away he took so many of the troops about Arlington that the camps and forts are rather denuded of men. I do not give, as may be observed, the names of regiments, unless in special cases—first, because they possess little interest, I conceive, for those in Europe who read these letters; and, secondly, because there is an exceedingly complex system—at least, to a foreigner—of nomenclature in the forces, and one may make a mistake between a regiment of volunteers and a regiment of State militia of the same number, or even of regulars in the lower figures. The soldiers lounging about the forts and over the Longbridge across the Potomac were an exceedingly unkempt,

17

"loafing" set of fellows, who handled their firelocks like pitchforks and spades, and I doubt if some of those who read or tried to read our papers could understand them, as they certainly did not speak English. The Americans possess excellent working materials, however, and I have had occasion repeatedly to remark the rapidity and skill with which they construct earthworks. At the Virginia side of the Long-bridge there is now a very strong *tête de pont*, supported by the regular redoubt on the hill over the road. These works did not appear to be strongly held, but it is possible men were in the tents near at hand, deserted though they seemed, and at all events reinforcements could be speedily poured in if necessary.

The long and weary way was varied by different pickets along the road, and by the examination of our papers and passes at different points. But the country looked vacant in spite of crops of Indian corn, for the houses were shut up, and the few indigenous people whom we met looked most blackly under their brows at the supposed Abolitionists. This portion of Virginia is well wooded, and undulating in heavy regular waves of field and forest; but the roads are deeply cut and filled with loose stones, very disagreeable to ride or drive over. The houses are of wood, with the usual negro huts adjoining them, and the specimens of the race which I saw were well dressed and not ill-looking. On turning into one of the roads which leads to Fairfax Court-house and to Centreville beyond it the distant sound of cannon reached us. That must have been about 9.30 a.m. It never ceased all day; at least, whenever the rattle of the gig ceased the booming of guns rolled through the woods on our ears. One man said it began at 2 o'clock, but the pickets told us it had really become continuous about half-past 7 or 8 o'clock. In a few minutes afterwards a body of men appeared on the road, with their backs towards Centreville and their faces towards Alexandria. Their march was so disorderly that I could not have believed they were soldiers in an enemy's country—for Virginia hereabout is certainly so—but for their arms and uniform. It soon appeared that there was no less than an entire regiment marching away, singly or in small knots of two or three, extending for some three or four miles along the road. A Babel of tongues rose from them, and they were all in good spirits, but with an air about them I could not understand. Dismounting at a stream, where a group of thirsty men were drinking and halting in the shade, I asked an

18

officer "Where are your men going, Sir?" "Well, we're going home, Sir, I reckon, to Pennsylvania." It was the 4th Pennsylvania Regiment, which was on its march, as I learnt from the men. "I suppose there is severe work going on behind you, judging from the firing?" "Well, I reckon, Sir, there is." "We're going home," he added after a pause, during which it occurred to him, perhaps, that the movement required explanation,—"because the men's time is up. We have had three months of this work." I proceeded on my way, ruminating on the feelings of a General who sees half a brigade walk quietly away on the very morning of an action, and on the frame of mind of the men, who would have shouted till they were hoarse about their beloved Union—possibly have hunted down any poor creature who expressed a belief that it was not the very quintessence of everthing great and good in government and glorious and omnipotent in arms,—coolly turning their backs on it when in its utmost peril because the letter of their engagement bound them no further. Perhaps the 4th Pennsylvania were right, but let us hear no more of the excellence of three months' service volunteers. And so we left them. The road was devious and difficult. There were few persons on their way, for most of the Senators and Congress men were on before us. Some few commissariat waggons were overtaken at intervals. Wherever there was a house by the roadside the negroes were listening to the firing.

All at once a terrific object appeared in the wood above the trees—the dome of a church or public building, apparently suffering from the shocks of an earthquake, and heaving to and fro in the most violent manner. In much doubt we approached as well as the horses' minds would let us, and discovered that the strange thing was an inflated balloon attached to a car and waggon, which was on its way to enable General M'Dowell to reconnoitre the position he was then engaged in attacking—just a day too late. The operators and attendants swore as horribly as Anna's warriors in Flanders, but they could not curse down the trees, and so the balloon seems likely to fall into the hands of the Confederates. About 11 o'clock we began to enter on the disputed territory which had just been abandoned by the Secessionists to the Federalists in front of Fairfax Court-house. It is not too much to say that the works thrown up across the road were shams and makebelieves, and that the Confederates never intended to occupy the position at all, but sought to lure on the Federalists to Manassas Gap, where they were prepared to meet them. Had it been otherwise the earthworks would have been of a different character, and the troops would have had regular camps and tents, instead of bivouac huts of branches of trees. Of course the troops of the enemy did not wish to be cut off, and so they had cut down trees to place across the road, and put some field-pieces in their earthworks to command it. On no side could Richmond be so well defended. The Confederates had it much at heart to induce their enemy to come to the strongest place and attack them, and they succeeded in doing so. But, if the troops behaved as ill in other places as they did at Manassas, the Federalists could not have been successful in any attack whatever. In order that the preparations at Manassas may be understood, and that General Beauregard, of whose character I gave some hint at Charleston, may be known at home as regards his fitness for his work, above all as an officer of artillery and of skill in working it in field or in position, let me insert a description of the place and of the man from a Southern paper:—

"Manassas Junction, Virginia, June 7.
"This place still continues the head-quarters of the army of the Potomac. There are many indications of an intended forward movement, the better to invite the enemy to an engagement, but the work of fortification still continues. By nature the position is one of the strongest that could have been found in the whole State. About halfway between the eastern spur of the Blue Ridge and the Potomac, below Alexandria, it commands the whole country between so perfectly that there is scarcely a possibility of its being turned. The right wing stretches off towards the head-waters of the Occoquan, through a wooded country, which is easily made impassable by the felling of trees. The left is a rolling table-land, easily commanded from the successive elevations, till you reach a country so rough and so rugged that it is a defence to itself. The key to the whole position, in fact, is precisely that point which General Beauregard chose for his centre, and which he has fortified so strongly that, in the opinion of military men, 5,000 men could there hold 20,000 at bay. The position, in fact, is fortified in part by Nature herself. It is a succession of hills, nearly equidistant from each other, in front of which is a ravine so deep and so thickly wooded that it is

passable only at two points, and those through gorges which 50 men can defend against a whole army. It was at one of these points that the Washington Artillery (of New Orleans) were at first encamped, and though only half the battalion was then there, and we had only one company of infantry to support us, we slept as soundly under the protection of our guns as if we had been in a fort of the amplest dimensions. Of the fortifications superadded here by General Beauregard to those of Nature it is, of course, not proper for me to speak.

The general reader, in fact, will have a sufficiently precise idea of them by conceiving a line of forts some two miles in extent, zigzag in form, with angles, salients, bastions, casemates, and everthing that properly belongs to works of this kind. The strength and advantages of this position at Manassas are very much increased by the fact that 14 miles further on is a position of similar formation, while the country between is admirably adapted to the subsistence and intrenchment of troop in numbers as large as they can easily be manoeuvred on the real battle-field. Water is good and abundant, forage such as is everywhere found in the rich farming districts of Virginia, and the communication with all parts of the country easy. Here, overlooking an extensive plain, watered by mountain streams which ultimately find their way to the Potomac, and divided into verdant fields of wheat, and oats, and corn, pasture and meadow, are the headquarters of the advanced forces of the army of the Potomac. They are South Carolinians, Louisianians, Alabamians, Mississippians, and Virginians, for the most part; the first two, singular enough, being in front, and that they will keep it their friends at home may rest assured. Never have I seen a finer body of men—men who were more obedient to discipline, or breathed a more self-sacrificing patriotism. As might be expected from the skill with which he has chosen his position, and the system with which he encamps and moves his men, General Beauregard is very popular here. I doubt if Napoleon himself had more the undivided confidence of his army. By nature, as also from a wise policy, he is very reticent. Not an individual here knows his plans or a single move of a regiment before it is made, and then only the colonel and his men know where it goes to. There is not a man here who can give anything like a satisfactory answer how many men he has, or where his exact lines are. For the distance of 14 miles around you see tents everywhere, and from them you can make a rough estimate of his men; but how many more are encamped on the by-roads and in the forests none can tell. The new-comer, from what he sees at first glance, puts down the numbers at about 30,000 men; those who have been here longest estimate his force at 40,000, 50,000 and some even at 60,000 strong. And there is the same discrepancy as to the quantity of his artillery. So close does the General keep his affairs to himself that his left hand hardly knows what his right hand doeth, and so jealous is he of this prerogative of a commanding officer that I verily believe, if he suspected his coat of any acquaintance with the plans revolving within him, he would cast it off."

It was noon when we arrived at Fairfax Courthouse—a poor village of some 30 or 40 straggling wooden and brick houses, deriving its name from the building in which the Circuit Court of the county is held, I believe, and looking the reverse of flourishing—and one may remark, *obiter*, that the state of this part of Virginia cannot be very prosperous, inasmuch as there was not a village along the road up to this point, and no shops or depôts, only one mill, one blacksmith and wheelwright. The village was held by a part of the reserve of M'Dowell's force, possibly 1,000 strong. The inhabitants were, if eyes spoke truth, Secessionists to a man, woman, and child, and even the negroes looked extra black, as if they did not care about being fought for. A short way beyond this village, Germantown, the scene of the recent excesses of the Federalists, afforded evidence in its blackened ruins that General M'Dowell's censure was more than needed. Let me interpolate it if it be only to show that General Beauregard and his rival are at least equal in point of literary power as masters of the English tongue:—

"Head-quarters Department of Virginia,
Fairfax Court-house, July 18.

"GENERAL ORDERS, No. 18.

"It is with the deepest mortification the General Commanding finds it necessary to reiterate his orders for the preservation of the property of the inhabitants of the district occupied by the troops under his command. Hardly had we arrived at this place, when, to the horror of every right-minded person, several houses were broken open, and others were in flames, by the act of some of those who, it has been the boast of the loyal, came here to protect the oppressed and free the country from the domination of a hated party. The property of this people is at the mercy of troops who, we rightly say, are the most intelligent, best educated, and most law-abiding of any that ever were under arms. But do not, therefore, the acts of yesterday cast the deepest stain upon them? It was claimed by some that their particular corps were not engaged in these acts. This is of but little moment; since the individuals are not found out, we are all alike disgraced. Commanders of regiments will select a commissioned officer as a provost marshal, and ten men as a police force under him, whose special and sole duty it shall be to preserve the property from depredations, and to arrest all wrongdoers of whatever regiment or corps they may be. Any one found committing the slightest depredation, killing pigs or poultry, or trespassing on the property of the inhabitants, will be reported to head-quarters, and the least that will done to them will be to send them to the Alexandria gaol. It is again ordered that no one shall arrest, or attempt to arrest, any citizen not in arms at the time, or search or attempt to search any house, or even to enter the same without permission. The troops must behave themselves with as much forbearance and propriety as if they were at their own homes. They are here to fight the enemies of the country, not to judge and punish the unarmed and defenceless, however guilty they may be. When necessary, that will be done by the proper person.

"By command of General M'Dowell

JAMES B. FRY, Assistant-Adjutant-General."

The chimney stacks being of brick are the sole remains of the few good houses in the village. Here our driver made a mistake, which was the rather persisted in that a coloured chattel informed us we could get to Centreville by the route we were pursuing, instead of turning back to Germantown, as we should have done. Centreville was still seven miles ahead. The guns sounded, however, heavily from the valleys. Rising above the forest tops appeared the blue masses of the Alleghanies, and we knew Manassas was somewhere on an outlying open of the ridges, which reminded me in colour and form of the hills around the valley of Baidar. A Virginian who came out of a cottage, and who was assuredly no descendant of Madame Esmond, told us that we were "going wrong right away." There was, he admitted, a by-road somewhere to the left front, but people who had tried its depths had returned to Germantown with the conviction that it led to any place but Centreville. Our driver, however, wished to try "if there were no Sechesers about?" "What did you say?" quoth the Virginian. "I want to know if there are any Secessionists there." "Secessionists!" (in a violent surprise, as if he had heard of them for the first time in his life) "No Sir-ree! Secessionists, indeed!" And all this time Beauregard and Lee were pounding away on our left front some six or seven miles off. The horses retraced their steps, the coloured youth who bestrode my charger complaining that the mysterious arrangement which condemns his race to slavery was very much abraded by the action of that spirited quadruped, combined or rather at variance with the callosities of the English saddle. From Germantown onwards by the right road there was nothing very remarkable. At one place a group of soldiers were buying "Secession money" from some negroes, who looked as if they could afford to part with it as cheaply as men do who are dealing with other people's property. Buggies and waggons (Anglicé, carriages) with cargoes of senators were overtaken. The store carts became more numerous. At last Centreville appeared in sight—a few houses on our front, beyond which rose a bald hill, the slopes covered with bivouac huts, commissariat carts, and horses, and the top crested with spectators of the fight.The road on each side was full of traces of Confederate camps; the houses were now all occupied by Federalists. In the rear of the hill was a strong body of infantry—two regiments of foreigners, mostly Germans, with a battery of light artillery. Our buggy was driven up to the top of the hill. The coloured boy was despatched to the village to look for a place to shelter the horses while they were taking a much required feed, and to procure, if possible, a meal for himself and the driver. On the hill there were carriages and vehicles drawn up as if they were attending a small country race. They were afterwards engaged in a race of another kind. In one was a lady with an opera glass; in and around and on others were legislators and politicians. There were also a few civilians on horseback, and on the slope of the hill a regiment had stacked arms, and was engaged in looking at and commenting on the battle below. The landscape in front was open to the sight as far as the ranges of the Alleghanies, which swept round from the right in blue mounds, the colour of which softened into violet in the distance. On the left the view was circumscribed by a wood, which receded along the side of the hill on which we stood to the plain below.

Between the base of this hill, which rose about 150ft. above the general level of the country, and the foot of the lowest and nearest elevation of the opposite Alleghanies extended about five miles, as well as I could judge, of a densely-wooded country, dotted at intervals with green fields and patches of cleared lands. It was marked by easy longitudinal undulations, indicated by the form of the forests which clothed them, and between two of the more considerable ran small streams, or 'runs,' as they are denominated, from the right to the left. Close at hand a narrow road, descending the hill, went straight into the forest, where it was visible now and then among the trees in cream-coloured patches. This road was filled with commissariat waggons, the white tops of which were visible for two miles in our front.

On our left front a gap in the lowest chain of the hills showed the gap of Manassas, and to the left and nearer to us lay the 'Junction' of the same name, where the Alexandria Railway unites with the rail from the west of Virginia, and continues the route by rails of various denominations to Richmond. The scene was so peaceful a man might well doubt the evidence of one sense that a great contest was being played out below in bloodshed, or imagine, as Mr. Seward sometimes does, that it was a delusion when he wakes in the morning and finds there is civil war upon him. But the cannon spoke out loudly from the green bushes, and the plains below were mottled, so to speak, by puffs of smoke and by white rings from bursting shells and capricious howitzers. It was no review that was going on beneath us. The shells gave proof enough of that, though the rush of the shot could not be heard at the distance. Clouds of dust came up in regular lines through the tree-tops where infantry were acting, and now and then their wavering mists of light blue smoke curled up, and the splutter of musketry broke through the booming of the guns. With the glass I could detect now and then the flash of arms through the dust clouds in the open, but no one could tell to which side the troops who were moving belonged, and I could only judge from the smoke whether the guns were fired towards or away from the hill. It was evident that the dust in the distance on our right extended beyond that which rose from the Federalists. The view towards the left, as I have said, was interrupted, but the firing was rather more heavy there than on the front or right flank, and a glade was pointed out in the forest as the beginning of Bull's or Poole's Run, on the other side of which the Confederates were hid in force, though they had not made any specific reply to the shells thrown into their cover early in the morning. There seemed to be a continuous line, which was held by the enemy, from which came steady solid firing against what might be supposed to be heads of columns stationed at various points or advancing against them. It was necessary to feed the horses and give them some rest after a hot drive of some 26 or 27 miles, or I would have proceeded at once to the front. As I was watching the faces of the Senators and Congressmen, I thought I had heard or read of such a scene as this—but there was much more to come. The soldiers who followed each shot with remarks in English or German were not as eager as men generally are in watching a fight. Once, as a cloud of thick smoke ascended from the trees, a man shouted out "That's good; we've taken another battery; there goes the magazine." But it looked like and I believe was the explosion of a caisson. In the midst of our little reconnaissance Mr. Vizetelly, who has been living and, indeed, marching with one of the regiments as artist of the *Illustrated London News,* came up and told us the action had been commenced in splendid style by the Federalists, who had advanced steadily, driving the Confederates before them—a part of the plan, as I firmly believe, to bring them under the range of their guns. He believed the advantages on the Federalist side were decided, though won with hard fighting, and he had just come up to Centreville to look after something to eat and drink, and to procure little necessaries, in case of need, for his comrades. His walk very probably saved his life. Having seen all that could be discerned through our glasses, my friend and myself had made a feast on our sandwiches in the shade of the buggy; my horse was eating and resting, and I was forced to give him half an hour or more before I mounted, and meantime tried to make out the plan of battle, but all was obscure and dark. Suddenly up rode an officer, with a crowd of soldiers after him, from the village. "We've whipped them on all points!" he shouted, "We've taken their batteries, and they're all retreating!" Such an uproar as followed. The spectators and the men cheered again and again, amid cries of "Bravo!" "Bully for us!" "Didn't I tell you so?" and guttural "hochs" from the

Deutschland folk and loud "hurroos" from the Irish. Soon afterwards my horse was brought up to the hill, and my friend and the gentleman I have already mentioned set out to walk towards the front—the latter to rejoin his regiment if possible, the former to get a closer view of the proceedings. As I turned down into the narrow road, or lane, already mentioned, there was a forward movement among the large four-wheeled tilt waggons, which raised a good deal of dust. My attention was particularly called to this by the occurrence of a few minutes afterwards. I had met my friends on the road, and after a few words rode forward at a long trot as well as I could past the waggons and through the dust, when suddenly there arose a tumult in front of me at a small bridge across the road, and then I perceived the drivers of a set of waggons with the horses turned towards me, who were endeavouring to force their way against the stream of vehicles setting in the other direction. By the side of the new set of waggons there were a number of commissariat men and soldiers, whom at first sight I took to be the baggage guard. They looked excited and alarmed, and were running by the side of the horses—in front the dust quite obscured the view. At the bridge the currents met in wild disorder. "Turn back! Retreat!" shouted the men from the front, "We're whipped, we're whipped!" They cursed and tugged at the horses' heads, and struggled with frenzy to get past. Running by me on foot was a man with the shoulder-straps of an officer. "Pray what is the matter, Sir?" "It means we're pretty badly whipped, and that's a fact," he blurted out in puffs, and continued his career. I observed that he carried no sword. The teamsters of the advancing waggons now caught up the cry. "Turn back—turn your horses" was the shout up the whole line, and, backing, plunging, rearing, and kicking, the horses which had been proceeding down the road reversed front and went off towards Centreville. Those behind them went madly rushing on, the drivers being quite indifferent whether glory or disgrace led the way, provided they could find it. In the midst of this extraordinary spectacle an officer, escorted by some dragoons, rode through the ruck with a light cart in charge. Another officer on foot, with his sword under his arm, ran up against me. "What is all this about?" "Why we're pretty badly whipped. We're all in retreat. There's General Tyler there badly wounded." And on he ran. There came yet another, who said, "We're beaten on all points. The whole army is

27

in retreat." Still there was no flight of troops, no retreat of an army, no reason for all this precipitation. True, there were many men in uniform flying towards the rear, but it did not appear as if they were beyond the proportions of a large baggage escort. I got my horse up into the field out of the road, and went on rapidly towards the front. Soon I met soldiers who were coming through the corn, mostly without arms; and presently I saw firelocks, cooking tins, knapsacks, and greatcoats on the ground, and observed that the confusion and speed of the baggage-carts became greater, and that many of them were crowded with men, or were followed by others, who clung to them. The ambulances were crowded with soldiers, but it did not look as if there were many wounded. Negro servants on led horses dashed frantically past; men in uniform, whom it were a disgrace to the profession of arms to call "soldiers," swarmed by on mules, chargers, and even draught horses, which had been cut out of carts or waggons, and went on with harness clinging to their heels, as frightened as their riders. Men literally screamed with rage and fright when their way was blocked up. On I rode, asking all "What is all this about?" and now and then, but rarely, receiving the answer, "We're whipped;" or, "We're repulsed." Faces black and dusty, tongues out in the heat, eyes staring—it was a most wonderful sight. On they came like him—

> —who having once turned round goes on,
> And turns no more his head,
> For he knoweth that a fearful fiend
> Doth close behind him tread.

But where was the fiend? I looked in vain. There was, indeed, some cannonading in front of me and in their rear, but still the firing was comparatively distant, and the runaways were far out of range. As I advanced the number of carts diminished, but the mounted men increased, and the column of fugitives became denser. A few buggies and light waggons filled with men, whose faces would have made up "a great Leporello" in the ghost scene, tried to pierce the rear of the mass of carts, which were now solidified and moving on like a glacier. I crossed a small ditch by the roadside, got out on the road to escape some snake fences, and, looking before me, saw there was still a crowd of men in uniforms coming along. The road was strewn with articles of clothing—firelocks, waist-belts, cartouch-boxes, caps, great coats, mess-tins, musical instruments, cartridges, bayonets and sheaths, swords and pistols—even biscuits, water-bottles, and pieces of meat. Passing a white house by the road-side, I saw, for the first time, a body of infantry with sloped arms-marching regularly and rapidly towards me. Their faces were not blackened by powder, and it was evident they had not been engaged. In reply to a question a non-commissioned officer told me in broken English, "We fall back to our lines. The attack did not quite succeed." This was assuring to one who had come through such a scene as I had been witnessing. I had ridden, I suppose about three or three and a-half miles from the hill, though it is not possible to be sure of the distance; when, having passed the white house, I came out on an open piece of ground, beyond and circling which was forest. Two field pieces were unlimbered and guarding the road; the panting and jaded horses in the rear looked as though they had been hard worked, and the gunners and drivers looked worn and dejected. Dropping shots sounded close in front through the woods; but the guns on the left no longer maintained their fire. I was just about to ask one of the men for a light, when a sputtering fire on my right attracted my attention, and out of the forest or along the road rushed a number of men. The gunners seized the trail of the nearest piece to wheel it round upon them; others made for the tumbrils and horses as if to fly, when a shout was raised, "Don't fire; they're our own men;" and in a few minutes on came pell-mell a whole regiment in disorder. I rode across one and stopped him. "We're pursued by cavalry," he gasped; "They've cut us all to pieces." As he spoke a shell burst over the column; another dropped on the road, and out streamed another column of men, keeping together with their arms, and closing up the stragglers of the first regiment. I turned, and to my surprise saw the artillerymen had gone off, leaving one gun standing by itself. They had retreated with horses. While we were on the hill I had observed and pointed out to my companions a cloud of dust which rose through the trees on our right front. In my present position that place must have been on the right rear, and it occurred to me that after all there really might be a body of cavalry in that direction, but Murat himself would not have charged these waggons in that deep, well fenced lane. If the dust came, as I believe it did, from field artillery, that would be a different matter. Any way it was now well established that the retreat had really commenced, though I saw but few wounded men, and the regiments which were falling back had not

29

suffered much loss. No one seemed to know anything for certain. Even the cavalry charge was a rumour. Several officers said they had carried guns and lines, but then they drifted into the nonsense which one reads and hears everywhere about "masked batteries." One or two talked more sensibly about the strong positions of the enemy, the fatigue of their men, the want of a reserve, severe losses, and the bad conduct of certain regiments. Not one spoke as if he thought of retiring beyond Centreville. The clouds of dust rising above the woods marked the retreat of the whole army, and the crowds of fugitives continued to steal away along the road. The sun was declining, and some 30 miles yet remained to be accomplished ere I could hope to gain the shelter of Washington. No one knew whither any corps or regiment was marching, but there were rumours of all kinds—"The 69th are cut to pieces;" "The Fire Zouaves are destroyed," and so on. Presently a tremor ran through the men by whom I was riding, as the sharp reports of some field-pieces rattled through the wood close at hand. A sort of subdued roar, like the voice of distant breakers, rose in front of us, and the soldiers, who were, I think, Germans, broke into a double, looking now and then over their shoulders. There was no choice for me but to resign any further researches. The mail from Washington for the Wednesday steamer at Boston leaves at 2.30 on Monday, and so I put my horse into a trot, keeping in the fields alongside the roads as much as I could, to avoid the fugitives, till I came once more on the rear of the baggage and store carts, and the pressure of the crowd, who, conscious of the aid which the vehicles would afford them against a cavalry charge, and fearful, nevertheless, of their proximity, clamoured and shouted like madmen as they ran. The road was now literally covered with baggage. It seemed to me as if the men inside were throwing the things out purposely. "Stop," cried I to the driver of one of the carts, "everthing is falling out." "— you," shouted a fellow inside, "if you stop him I'll blow your brains out." My attempts to save Uncle Sam's property were then and there discontinued. On approaching Centreville a body of German infantry of the reserve came marching down and stemmed the current in some degree; they were followed by a brigade of guns and another battalion of fresh troops. I turned up on the hill half a mile beyond. The vehicles had all left but two—my buggy was gone. A battery of field guns was in position where we had been standing. The men looked well. As yet there was nothing to indicate more than a retreat and some ill-behaviour among the waggoners and the riffraff of different regiments. Centreville was not a bad position properly occupied, and I saw no reason why it should not be held if it was meant to renew the attack, nor any reason why the attack should not be renewed, if there had been any reason why it should have been made. I swept the field once more. The clouds of dust were denser and nearer. That was all. There was no firing—no musketry. I turned my horse's head, and rode away through the village, and after I got out upon the road the same confusion seemed to prevail. Suddenly the guns on the hill opened, and at the same time came the thuds of artillery from the wood on the right rear. The stampede then became general. What occurred at the hill I cannot say, but all the road from Centreville for miles presented such a sight as can only be witnessed in the track of the runaways of an utterly demoralized army. Drivers flogged, lashed, spurred, and beat their horses, or leaped down and abandoned their teams, and ran by the side of the road; mounted men, servants, and men in uniform, vehicles of all sorts, commissariat waggons thronged the narrow ways. At every shot a convulsion as it were seized upon the morbid mass of bones, sinew, wood, and iron, and thrilled through it, giving new energy and action to its desperate efforts to get free from itself. Again the cry of "Cavalry" arose. "What are you afraid of?" said I to a man who was running beside me. "I'm not afraid of you," replied the ruffian, levelling his piece at me and pulling the trigger. It was not loaded or the cap was not on, for the gun did not go off. I was unarmed, and I did go off as fast I could, resolved to keep my own counsel for the second time that day. And so the flight went on. At one time a whole mass of infantry, with fixed bayonets, ran down the bank of the road, and some falling as they ran must have killed and wounded those among whom they fell. As I knew the road would soon become impassable or blocked up, I put my horse to a gallop and passed on towards the front. But mounted men still rode faster, shouting out, "Cavalry are coming." Again I ventured to speak to some officers whom I overtook, and said, "If these runaways are not stopped the whole of the posts and pickets into Washington will fly also!" One of them, without saying a word, spurred his horse and dashed on in front. I do not know whether he ordered the movement or not, but the van of the fugitives was now suddenly checked, and, pressing on through the wood at the roadside, I saw a regiment of infantry blocking up the way, with their front towards Centreville. A musket was levelled at my head as I pushed to the front:—"Stop, or I'll fire." At the same time the officers were shouting out, "Don't let a soul pass." I addressed one of them and said, "Sir! I am a British subject, I am not, I assure you, running away. I have done my best to stop this disgraceful rout (as I had) and have been telling them there are no cavalry within miles of them." "I can't let you pass, Sir!" I bethought me of General Scott's pass. The adjutant read it, and the word was given along the line, "Let that man pass!" and so I rode through, uncertain if I could now gain the Long-bridge in time to pass over without the countersign. It was about this time I met a cart by the roadside surrounded by a group of soldiers some of whom had "69" on their caps. The owner, as I took him to be, was in great distress, and cried out as I passed, "Can you tell me, Sir, where the 69th are? These men say they are cut to pieces." "I can't tell you." "I'm in charge of the mails, Sir, and I will deliver them if I die for it. You are a gentleman and I can depend on your word. Is it safe for me to go on?" Not knowing the extent of the *débâcle*, I assured him it was, and asked the men of the regiment how they happened to be there, "Shure, the Colonel himself told us to go off every man on his own hook, and to fly for our lives," replied one of them. The mail agent, who told me he was an Englishman, started the cart again. I sincerely hope no bad result to himself or his charge followed my advice. I reached Fairfax Court-house; the people, black and white, with anxious faces, were at the doors, and the infantry were under arms. I was besieged with questions, though hundreds of fugitives had passed through before me. At one house I stopped to ask for water for my horse; the owner sent his servant for it cheerfully, the very house where we had in vain asked for something to eat in the forenoon. "There's a fright among them," I observed, in reply to his question respecting the commissariat drivers. "They're afraid of the enemy's cavalry." "Are you an American?" said the man. "No, I am not." "Well, then," he said, "there will be cavalry on them soon enough. There's 20,000 of the best horsemen in the world in Virginny!" Washington was still 18 miles away. The road was rough and uncertain, and again my poor steed was under way; but it was no use trying to outstrip the runaways. Once or twice I imagined I heard guns in the rear, but I could not be sure of it in consequence of the roar of the flight behind me. It was most surprising to see how far the foot soldiers had contrived to get on in advance. After sunset the moon rose, and amid other acquaintances I jogged alongside an officer who was in charge of Colonel Hunter, the commander of a brigade, I believe, who was shot through the neck, and was inside a cart, escorted by a few troopers. This officer was, as I understood, the major or second in command of Colonel Hunter's regiment, yet he had considered it right to take charge of his chief, and to leave his battalion. He said they had driven back the enemy with ease, but had not been supported, and blamed—as bad officers and good ones will do—the conduct of the General:—"So mean a fight I never saw." I was reminded of a Crimean General who made us all merry by saying after the first bombardment, "In the whole course of my experience I never saw a siege conducted on such principles as these." Our friend had been without food, but not, I suspect, without drink—and that, we know, affects empty stomachs very much—since 2 o'clock that morning. Now, what is to be thought of an officer—gallant, he may be, as steel—who says, as I heard this gentleman say to a picket who asked him how the day went in front, "Well, we've been licked into a cocked hat; knocked to —." This was his cry to teamsters, escorts, convoys, the officers, and men on guard and detachment, while I, ignorant of the disaster behind, tried to mollify the effect of the news by adding "Oh, it's a drawn battle. The troops are re-occupying the position from which they started in the morning." Perhaps he knew his troops better than I did. It was a strange ride through a country now still as death, the white road shining like a river in the moonlight, the trees black as ebony in the shade; now and then a figure flitting by into the forest or across the road—frightened friend or lurking foe, who could say? Then the anxious pickets and sentries all asking, "What's the news?" and evidently prepared for any amount of loss. Twice or thrice we lost our way, or our certainty about it, and shouted at isolated houses and received no reply, except from angry watch dogs. Then we were set right as we approached Washington by teamsters.

For an hour, however, we seemed to be travelling along a road which in all its points far and near was "12 miles from the Long-bridge". Up hills, down into valleys, with the silent grim wood for ever by our sides. Now and then in the profound gloom, broken only by a spark from the horse's hoof, came a dull but familiar sound like the shutting of a distant door. As I approached Washington, having left the colonel and his escort at some seven miles on the south side of the Long-bridge, I found the grand guards, pickets' posts, and individual sentries burning for news, and the word used to pass along "What does that man say, Jack?" "Begorra, he tells me we're not het at all—only retraiting to the ould lines for convaniency of fighting to-morrow again. Oh, that's iligant!" On getting to the *tête de pont*, however, the countersign was demanded; of course, I had not got it. But the officer passed me through on the production of General Scott's safeguard. The lights of the city were in sight and reflected on the waters of the Potomac, just glistened by the clouded moon, shone the gay lamps of the White House, where the President was probably entertaining some friends. In silence I passed over the Long-bridge. Some few hours later it quivered under the steps of a rabble of unarmed men. At the Washington end a regiment with piled arms were waiting to cross over into Virginia, singing and cheering. Before the morning they received orders, I believe, to assist in keeping Maryland quiet. For the hundredth time I repeated the cautious account, which to the best of my knowledge was true. There were men, women, and soldiers to hear it. The clocks had just struck 11 p.m. as I passed Willard's. The pavement in front of the hall was crowded. The rumours of defeat had come in, but few of the many who had been fed upon lies and the reports of complete victory which prevailed could credit the intelligence. Seven hours had not elapsed before the streets told the story. The "Grand Army of the North", as it was called, had representatives in every thoroughfare, without arms, orders, or officers, standing out in the drenching rain. When all these most unaccountable phenomena were occurring I was fast asleep, but I could scarce credit my informant in the morning, when he told me that the Federalists, utterly routed, had fallen back upon Arlington to defend the capital, leaving nearly five batteries of artillery, 8,000 muskets, immense quantity of stores and baggage, and their wounded and prisoners in the hands of the enemy!

Let the American journals tell the story their own way. I have told mine as I know it. It has rained incessantly and heavily since early morning, and the country must be unfit for operations; otherwise, if Mr. Davies desired to press his advantage, he might now be very close to Arlington Heights. He has already proved that he has a fair right to be considered the head of a "belligerent *power.*" But, though the North may reel under the shock, I cannot think it will make her desist from the struggle, unless it be speedily followed by blows more deadly even than the repulse from Manassas. There is much talk now (of "masked batteries," of course) of outflanking, and cavalry, and such matters. The truth seems to be that the men were overworked, kept out for 12 or 14 hours in the sun exposed to long-range fire, badly officered, and of deficient regimental organization. Then came a most difficult operation—to withdraw this army, so constituted, out of action in face of an energetic enemy who had repulsed it. The retirement of the baggage, which was without adequate guards, and was in the hands of ignorant drivers, was misunderstood and created alarm, and that alarm became a panic, which became frantic on the appearance of the enemy and on the opening of their guns on the runaways. But the North will be all the more eager to retrieve this disaster, although it may divert her from the scheme, which has been suggested to her, of punishing England a little while longer. The exultation of the South can only be understood by those who may see it, and if the Federal Government perseveres in its design to make Union by force it may prepare for a struggle the result of which will leave the Union very little to fight for. More of the "battle" in my next. I pity the public across the water, but they must be the victims of hallucinations and myths it is out of my power to dispel or rectify just now. Having told so long a story, I can scarcely expect your readers to have patience, and go back upon the usual diary of events; but the records, such as they are, of this extraordinary repulse must command attention. It is impossible to exaggerate their importance. No man can predict the results or pretend to guess at them.

According to the Saturday Review *in 1858, 'the compilers of the City articles [in* The Times] *would have commanded the respect of Adam Smith.' Their master spirit throughout this period was M. B. Sampson, in whom Delane reposed an absolute trust, to the extent of giving him an absolutely free hand. In the end (1875) he abused his trust by involving himself and the paper in a murky City scandal. But no-one ever questioned his ability. He must have passed, when he had not written, all the copy about American affairs that appeared on the City page during the Civil War; but his assistant, a Mr. Page, who was an authority on the price of gold and the currency, presumably had a lot to do with the endless stream of unfavourable comment on American monetary policies.*

November 28th, 1861 *page 7*

MONEY-MARKET & CITY INTELLIGENCE

WEDNESDAY EVENING.

The news of the aggression upon the Royal Mail Company's steamer Trent by the United States' ship of war San Jacinto produced an indescribable effect in the city this morning. It transpired about the middle of the day, up to which time the English funds had shown great buoyancy, and after a few moments, during which it was deemed almost incredible, the result on the funds was a fall of one per cent. From this there was a rally of nearly a-half per cent., but the market closed with a very unsettled appearance, although the precise details of the act, which are calculated to increase to an intense point the feelings with which it will be regarded, had not up to that hour been published. The opening quotation of Consols for the account was 92⅝ ex dividend, at which there were afterwards buyers. At 1 o'clock the notice from the Royal Mail Company began to circulate, and a rapid fall ensued to 91⅝. An impression was then encouraged that the particulars of the transaction would, on their receipt, probably show some features of mitigation, and, as several of the parties by whom speculative sales had been effected were disposed to realize their profit, a recovery ensued to 92 to ⅛. A large portion of the public, however, continued to regard the act in the worst light, as a confirmation of the indications so long given by Mr. Seward of his desire to involve this country in a collision at any cost. Nevertheless, an unanimous confidence is expressed that our Government on this, as on former occasions, will maintain the national dignity too well to be betrayed into irritation, and will pursue with the most literal exactitude whatever course may be indicated by the precedents of international law and the natural rules for the

36

comity of nations. Although no one in the city to-day has been able to conceive it possible for any United States warrant to be served on board a British ship for the capture of peaceable passengers not charged with any recognized crime, the Cabinet will be fully supported even in tolerating that act, provided it can be shown to be in conformity with the reciprocal law between the two nations, or the nations of the world generally. On the other hand, should the proceeding be found unquestionably illegal, there will be no limit to the energy with which the country will respond to the demand for the requisite means for obtaining instant satis-faction, and upholding the common principles that regulate and render possible the intercourse of mankind. Bank Stock closed at 231 to 233; Reduced and New Three per Cents., $91\frac{3}{8}$ to $\frac{7}{8}$; India Stock, 226 to 228; India Five per Cents., $99\frac{1}{4}$ and $185\frac{1}{4}$; India Bonds, 12s. to 10s. premium; and Exchequer-bills (March), 7s. to 11s., (June), 10s. to 15s. premium.

The Liverpool cotton-market this afternoon closed in the midst of great uncertainty and agitation, the possibility of events that may lead to a speedy raising of the present imperfect block-ade of the cotton ports being among the contingencies recognized by the operators.

Great attention has been aroused in Mincing-lane to-day by the fact of the news of the attack on the Trent having arrived at a period when the market for saltpetre had been singularly affected by some recent transactions on American account. Since Friday last about 8,000 tons of saltpetre have been purchased on terms which have caused a rise of from 36s. to 40s. per cwt. This quantity is about equal to the entire stock in London and, as there was nothing in the position of the article to lead to the expectation of any particular movement, the affair caused sur-prise and curiosity. The buyers gave out that, enormous as the quantity was, no portion of it was likely to be thrown back upon the market, and it now appears that they were acting for the Federal Government. As the whole could not be procured on the spot, a portion had to be bought for arrival; but the greatest urgency has been manifested to obtain immediate delivery of as much as possible, and about 1,000 tons are understood to be at this moment loading from London, while shipments are likewise being hurried off from Liverpool. Meanwhile a further advance has occurred, and the price now asked is 43s. Looking at the state of affairs now known, the remark this afternoon has been that such a sudden and, under ordinary circumstances, improvident mode of buying seems to denote that the intention of offering an outrage to England, such as might render it difficult to obtain supplies hereafter, was the cause of the hasty despatch of this extraordinary order. Under any circumstances it is now assumed to be likely that the British Government will summarily prohibit the clearance of such contraband of war. It has also become known that for several months past large quantities of rifles and other fire-arms, amounting to some hundred thousand, have been shipped hence to the United States under the designation "hardware," and that the business is still going on. Henceforth, however, the public will not be satisfied unless the most stringent measures are taken to prevent this breach of neutrality in favour of the Northern belligerents.

At Lloyd's to-day, in consequence of the news by La Plata, war risks of five guineas were demanded on vessels from New York.

The Trent is one of the steamers employed by the Royal Mail Company in their Mexican and intercolonial service, and at the time of her stoppage was on the way to St. Thomas, to transfer her passengers and freight to la Plata, for England. She is registered 1,856 tons, with 439-horse power.

The foreign stock-market this morning was rather dull at the opening, and on the announcement of the American news a general decline took place, from which there was only a partial recovery. . . .

December 14th, 1861   *page 7*

TO THE EDITOR OF THE TIMES

Sir,—The intimation in yesterday's *Times* of "a yearning in this country after" American views upon the new complication of our relations with England, followed this morning by relaxing and even kindlier strictures, tempts me to submit briefly some thoughts which an occurence profoundly embarrassing suggest; not, however, upon "international law," for, as an humble journalist, I have been accustomed only to the common-sense interpretations of public questions; and, were I at all qualified to enter into the legal argument, I should be inclined to accept your own view of the question—viz., that time and circumstances have so far changed the practice and reformed the principles of international maritime law as to render the earlier precedents and authorities largely inapplicable to existing cases; and, further, while the concession, in proving my candour may impeach my patriotism, I am constrained to admit that in the ventilation of the Laurens seizure, as cited by Mr. George Sumner, the bottom has fallen out of our strongest precedent.

Dismissing, therefore, the legal considerations of the Trent and San Jacinto question, I confess to a very strong "yearning" that the English Government, its press, and its people, may be disabused of an impression which has so generally obtained, that our Government seeks occasions for disagreement, or cherishes other than such feelings as belong to the relations of interest and amity that blend and bind us together. I am even less surprised at the belligerent sensibility which the Trent affair has awakened here, than with the pervading antecedent impression that our Government entertains hostile purposes towards England, and that our Secretary of State has actually designed the disruption of relations which I had supposed, and still believe, almost universally regarded as essential to the welfare of our country and the happiness of our people.

An alleged conversation of Secretary Seward with the Duke of Newcastle, referred to in *The Times*, conflicts with these assurances. Without precise information as to the language used by Mr. Seward, I cannot be mistaken in assuming that its spirit was misapprehended. The conversation occurred, I believe at a dinner given by Governor Morgan to the Prince of Wales. The avowal of a prominent senator, who had reason to suppose that he might be called to a more responsible position in the Government, of a deliberate intention to "*insult your* (the Duke's) *Government*," could not but have been highly offensive. But while I can readily excuse an English nobleman for misinterpreting idle or "loose talk" in an American statesman, to all Americans the *badinage* of Mr. Seward would have been readily understood. Perhaps it would have been wiser not to attempt to "play with edged tools." Indeed, from the mischief an attempted pleasantry has occasioned, any departure from the gravities of conversation is certainly to be regretted. After disclaiming, as I feel quite authorized in doing, for Mr. Seward, unfriendly intentions and feelings towards England, I beg to refer such

English gentlemen as have acquaintance with, or opportunities for consulting, Mr. Adams, our resident Minister, for a true reflex of American sentiment and sympathies. That distinguished statesman, whose eminent father and grandfather at different epochs represented our country—first at the Court of St. James's, and subsequently as President of the United States,—enjoys, in the best and broadest sense of the term, the confidence of his Government; and, resigning his seat in Congress to assume diplomatic responsibilities, he is also familiar with the views and feelings of our public men.

Until I saw the accusation against Secretary Seward standing out prominently in the London press the idea had not entered my mind, nor can I now persuade myself that it has any real foundation to stand upon. After the settlement of the Maine and Vancouver boundary questions, in their final action upon both of which the course of the English Government was characterized by enlightened justice and wisdom, I had supposed that no cause of misunderstanding remained, and that we might look forward to a long period of exemption from conflict or dissension. Subsequently incidental occasions for interchanges of national courtesies occurred calculated and tending to confirm and strengthen feelings of good will. These were succeeded by that memorable visit of the Prince of Wales, whose advent among us afforded to the American people an opportunity to mark, in heartfelt ovations, both their regard for the future monarch of Great Britain and their high estimate of, and their personal admiration for, a *Queen* whose eventful and illustrious reign, in advancing civilization, in promoting public and private virtue, and in hallowing household shrines, will enrich the archives and brighten the pages of England's history. I often thought, while witnessing, as I did, in several of our cities, the spontaneous demonstrations of unmistakable regard from hundreds of thousands of hearts warmed by remembrances of Saxon descent, that if all England could be "there to see," we should thenceforth, as nations, dwell together in peace and friendship. In that triumphal journey, extending many thousand miles, through cities, towns, villages, hamlets, and wilderness, nothing occurred to jar its enjoyment. The American people, though enthusiastic, were considerate and respectful. The Prince, either from intuitive or inherited good sense and taste, while observing all the proprieties of his position, was so naturally gracious as to win nothing but "golden opinions," and to leave everywhere agreeable and enduring impressions; and even now, so universal is the homage of our people for the Queen, that were Her Majesty to deign us a visit, Earl Russell and Secretary Seward, were either or both of these eminent statesmen disposed to perpetrate a great national wrong, would find the bonds of affection stronger than ambition or strategy.

Upon the course which our Government shall deem wise or expedient in this abrupt emergency it is scarcely necessary to speculate. We shall not remain long in suspense. Nor could I add to the calm, well-considered views contained in the letter of Lieutenant-General Scott, in whom America has no more devoted patriot, nor England a more sincere friend. That distinguished and veteran General led our army creditably through one war with England. I, in humble positions, shared in that conflict; and I speak for both—enjoying the confidence and friendship of our great Chieftain—in saying that neither cares to survive another struggle so revolting to all who rejoice in a common ancestry and commingled blood, with kindred memorials and associations.

Of the exact nature of the despatch from the English Government I am ignorant; but, I am constrained to express the opinion, that if that despatch has taken the form of a peremptory demand it will be met by as peremptory a refusal; for in temper and pride we are as unreasoning as the bad examples of our mother country, absurdly intensified, can make us. But I devoutly hope that the mastiff mode of diplomacy will not, on either side, be resorted to. There are no real interests of either country to be promoted or protected by a contest for the championship. Nor is it necessary to determine questions of relative prowess or courage. The battle of Lundy's-lane, in Canada, fought upon a fair field, with forces nearly equal, which consigned the remains of 700 British and 700 American soldiers to "dead men's beds," should be accepted as a satisfactory solution by both nations. This Slidell and Mason *imbroglio*, which has been sprung upon us, places both Governments in false position. England is running upon all fours across the track of her lifelong practices and precepts, while America is forced, in maintaining the act of Com. Wilkes, to ignore a policy earnestly insisted upon—a policy which, at the conclusion of the war of 1812, was left to be determined by the future good sense and forbearance of both Governments. In this "muddle," should either nation be too tenacious? I do not say or think that in this matter we have done quite right, or that we are wholly wrong. The temptations in this case were far greater than can be understood abroad. Messrs. Slidell and Mason were responsible leaders in the unnatural and causeless rebellion which set brother against brother in fierce and brutish civil war. As senators in the Congress of the United States, while unanimous millions supposed men incapable of such perfidy, they committed acts of treason far more flagrant than the offences which have consigned the heads of British noblemen, through the Tower, to the block. It will require, therefore, calm deliberation and a large measure of forbearance in our Government and people to bring them to an acquiescence in the views taken of this question here—views which, I am compelled to admit, have obtained across the Channel.

But if events are not precipitated; if time is given for reflection, so that the cost and consequences of war may be calculated, my apprehensions would be greatly relieved. I quite concur with the *New York Tribune* in the opinion that these rebel emissaries are not worth a war, and, individually, would not hesitate to make large concessions, in feeling, for peace. With England whose canvass whitens every ocean and sea "catching the dawning rays of the rising and mellowed by the departing beams of the setting sun," the honour of her flag is everything. In defence of this flag England, with her blood heated, will not sacrifice the "avoirdupois of a hair." Surely, then, if appealed to in a neighbourly spirit we can afford to do for England what we should, touched in the same tender point, expect England to do for America.

Respectfully, your obedient servant,

THURLOW WEED.

London, Dec. 12.

It was all very well for Thurlow Weed (1797-1882) to describe himself as 'an humble journalist'; he was in fact one of the most successful journalists in America, and a leading Republican politician. He was one of the chief founders of the Whig Party, and W.H. Seward's closest political ally for over thirty years.

AN AMERICAN IN MANCHESTER

(From the Manchester Guardian.)[1]

The *Boston* (United States) *Daily Courier* publishes a diary penned by Mr. H. Adams, son of the American Minister in London, during a recent visit to this city. Mr. Adams came down to Manchester in November last for the purpose of ascertaining the feeling of our merchants and manufacturers on the American question. He was particularly anxious to know whether there was any disposition to urge the Government to break the Southern blockade in order to obtain cotton. On Friday, the 8th of November, he had interviews with several gentlemen, and thus sums up the result of his inquiries:—"So far as the cotton interests in Manchester are concerned, our Government will have two months more full swing over the South. At the end of that time a party will arise in favour of ending the war by recognizing the insurgents, and, if necessary, breaking the blockade or declaring it ineffective. The Radicals, the Indian and colonial interests, and some others, will oppose the step, and there will be a severe contest; all supposing that affairs on our side remain in about their present position." We may here state that he remarks, towards the close of his diary, that this conclusion was strengthened by all he subsequently heard.

On Saturday he renewed his inquiries, and he states the substance of a conversation he had with a member of a large spinning firm:—"I brought up the question of the blockade again, mentioning the fact that the belief in America was very general that England meant to break it, and that this belief had caused most of the irritation that existed there against England. It was the lowness of the motive that had disgusted us. He declared that the idea was ridiculous, and that no one contemplated it in the present position of affairs. But, then, if the war drags itself out indefinitely, to the loss and suffering of the rest of the world, and it becomes evident that neither party will yield, and that a settlement is hopeless, then an intervention may take place for the benefit of foreign nations and mankind. I remarked

[1] It was common practice for articles from provincial as well as American newspapers to be reprinted in *The Times*.

43

that this was a dangerous latitude to allow, when the same party who judged the cause was to profit by the decision. He went on, 'But such a latitude is a necessity. The world must, of course, have a right to decide where it considers its interests to over-balance those of a single nation. Suppose that the Southerners, instead of a partial monopoly of cotton, had a complete mono-poly of grain of all kinds, and the world were to be famished by the blockade, would not intervention be justifiable? Suppose that it was England, instead of the North, who maintained the block-ade, would not France interfere, and could England soberly blame her for doing so? There is no disposition in England to refuse to the Union a full and fair trial; but if, after what is evident to be such a trial, no step has been gained towards a settlement, foreign nations have a right to interfere, at least by a recognition of the South.' This is not to be denied, I believe, in law, and yet it practically leaves the whole question as unsettled as ever. 'Most Englishmen,' he stated, 'would, no doubt, prefer to see a separation accomplished, yet this neither implies sym-pathy with the South nor hostile measures towards the North. It is a mere matter of private opinion.' I assured him that on that point England was perfectly welcome to think what she liked. Her opinions were of no consequence to us, except as they indicated her actions. She had thought it her interest to weaken France and strengthen Austria, but instead of that it was Austria that was falling to pieces and France that was stronger than ever, and I saw no reason why her policy should be more successful in America than in Europe. He talked of the Surat cotton, and stated that since the cotton pressure had begun much more attention had been paid to it, and the spinners had been surprised to find how well it answered their purposes. He was confident that already, whatever might be the fate of the American crop, Indian cotton had obtained a position and a hold upon the market that it would not lose. Whatever might happen, the cotton trade never would go back to the old channels."

Again, we find Mr. Adams in conversation with "Mr. —, one of the M.P.'s for —," who gave him the strongest assurance of English sympathy with the North. "He assured me that he believed the feeling in Manchester to be one of sympathy with the Union, and of regret that the effort at dissolution had ever been made. He knew of no party in Manchester forming to bring about the infraction of the blockade by Great Britain, nor did he believe that such a party could be created here or elsewhere. On the contrary, he believed he might tell me that within a short time it had been proposed, among some of the men of position in the city, to make a public demonstration of sympathy with the North. The disposition was one of goodwill towards us. I replied that it was very agreeable to hear this statement on such good authority, and I was sure that any public declaration of good will would have a great effect in America, where precisely the contrary belief had been preached, until it was looked upon as a matter of fact, beyond a shadow of doubt, that Manchester was bitterly hostile to us. The conversation lasted about 15 minutes, and nothing could be more distinct than the statement which he made; nor do I know where to go for better authority on such a question."

Mr. Adams found a strong feeling in favour of Indian cotton, and he seems to have been satisfied that, rather than go to war for the purpose of obtaining the raw material from the Southern States of America, "the Radicals, the anti-slavery interest, and the colonies would unite in preferring a prohibitive duty" on slave-grown cotton—a measure which, in his opinion, would have the effect of bringing in supplies from all parts of the world. He adds:—"It cannot be doubted that if the blockade continues spring will find England nearly independent of America for this article, and we shall see the steady advance of a great revolution in the world's condition. Matters can never go back to where they were a year ago. Yet America can always compete with any country in the production of this staple, and no one wishes to see her unable to do so. All that is wanted is to open competition, and then the slave power may again be curbed to its due position in politics, while the shores of Africa may be made the scene of a new civilization, and India may rise again to her old wealth and glory. Some persons complain that such an event would be the ruin of the United States, that it would destroy the balance of trade, and make America hopelessly the debtor of Europe. Why this should be so does not appear. A nation, like a private person, is wealthy and prosperous, not in proportion to what it receives, but to what it spends. If our civil war has taught us one fact with certainty, it is this—that our imports may be cut down with safety, and even advantage, 100 millions of dollars. If our receipts from cotton were lowered 50 millions we might still be rich; but, though we exported cotton enough to pave our streets with gold, we should still be poor if we went on in that reckless extravagance which has already three times thrown the nation into bankruptcy."

Mr. Adams speaks of the objection of our manufacturers to a too curious inspection of their improved machinery; and in one mill he visited he found the operatives "dirty, very coarsely dressed, and very stupid in look—altogether much inferior to the American standard."

Of Manchester society he says:—"Manchester society seems to be much more like what one finds in American cities than like that of London. In Manchester, as in America, it seems to have fallen, or be falling, wholly into the hands of the young, unmarried people. In London the Court gives it dignity and tone, and the houses into which an admission is thought of most value are generally apt to slight dancing. In Manchester, I am told, it is still the fashion for the hosts to see that their guests enjoy themselves. In London the guests shift for themselves, and a stranger had better depart at once as soon as he has looked at the family pictures. In Manchester one is usually allowed a dressing-room at an evening party. In London a gentleman has to take his chance of going into the ball-room with his hair on end or his cravat untied. In Manchester it is still the fashion to finish balls with showy suppers, which form the great test of the evening. In London one is regaled with thimblefuls of ice-cream and hard seed-cakes. I presume the same or similar differences run through all the great provincial towns. London society is a distinct thing, which the provinces are sensible not to try to imitate."

January 9th, 1862 page 8

Twenty four hours after the Message from Washington which we reported yesterday the Cabinet of the Federal States' Government broke its silence, and the Old World is no longer at enmity with the New. In the afternoon of the 27th of December Lord Lyons received an announcement from the United States' Government that they consented to deliver to him the four prisoners when and where he pleased. We draw a long breath, and are thankful. The suspense which has endured so long, and has weighed so heavily upon our peaceful avocations, has at last terminated. We are once more able to subside from the bustle of preparation, to withdraw our attention from the mustering of squadrons and the equipment of vast engines of destruction, and to busy ourselves about our own domestic affairs. With a clear conscience and a placid self-respect we can congratulate ourselves that in doing what is right we have done also what was expedient. The straightforward course of honour and of duty always has its compensations, but in this case it has had the unusual reward of a signal and immediate success. Crotchet-mongers and charlatans of every kind have hung upon the footsteps of the men who conducted this great affair, and have attempted to force upon their attention their importunate conceits. The owls of wisdom and the bats of ill augury filled the atmosphere with their shrill cries and dull flappings. But, keeping within the circle of manly sense and international precedent, the trusted chiefs of the British people have succeeded in conjuring away this storm and in bringing back a tranquil sky. Thanks, under PROVIDENCE, to them, we have come out of this trial with our honour safe and no blood spilt.

It is a great victory though it is but an escape from being obliged to conquer. We are but where we were before we were so grossly insulted. We have but curbed for a moment the insolence of a neighbour who took pleasure in continually provoking us, and had permitted himself at last to go beyond the possibility of sufferance. We have done nothing to set up monuments to commemorate; we have only held our own in the great community of nations, and read a necessary lesson to an ill-mannered companion. There have been times in our history—times when we had not the strength we could now put forth—when we should have had no such real joy as we now feel in the hinderance of such a conflict. There are other nations which even at this age of the world would not have thought it consistent with their renown to manifest such patience and long suffering under outrage as we have exhibited. If the same experiment had been tried upon France, we question whether the same forbearance would have been afforded to the aggressor, or the same readiness to receive a tardy and grudging reparation. We have manifested a deliberation and tranquillity under insult which even we could not have shown towards a people for whom we thought it right to make fewer allowances, or whom we feared more. The Government of the Federal States had done in mere wantonness what no nation of the Old World had ever dared to do. They had invaded the sanctuary which England extends to all political exiles who seek her protection; and to this wound, inflicted on her most sensitive pride, they had added an insult to her maritime flag and a menace to her security in traversing the seas. On all hands it is now admitted that the offence was at once insult and wrong, and it is no great triumph, therefore, that it should have been followed by reparation. If we had had to deal with a friendly and courteous people, we should have had no occasion for preparations of war. If a French or an English captain, while the two nations are upon their present terms, were to gratify a crack-brained freak or an insane thirst of notoriety by some piratical outrage against the foreign flag, neither Government would wait to see whether any miserable advantage could be gained by the circumstance. The act would be at once disavowed, and the booty returned, with apologies and compensation. This was the course which, if Federal America had been courteous or even shrewd, Federal America would have pursued. Mr. SEWARD missed a great opportunity when he failed to act as a European statesman would have acted under similar circumstances. At this moment there is no great sympathy here for either party. The attraction we feel towards a weaker nation invaded by a stronger and a richer nation is repelled by the very general detestation of slavery; and, if Mr. SEWARD had seized the opportunity for a graceful and courteous act we would not answer for how far our countrymen might have been tempted from their rigorous neutrality. It was a gross blunder for the shrewd Minister of a shrewd people to miss the chance of a great advantage only to do the same act at last under circumstances of unavoidable humiliation.

But we are told that a very elaborate Note of protest accompanies this surrender. This voluminous gloss upon a very simple fact is still upon its way from Queenstown. We cannot say we are very impatient for it. We have long since learnt to value Transatlantic statesmen less for what they say than for what they do. It is by deeds, and not by arguments, that the fact we to-day announce has been brought about. It is not VATTEL and BYNKERSHOEK, and STOWELL and DE HAUTEVILLE, who have influenced this controversy, but the promptitude with which we reinforced Admiral MILNE's fleet, and poured battalion after battalion into Canada. They loudly proclaim this in America, and Mr. SEWARD's Note will very probably be found to bear marks of the same sentiment. We make up our minds in advance, therefore, to accept with unruffled equanimity any quantity of words. Even if there should be muffled threats and expressions of ill will we shall humbly hope to outlive them. The aggressor is making retribution. It never has been held of much consequence whether he does it with a good grace or no. The substantial apology lies in the fact of the surrender of the thing taken. We hope to find in Mr. SEWARD's Note an expression of regret that he should ever have employed so inconsiderate a commander as Captain WILKES, or should have been so ill-advised as to persevere in a tacit recognition of his act; but we shall be neither surprised or discomfited if this hope is not fulfilled.

To-day, however, it is enough that we congratulate ourselves that the danger is past, and all present apprehension of war at an end. Let us also especially congratulate ourselves that the crisis found this united nation and her loyal Colonies so well prepared, and that it leaves us so well protected. We have every reason to be satisfied with the position which this country has held throughout. We have never deviated from grave and courteous discussion, and have never descended to retort the wild invectives which came from the other side of the Atlantic. The War Departments have manifested an efficiency which gives us confidence in ourselves, and will give us security from future insult. The Government have acted with a rare courtesy and temper, but have displayed, together with dignified deliberation, firmness, promptitude, and courage. Nor will we refrain from adding, what every one will feel while he reads this news, that the man upon whom the nation instinctively relied while the crisis lasted deserves our warmest gratitude now that the peril is overcome. It is indeed a rare triumph to grace the latter years of a life so happily prolonged, that Lord PALMERSTON has found, and has used, the opportunity to curb the arrogance of the only people which has in this generation entered systematically upon a course of offence towards England.

January 25th, 1862 pages 8-9

Under the technical designation of "Military Hygiene", a science of the utmost importance has recently been introduced to the notice of the public. Its object is nothing less than the preservation of the life and health of the soldier. It seeks to protect him from disease, to economize his strength, and to sustain his efficiency both at home and abroad, in barracks as well as in camp, in hospital as well as in the field. What could be accomplished by its agency was shown in the expedition to Pekin, but we have now a later and more extraordinary example of its application in the history of the American War. The Americans have indeed gone to work with a will upon the new theory, and never, we suppose, was the hyperbolic turn of the Transatlantic mind more signally illustrated than in the proceedings of the Sanitary Commission on the Potomac. The Federals did not wait, as we did in the Crimean War, for the mischief to begin. They actually appointed a Commission to inquire into the health of the army before that army had assembled, and not a minute was lost by the Commissioners in entering upon their duties. Under the presidency of a Doctor, not of Medicine, but of Divinity, they have been at work seven months. In that time they have received from their subordinate officers upwards of 400 Reports, each containing 360 questions and answers; they have favoured Government with 40 Reports of their own, and they have distributed 150,000 copies of their "publications" through-out the loyal States. When we come, indeed, to see what they proposed to themselves, and what objects they included in their inquiry, we cannot be surprised at, their voluminous issues. Never, except in a French "Act of Accusation," was so complete a compilation of facts attempted. The Rev. Dr. BELLOWS seems to have taken his men or his regiments, and ascertained all their "antecedents" with the accuracy of a German police agent. We learn everthing about the troops—where they came from, how they came, how long they were coming, and what kind of men they were, as well as how they were lodged, fed, paid, clothed, entertained, and doctored. It may well be supposed that this information is valuable. We must say that we never met with a more exhaustive report. The Commission appears to have been of great benefit to the army, and it will now enable the world to observe how that singular army has been constituted.

In the months of September and October last 200 regiments in a batch, taken proportionately from the Eastern, Western, and Middle States of the Federal territories, were severally inspected and catechized. Upon an average, we are told, every one of these regiments had been raised within a space of six weeks. Some had actually been formed in ten days' time, but these, we must needs presume, had some previous organization. It will surprise the public to learn, after what has been said on the subject, that native Americans were found to constitute the majority in $76\frac{1}{2}$ per cent. of all the battalions inspected, and that in 5 or 6 per cent. only was the majority formed of Germans or Irish. The average age of the Volunteers is supposed to be " a little below 25," about half the whole number being under 23; but on this point the evidence is incomplete. Considering the precipitation with which this enormous army was sent into the field, it is not surprising that the previous inspection of the recruits was but imperfectly conducted. In 58 per cent. of the regiments there had been no pretence of such preliminary examination, and when a wholesale discharge took place in October it was found that half of the non-effectives dismissed ought never, under a good system, to have been enlisted at all. Dr. BELLOWS reckons that Government lost a good 16,000 on this batch only. Herein, too, we must observe that the Commisioners apply their probes to the moral as well as the physical man, and pronounce as sternly against the admission of incorrigibly vicious characters as against the enrolment of infirm or debilitated Volunteers. The point is not undeserving our notice.

When we get at length to the Sanitary Report proper, the information afforded is equally interesting, though not quite so novel. The clothing of the soldiers in general bore inspection so well that the Commisioners think no army was ever better supplied "at a similar period" of a great war. In 94 per cent. of the regiments the men had two shirts each; in 82 per cent. they had good overcoats; in 75 per cent. they had good bodycoats and to a similar extent they had one good blanket each. The rations were abundant, and of a satisfactory quality; nor was cooking complained of. In six regiments only out of the 200 was intoxication notoriously common, while in 163, as the Inspectors were assured, "and had no reason to doubt," it was "very rare." This is certainly not a bad report of things, and other traits of American character peep out as we proceed. In as many as 57 per cent. of the regiments the men were in the practice of sending home between half and three-fourths of their pay, and the proportion would probably have been larger still but that in many cases the pay at the time of inspection had not been received. The correspondence, too, maintained between the troops and their friends is characteristically voluminous. In some regiments of 1,000 men as many as 600 soldiers posted a letter a day each for weeks together, which the Commisioners accept as "a

51

delightful indication of a fact which should remove all fear of a permanent military despotism in this country."

In the army thus constituted the average constant number of sick during the months of August, September, and October was about 77 per 1,000, the invaliding being considerably greater in Western Virginia than on the Potomac. In the latter position the average mortality through the summer is computed at $3\frac{1}{2}$ per cent., or at 5 per cent. if the remoter camps are included in the reckoning. The chief evil was occasioned by the injudicious choice of sites for encampments, which were often formed on unhealthy ground, insufficiently provided with drainage, and kept on the same spot too long. The tents, too, were "seldom tolerably ventilated at night;" and, though the daily removal of refuse was pretty well attended to, the troops in general had not such habits of personal cleanliness as we might expect from men of their stamp. The Commissioners observe, however, that "slovenliness is our characteristic national vice," so that military service may answer the purposes of education in this respect. The tents, besides being in many cases indifferently adapted for ventilation, were very variously supplied with flooring. Sometimes the men slept on wooden boards, sometimes on indiarubber cloth, sometimes on boughs or straw, and sometimes on the bare ground. The liabilities attaching to each of these cases were curiously noted. The largest proportion of fever was found with indiarubber blankets, the least with straw or boughs. Boughs and straw had again all the advantage in the case of rheumatism, which was most frequent where the flooring was of board. Board also was the worst thing for throat affections, which were fewest where the men slept on the ground. In this situation, however, they were most exposed to malaria, which, like fever and rheumatism, was most commonly escaped by the aid of branches or straw. It is remarked at the close of the Report that typhus fever, instead of vanishing with the approach of winter, is "decidedly on the increase"; but the Commissioners hit upon the right explanation of the paradox. Cold drives the men to "burrow or seal themselves in their lodgings"; the atmosphere of the tent becomes vitiated from the careful exclusion of the air without, and typhus follows. Smallpox also creates a little uneasiness, but Dr. BELLOWS and his colleagues have "improved the occasion" by vaccination, in the way of military duty, upwards of 20,000 citizens, who would otherwise have dispensed with the operation.

It will be seen that we may learn something from American practice; but, if we appear to have fallen short of such efficiency in our own doings, it should be remembered in fairness that the case of the Federals is an exceptional one. Their army is close at home. The men stand, as it were, at their own doors. They can be looked after as easily as our own troops at Aldershott. It will be a very different thing when they advance, if ever they do, into the enemy's country, as we see, indeed, from the greater mortality which prevails already in the remoter camps of the West. Still, we may expect that these seven months of sanitary schooling will leave good results behind them, for officers and men have now been taught what to do for their own preservation, and it is not probable that, under any ordinary circumstances, they will forget the lesson.

John Bright (1811-1889), in both his strengths and weaknesses, was the representative, as well as the most conspicuous, radical of the mid-nineteenth century. He fought against the Corn Laws in the 'forties and the Crimean War in the 'fifties; he was the principal leader of the friends of the North in the 'sixties, and as such irritated The Times *more than any other public figure.*

February 18th, 1862   *pages 6-7*

HOUSE OF COMMONS, Monday, Feb. 17th
The SPEAKER took the chair a few minutes before 4 o'clock.

THE SUPPLEMENTARY ESTIMATES.
REINFORCEMENTS FOR CANADA.
On the motion for going into Committee of Supply

... Mr. BRIGHT.—Sir, before you leave the chair I should like to make two or three observations on this vote. I am not going to object to the vote, of course. I have had too much experience of such matters to attempt any such thing (a laugh); but after the prodigious sums voted last year, and the year before, I think we are now driven to consider whether the expenditure of an additional million is necessary or wise. Now, I am not about to find fault with Her Majesty's Government as regards the recent transaction with the Government of the United States, so far as I see anything, or expect to see anything, in the blue-books, containing the correspondence between the Foreign-office in

53

England and that department of the State at Washington. So far as the despatches signed by Lord Russell go, I make no complaint about them. It does not appear to me that the request made to the American Government was one which they could reasonably have objected to, or the language in which it was couched such as they were entitled to complain of. Therefore, so far as that goes, I have no charge to bring against Her Majesty's Government; but it does appear to me clear that there was great inconsistency between the conduct of the Foreign-office, as exhibited in those documents, and the conduct of certain other departments of the Government. It is not customary in ordinary life for a person to send a polite messenger with a polite message to a friend or neighbour or acquaintance, and at the same time to send a man of portentous strength, wielding a gigantic club, and making every kind of ferocious gesticulation, and still to profess that all this is done in the most friendly and courteous manner. That is what has been done by Her Majesty's Government in this case; and I am about to explain for a moment why I think this million has been worse than thrown away. Besides being thrown away, it leaves behind it consequences of much more value or much more harm than the million itself. The House will recollect that at the very time when the Cabinet was said to be meeting to discuss the form of despatch to be sent by the Saturday boat to America, there appeared in the newspapers which are the especial organs of the Government language of the most violent and offensive character; and that instantaneously—probably the very day the despatch was written—steps were taken, both as regarded the army and the navy, exactly as if the despatch itself had not been a courteous demand for compliance with a just request, but rather a declaration of war. Now, the effect of that in this country must be very obvious. It created an almost universal impression that there was something which the Government knew and which the country did not know. Though nobody but the Government could imagine that a cause of war could arise out of that question, it was supposed that the Government knew war to be inevitable, or that they intended war if war could by any possibility be made out of it. Looking to what occured at the time, I suppose that the answer to be given to me will be based on either of two theories, which I venture to say are about as false and about as ignorant as any ever offered to Parliament in justification of any proceedings. Certain organs which affect to represent the Government—and which are sometimes the slave of the Government and sometimes its master—stated that the Government at Washington, and Mr. Seward especially, were anxious to get into a war or difficulty with this country if they could do so, in order to enable them to get out of the war with the South, and under cover of war with England to make a peace or terms of some kind—I suppose by acknowledging the independence of the Southern States. That is one of the theories. Nothing could be offered to rational men more absurd or more impossible. Mr. Seward cannot make war. The President himself cannot make war. Mr. Seward and the President together cannot make war; but the President and Congress can make war. Therefore we may be perfectly certain that it did not rest in the brain of any one man, however eminent or however ingenious, to consent to the dismemberment of the United States under cover of a war with us. Then it was stated again that the Government of America were so entirely under the influence and direction of the mob that they could not listen to the courteous demand of the English Government; that, in fact, what we wanted was not to overawe the Government, but to overawe that mob which in the United States may be supposed to overrule and overawe the Government. (Hear hear.) I see that I have hit the point exactly which hon. gentlemen have imagined to themselves; but hon. gentlemen who have watched the history of the United States from the beginning to this hour must know that there never has been a great nation in which what is familiarly termed "mob law" is less known or has less influence. ("Oh, oh!") Wherever men have votes, club law and mob law necessarily disappear. ("Oh, oh!") I confine my observations entirely to the free States of the North; but if any hon. gentleman thinks that I am not fairly describing the facts of the case, I ask him to look at the circumstances that have occurred. He must know that the Government at Washington, whether in the removal of a distinguished and popular General, or in the removal of a Minister, or in the recognition of the fairness of the demand of our Government for the surrender of two men, perhaps more hateful to them than any other two individuals in the world, have not hesitated to do what they considered to be right. I say that, looking at these things, the man must be prejudiced beyond all power of conviction who thinks that the Government of North

55

America have been influenced by the action of the mob to any extent beyond that which is found to prevail in this country, and in almost every other country in Europe. Now, the noble lord at the head of the Government will have this advantage over me of course, and so will any of his friends who may take a different view of this affair,—they will say, and I cannot prevent them from saying, that whether they were wrong or not in their policy, that policy has been crowned with a certain success. (Hear, hear.) But that is not always conclusive of a policy being right. I have not the smallest doubt that what made it a question whether those men would be surrendered and war avoided was, not the tenour of the despatch, but the articles in the press known to represent a section of of the Government, and the movement and operations of troops and ships, which were understood as a menace to Washington. Every man who has access to the shelves of the Foreign-office knows that when the question as to the right to take those men came to be considered, whatever use might be made of English precedents, nothing whatever could be said if you adhered to American practices and principles. And it is clear to any man who read the speech of Mr. Sumner in the American Senate—in which speech he collected the authorities on both sides, all of which must be known at our Foreign-office—that the American Government would have been utterly unable to resist the demand of the English Government, in accordance with American practices and principles, however courteously that demand might have been made. It was, indeed, very well known to those who were at Washington at the time, that the influence of those military preparations was not felt upon the Government and people of the United States, but on the Ministers who represented the European Powers; for I have reason to know that there were not fewer than two of the Ministers of the European Powers at Washington who expressed their decided opinion that there was an intention on the part of some section of the Government, or of some powerful classes in this country, if the opportunity offered, to engage in war with the United States (a cry of "No! no!"), and the effect of that statement and opinion was this, that every man who felt himself aggrieved or humiliated by the course taken by Her Majesty's Government asked himself, "Shall I gain anything by this surrender, or shall I wait for some other opportunity for the action of hostility so apparent?" I do not bring this charge against the

Government of this country, or say that they intended war; but there were many persons in this country who were led to that conclusion. I think it likely that the noble lord at the head of the Government, bringing down his traditions from a time of past war, when right and justice were little regarded by the most civilized nations of Europe, thought that the only mode of securing what he wished was by this great demonstration of force. Now, I believe that on this question, as on some others, and on this more than others, there is no other powerful Government in the world that is so uniformly disposed to abide as far as possible by known and defined law as the Government of the United States; and when I heard that this demand had been made with my knowledge of their previous course in respect to these questions, I had no doubt whatever that the matter would be amicably arranged, except that the menaces from this side might make it difficult for them to concede the demand of Her Majesty's Government. As to the effect of these demonstrations on English interests I wish to say one word. I will not count up how much the fall in stocks, railway shares, and other securities amounted to, but in one market alone, that of Liverpool, the effect of what was done, not on board the Trent, not by the despatches of the Foreign-office, but by the warlike preparations of the Government, was to reduce the value of one article alone to the extent of 3,000,000*l*. sterling. I have not seen it myself, but I have heard of a letter from Bombay or Calcutta, which states that on a certain day, when the news arrived that war between England and the United States was imminent, a complete paralysis took place in the trade of Bombay and Calcutta; and from that time up to the period of the latest advices that paralysis continued, to the great loss and inconvenience of persons engaged in the commerce of that country. And when the news arrives from Australia we shall doubtless hear that from the moment when war appeared to be likely or possible not an ounce of gold was shipped to this country. No man could know that an Australian ship would not meet with an American man-of-war or privateer, and doubtless the panic that prevailed in India would also be felt in Australia. This is a view of the question worth looking at. Your people are employed by the operation of this commerce and the security of the capital embarked in it; and when there arises between two friendly countries any transaction like this unhappy accident of the Trent (a laugh),—I do not know whether any one on the Treasury bench laughs because I call it so. (A pause, during which the hon. gentleman directed his gaze upon the front Ministerial bench.) I say it was an unhappy accident. As regards the United States' Government and our own Government, it was nothing but an accident; and no one knows this better than the noble lord at the head of the Government. And when accidents of this or any other kind arise that can possibly cause jarring between the two countries, it is the policy and the duty of the Government, in the first place certainly, to try all those moderate and courteous means which it would like to have tried itself before it has recourse to measures which send a paralysis through all the ramifications of the greatest commerce of the world, and create immense loss among almost all classes of the people. Now, I may say with the utmost satisfaction and truth that the noble lord at the head of the Government was not more pleased than I was at the favourable termination of that untoward event. If the noble lord believed that there was no course by which war could be prevented but that which he took it would be very harsh and unfair to blame him. But, knowing how much the United States' Government are bound up and connected with the humane principle of international maritime law, he might have trusted much more to their desire to act in accordance with international law than to the force that had been brought against them. We shall do well to remember that the Power which is for a moment partially disabled and crippled, yet which gives its support to the Washington Government, consists at the present moment of 22,000,000 of people. Those Northern States, 10, 20, and 30 years hence, will increase as rapidly as they have ever done before in population and power. They are our countrymen to a great extent. We have few enemies there, except those who left these shores with feelings of discontent against this Government because their grievances were not removed. And it is worth our while, on all moral grounds and on grounds of self-interest, that we should in all our transactions acknowledge our alliance and kinship with such a nation, and not leave behind an ineradicable and undying sting, which it would take many years, perhaps a generation or two, to remove. The War of Independence 80 years ago left such a sting; the war of 1812 inflicted similar mischief. The course taken by the Government, not in the demand made, not in the despatch by which that demand was accomplished, not in the courteous manner in which Lord Lyons managed the negotiations (cheers), but in the instantaneous and alarming menace of war, coupled with the offensive charges made every day by the press which supported the Government, tended to leave on the mind of every American a feeling that England had not treated the United States in that magnanimous and friendly manner which they had a right to expect from us. I am glad to see that a remarkable change has operated day by day, both in this House and out of it. It is obvious that since the course taken by the American Government has been known a great change has taken place in the opinion of this country. It has become more friendly to the Washington Government, for people now see that it is a real Government, not ruled by a mob or disregarding the law, but struggling to maintain the integrity of a great country. They see in that country the home of every man who wants a home, and, moreover, they believe that that greatest of all crimes, that any people in the history of the world has ever been connected with, the crime of keeping in slavery 4,000,000 of people, is, under the providence of a Power very much higher than that of a Prime Minister of England or the President of the United States, marching on, as I believe, to its entire abolition.

. . .

Lord PALMERSTON.—I am not going to answer the latter part of the speech of my hon. friend who has just sat down; that is a topic which will be more properly handled by my right hon. friend near me (Sir G. C. Lewis) when he comes to make his statement about the Estimates. But I am unwilling to let a longer time elapse without making some observations on what has fallen from the hon. member for Birmingham. I said on a former occasion that it was desirable in this House that we should not only pass laws and vote Estimates, but should be the organs of the opinions and feelings of large masses of the community. I go further, and I admit that it is sometimes useful that this House should hear the views and opinions of individuals, and to-night we have had an example of the singular opinions of one instead of the general opinion of many. (Laughter.) But I think it must be admitted that the opinions which my hon. friend has expressed are as nearly as possible confined to himself. (Laughter.) Sir, my hon. friend does justice to the course which the Government pursued in making their demand for redress from

the American Government. Upon that point there is no difference of opinion. (Hear, hear.) He has done full justice to the
considerations which influenced my noble friend at the head of
the Foreign-office when he instructed Lord Lyons to make the
communication, and to the delicacy, judgment, and good taste
with which Lord Lyons complied with his instructions. (Hear,
hear.) It is well, therefore, to know that the ground is cleared of
any objections upon those preliminary points. But my hon. friend
thinks that we were wrong in those military and naval preparations which have been made; that we were wrong in sending out
troops who went with what I think he called "ferocious gesticulations." (Laughter.) I do not know to what particular circumstance he alludes, but the weather was cold when they were
going, and if they did make "ferocious gesticulations" it must
have been for the purpose of warming their hands. (Laughter.)
But the point of my hon. friend's argument is this, that the
United States were bound by various obligations of international
law to give up those persons who were taken from on board the
Trent, and that in the course which they took they were not
swayed by mob influence. My hon. friend says where everybody
is a voter there can be no mob. I do not quite agree in that
theory. (Hear, hear.) But he contends that the United States
Government were bound by their own principles to do that
which we asked them, and that they were quite free, nor was any
control exercised over them by any class of the community. But,
now I would just ask him if the United States Government held
all along that they were bound by their own principles to disavow any act contrary to those principles, and, therefore, to afford
redress, why did they keep those four gentlemen in prison?
(Cries of "Hear, hear".) Was it because, as he states, those
gentlemen happened to be the objects of great hatred to the
United States Government, for that is not the reason why an act
of injustice should be committed? (Cheers.) Why should those
gentlemen be kept in prison, who, according to the acknowledged
principles of the Government, were entitled to their freedom
from the first moment? (Hear, hear.) It is to my mind true that
the United States Government had not come, in the earlier stages
of the matter, to the decision that this was an act which they
must disavow, and that they were bound to restore those persons.
(Hear, hear.) But my hon. friend says that no compulsion was
exercised upon the United States Government; that as to war,

Mr. Seward and Mr. Lincoln could not make it upon their own authority—we knew that very well; it requires the sanction of the Senate—and that therefore it was quite foolish and criminal in us to take measures calculated to provoke a war with the United States. But had we no ground for thinking that it was very doubtful whether our demand would be complied with? (Hear, hear.) And will any man tell me who remembers the indignant feeling that prevailed throughout the whole country at the insult and outrage which had been committed that the people of Great Britain would tamely have submitted to a refusal? (Cheers.) Well, then, if that refusal came we should be bound to extort by the usual means that compliance which had been refused to a more courteous application. (Hear, hear.) Well, what reason had we to think that a refusal would not be given? My hon. friend cannot have forgotten transactions so recent and events so fresh in the memory of every one. Why, what was the tone and temper of the Northern States? We knew that Captain Wilkes had done this act upon his own authority, and that the United States were quite at liberty to disavow it if they chose. Mr. Adams told my noble friend that in a despatch which he received from Mr. Seward it was stated that the United States were free to act as they pleased, and that its conduct might depend upon that which the British Government might think fit to follow. The despatch went no further.

Mr. BRIGHT.—It did go further.

Lord PALMERSTON.—I don't know that. Well, Captain Wilkes declared that he had done the act without authority and instructions. But did the people, did the public of the United States hesitate as to whether what had been done was right or wrong? (Hear, hear.) It is well known that Captain Wilkes was made a hero of; and for what? Why, the reason was distinctly avowed and put forward—viz., because he had had the courage to insult the British flag. (Hear, hear.) There was a great ovation at Boston, where, I believe, persons holding Judicial situations, among whom was a person in high office, the governor of the State, joined in the general chorus of approbation. (Hear, hear.) But you may say that that took place at a public meeting, and that we have heard many foolish speeches made at public meetings, and a great many opinions there expressed which were not backed or re-echoed by the rest of the country. ("Hear, hear," and laughter.) But did things stop there? When Captain

Wilkes went to the theatre in New York the whole audience rose, as they might have done at the entrance of a great liberator of his country; they rose in honour of Captain Wilkes, and cheered him, I believe. (Hear, hear.) Well, were the American Government entirely free from participation in such demonstrations? With respect to some Governments, it is said that one department does not know what another department does, and it is sometimes made a reproach here that departments conduct their affairs at cross-purposes; but in America, the Naval Department—the Secretary of the Admiralty actually approved Captain Wilkes's conduct, and thanked him, and only ventured to hint that Captain Wilkes had shown too great forbearance, and hoped that the example would not, in that respect, be brought into a precedent in future. (Hear, hear.) Then, the House of Representatives, if I mistake not, voted thanks to Captain Wilkes, and approved his conduct. (Hear, hear.) Here, then, were the American public, the Government, a branch of the Legislature, all approving the act committed. Well, with all these facts before our eyes, should we have been justified in supposing that a mere courteous application, asking the American Government to have the goodness to deliver the four captured persons into our hands, would have induced them to say, "The whole American people see that we have insulted your flag and are glad of it; but as you ask for the delivery of the prisoners as a favour, as a favour we assent to the delivery"? I really think that we should have been deserving of condemnation and censure as shortsighted men, not actively alive to the interests of the country, if we had simply rested our case on the demand. (Cheers.) Moreover, it is well known that it was generally said by persons in America, and also I believe by some Americans in this country, that the four prisoners were not to be delivered—"that they won't and shan't be given up." What was considered by the Americans to be our weak point, and what was the circumstance which made the United States always more difficult to deal with by England than by France? It was the thought that Canada and the British North American colonies were defenceless. (Cheers.) What, then, was it our duty to do? It was to strengthen them, and make the Americans see that we were able to defend ourselves on that point which they thought to be the most vulnerable and most easily accessible to them. (Hear, hear.) That was not "ferocious gesticulation." ("Hear, hear," and laughter.) It was simply a defensive measure (hear, hear), it was simply strengthening that part which had been weak and might be attacked, and the knowledge of the weakness of which might induce the Americans to maintain that position which they had up to that moment occupied—to retain these men in prison and refuse to comply with our demand for their restoration. (Hear, hear.) Therefore, so far from Her Majesty's Government being obnoxious to blame, I think that the Government are deserving of commendation for what they did; and, though they performed no more than their duty, they performed it promptly and efficiently, and have met with, I believe, the approbation of the country at large. (Cheers.) I think, then, that the censure of my hon. friend the member for Birmingham is not deserved, and that what we did was not at all calculated to provoke the Government of the United States. It was simply a measure which it was our bounden duty to take, seeing the uncertainty of the result of the communications carried out from this country. So far from any feeling of ineradicable irritation between the two countries being engendered by the course pursued, I believe that a contrary course would have produced such a result. If Her Majesty's Government had submitted to a declared insult, no doubt a vote of censure would have been passed on them. Still the act would have been done, and a sense of humiliation and degradation would have been perpetually in the minds of at least the present generation, on account of the gross and unatoned for insult committed against the country. I agree with my hon. friend who has just sat down, that the course actually pursued is one much more likely to produce peace between the two nations. There start up from time to time between countries antagonistic passions and questions of conflicting interest, which if not properly dealt with would terminate in the explosion of war. Now, if one country is led to think that another country, with which such questions might arise, is from fear disposed on every occasion tamely to submit to any amount of indignity, that is an encouragement to hostile conduct and to extreme proceedings which lead to conflict. It may be depended on that there is no better security for peace between nations than the conviction that each must respect the other, that each is capable of defending itself, and that no insult or injury committed by the one against the other would pass unresented. (Hear, hear.) Between nations, as between individuals, mutual respect is the best security for mutual goodwill and mutual courtesy; and therefore, in my opinion, the course pursued by the Government is one much more likely than that suggested by my hon. friend the member for Birmingham to secure the continuance of peace. (Loud cheers.)

The House then resolved itself into a Committee of Supply.

March 27th, 1862   *page 9*

THE CIVIL WAR IN AMERICA

(FROM OUR SPECIAL CORRESPONDENT.)

WASHINGTON, MARCH 11.

... And now about the most significant and important event in naval annals for many a year. I had the advantage of hearing a very animated description of the affair from a naval officer of the United States who saw part of the action, but the *Baltimore American* contains such an excellent account from another eyewitness, that I prefer sending it to running the risk of losing the mail by writing out the narrative of my friend. The statement already mentioned is as follows:—

"The dullness of Old Point was startled at 1 o'clock on Saturday by the announcement that a mysterious vessel, supposed to be the Merrimac, looking like a submerged house with the roof only visible above water, was running down from Norfolk by the channel in front of Sewell's Point batteries. Signal guns were immediately fired by the Cumberland and Congress to notify the Minnesota, St. Lawrence, and Roanoke of approaching danger, and all was excitement in and about Fortress Monroe. The monster steadily approached, and there was nothing protruding above the water but a flagstaff flying the rebel flag, and a short smoke stack. She moved along slowly until she passed Sewell's Point, and, turning into the channel leading to Newport News, steered direct for the Federal frigates Cumberland and Congress, which were lying at the mouth of James River. As soon as the Merrimac came within range of the Cumberland the latter opened on her with her heavy guns, but the balls struck and glanced off, having no more effect on her than peas from a popgun. The ports of the Merrimac were all closed, and she moved on in silence, but with a full head of steam. In the meantime as the Merrimac was approaching the two frigates on one side, the rebel iron-clad steamers Yorktown and Jamestown came down the James River and engaged our frigates on the other side. The batteries at Newport News also opened on the Jamestown and the Yorktown, and did all in their power to assist the Cumberland and the Congress, which, being sailing vessels, were at the mercy of the approaching steamers. The Merrimac, in the meantime, kept steadily on her course and slowly approached the Cumberland, when she and the Congress, at the distance of 100 yards, rained full broadsides on the iron-clad monster. The shot, however, took no effect, glancing upwards and flying off, having only the effect of checking her progress for the moment. After receiving the first broadside of the two frigates the Merrimac ran on to the Cumberland, striking her about midships, and literally laying open her side. She then drew off, fired a broadside into the disabled ship, and again dashed against her with her iron-clad prow, and, knocking in her side, left her to sink, while she moved off to engage the Congress, which lay about a quarter of a mile distant. The Congress had in the meantime kept up a sharp engagement with the Yorktown and Jamestown, and having no regular crew on board of her, and seeing the hopelessness of resisting the iron-clad monster, at once struck her colours. The crew had been discharged several days since, and three companies of the naval brigade had been put on board temporarily until she could be relieved by the St. Lawrence, which was to have gone up on Monday to take her position as one of the blockading vessels off James river. On the Congress striking her colours the Jamestown approached and took from on board of her all the officers as prisoners, and directed the crew to leave the vessel in the boats. The vessel being thus cleared was fired by rebels, when the Merrimac and her two iron-clad companions opened with shell and shot on the Newport News batteries. The firing was briskly returned. In the meantime the steam frigate Minnesota, having partly got up steam, was being towed up to the relief of the two frigates, but did not get up until too late to assist them. She was followed by the frigate St. Lawrence, which was taken in tow by several of the small harbour steamers. It is, however, rumoured that neither of these vessels had pilots on board of them, and after a short engagement both of them seemed to be, in the opinion of the pilots on the Point, aground. The Minnesota, either intentionally or from necessity, engaged the three steamers at about a mile distance, with only her two bow guns. The St. Lawrence also poured in shot from all the guns she could bring to bear, and it was the impression of the most experienced naval officers on the Point that both of them had been considerably damaged. In the meantime darkness approached, though the moon shone out brightly, and nothing but the occasional flashing of the guns could be seen. The Merrimac was also believed to be aground, as she remained stationary at the distance of a mile from the Minnesota, making no attempt to attack or run into her. The rebel battery at Pig's Point was also enabled to join in the combined attack on the Minnesota, and several guns were fired at her from Sewell's Point as she went up; none of the shot, however, struck her, but one or two of them passed over her. Previous to the departure of the steamer from Baltimore no guns had been fired for a half hour, the last being fired from the Minnesota. Fears were, of course, entertained for the safety of the Minnesota and St. Lawrence in such an unequal contest; but if the Merrimac was really ashore she could do no further harm to them. It was the intention of the Minnesota, with her picked and gallant crew, to have run into close quarters with the Merrimac, avoid her iron prow, and board her. This the Merrimac seemed not inclined to give her an opportunity to do, being afraid even to approach her at close quarters when aground. At 8 o'clock, when the Baltimore boat left, a fleet of steamtugs were being sent up to the relief of the Minnesota and St. Lawrence, and an endeavour was to be made to draw them off from the bar on which they had grounded. The loss of life could not be ascertained, and must be principally on board the Cumberland, from drowning. She received one broadside from the Merrimac, and was left sinking with all on board. She was not more than 200 yards from the shore, and it is probable that the greater portion of her officers and crew escaped. Of those on the Congress all escaped except the officers, who were taken prisoners. There was also probably some loss of life on the Minnesota and St. Lawrence, the latter vessel being commanded by Commander Purviance, of Baltimore. The Merrimac was understood to be under the command of Captain Buchanan, of Charles county, Maryland, who, after he had resigned, desired to withdraw his resignation and enter the Federal service against the rebellion.

"On Saturday night, after the above occurrences, Mr. Ericsson's iron-cased steamer Monitor, in command of Lieutenant Worden, arrived in Hampton Roads, and immediately went to the assistance of the Minnesota, then aground just below Newport News, in whose company she continued during the night, and was unsucessfully assailed the next morning by the Merrimac, Jamestown, and Yorktown, which had returned to engage the Minnesota. The Monitor, whose presence there must have greatly surprised the enemy, promptly took them in hand, paying her attentions especially to the Merrimac, which, after an exciting conflict of several hours, much of the time at very close quarters, was towed off by her consorts, aided by some tug boats, towards Norfolk. To what extent she is damaged is not known. Lieutenant Worden thinks she is seriously crippled. With the exception of Lieutenant Worden, who was injured, it is hoped not seriously, by the cement from the pilot house being driven into his eyes, no one on board the Monitor was hurt. It is reported that in the engagement of Saturday the Minnesota had about five killed and nine or ten wounded; no officers among either. The Cumberland had her chaplain (probably) drowned, master's mate Harrington and 20 men killed, and about 130 drowned, including some 50 who were wounded. On board the Congress Acting Commander Joseph Smith (a son of Commodore Joseph Smith) was killed. Paymaster Buchanan was her only officer not taken prisoner. None of the rest of her officers were killed or wounded. It is not known yet how many men she killed or wounded. Captain Radford, the commander of the Congress, happened to be absent on a court-martial, and thus escaped capture. Lieutenant Morris (who is safe) fought the Cumberland until she sunk—which she did with her flag flying—a worthy son of a glorious naval sire". . . .

April 5th, 1862   *page 5*

NAVAL AND MILITARY INTELLIGENCE

Yesterday, one of the finest ships in Her Majesty's navy was removed from her moorings up the harbour of Portsmouth, and placed alongside the dockyard. The necessary preparations were at once begun for cutting off her upper and main decks to convert her from a 131 screw three-decker to a 12-gun shield ship, on Captain Coles's plan. The order was received at the master-shipwright's office on Tuesday afternoon, and a body of men were sent to the ship at her moorings in the harbour at 3 p.m., but the work of conversion may be fairly said to have commenced yesterday morning, on the ship being lashed alongside the dock-yard. The ship thus selected to take the lead in this fresh regeneration of the navy is fitly named the Royal Sovereign. She was laid down in Portsmouth dockyard from designs furnished from the office of Sir W. Symonds, then Surveyor of the Navy. Previously to being launched she was lengthened and altered to a screw steamship, like the Marlborough, the Prince of Wales, and the Duke of Wellington, and was finally launched on the 24th of April, 1857. She is of 3,759 tons burden, builders' measurement; is 240 ft. 6in. long between perpendiculars, and has an extreme breadth of 60ft. Her engines are from the manufactory of Maudslay, Son, and Field, and are of 800 horse-power, nominal. On her trial of speed in Stokes-bay she realized a speed of 12.253 knots at light draught, with an indicated horse-power of 2,795.8, a displacement of 4,023 tons, and an area of midship section of 803ft. The resources of Portsmouth dockyard are now principally employed on iron-cased ships—the Black Prince, in No. 10 dock; the Royal Alfred, preparing for plating in No. 5 building slip, and the Royal Sovereign. All work by the shipwrights is for the present suspended on two out of the three wooden vessels building,—the Dryad, 50-gun frigate, and the Harlequin, 17-gun corvette. The third wooden vessel, the Helicon, one-gun paddle despatch steamer, has still a few hands employed in completing her frame for planking.

The Lords of the Admiralty have decided on converting the 91-gun line-of-battle steamer Bulwark, 3,716 tons, 1,000 horse-power, now on the stocks at Chatham Dockyard, into an armour-plated frigate similar to the Royal Oak, under construction at that establishment, as soon as the latter vessel is completed. The Bulwark has been on the stocks three years and is about three-fourths completed. She is a fine specimen of her class of two-decker screw steamers, and is admirably adapted for conversion into an armour-plated frigate. She will require to have one of her decks cut down, and to be lengthened amidships, and otherwise strengthened, to bear the heavy armour-plates with which she will be encased. It is probable that the screw frigate

Belvidera, 51 guns, 3,027 tons, building on the adjoining slip, will also be completed as an armour frigate, for which she is well suited, the alterations from her original designs being very trifling. She was commenced in April, 1860, and has remained some time in frame, the further progress of the works having been suspended for several months. There is also a 22-gun screw corvette partially completed at Chatham Dockyard, together with a 17-gun screw steamer, the whole of the hands from both of which have been withdrawn, in order to enable the Admiralty to decide what course should be taken with regard to the completion of these vessels according to the original designs. . . .

The following letter was part of the great 'battle of the guns' waged by Joseph Whitworth (1803-1887) against the Board of Ordnance. Whitworth was perhaps the greatest engineer of his day, being (among other things) one of the fathers of the modern machine tool industry. His genius earned him a large fortune which he chiefly devoted to educational and charitable purposes in the Manchester area. From the time of the Crimean War onwards he was deeply involved in projects for the improvement of English artillery and small arms, projects which, because of their brilliance and practical sense, were rejected by the War Office and adopted by Napoleon III, who gave him the Légion d'Honneur in 1868. The following year his charitable undertakings were rewarded by a baronetcy.

GUNS v. SHIPS

TO THE EDITOR OF THE TIMES

Sir,—The experience acquired from recent naval engagements shows that, as regards ships of war, the means of defence have progressed in advance of the means of attack at present employed. The possession of an iron-plated navy is confessedly proved to be a necessity; I venture to add that it is equally a necessity to arm that navy with artillery which iron-cased ships cannot set at defiance.

It has been said that this can only be done by using smooth-bore guns of large size, throwing shot of great weight, which will crush in the side of the iron ship, and this would seem to have become the conviction in some official quarters. But, whatever may have been the results of comparisons made by others between rifled guns and smooth bores, those made by me have led me to a very different conclusion. It is difficult to believe that the experience of rifled guns in the service has led to the advocacy of so retrograde a step as the re-adoption of the smooth bore in preference to the rifled gun, which, with elongated projectiles, made of the proper shape and material, and having the requisite velocity, will always prove incomparably more effective. The object to be effected is to force an entrance into the wrought-iron ship's side. To attempt to do this by firing *cast-iron* projectiles, in the vain hope of making the weaker material overcome the stronger, is manifestly absurd. No one would use a cast-iron punch to perforate a wrought-iron plate, nor would the head of the punch be made spherical. Wrought-iron should not be attacked with a metal inferior or only equal to itself, but with a metal superior in strength and hardness, formed into a shape suited for penetration, and propelled with the requisite velocity. To have recourse to huge round shot to smash in the ship's side is like employing brute force and neglecting the aids which science and mechanical experience have placed at our disposal.

If by the use of properly adapted projectiles we can make the iron-sided ship vulnerable without employing guns of inordinately increased size, we shall in an efficient manner restore to attack its supremacy over defence. That this may be done I confidently assert, and my experiments justify me in stating that not only solid, but also hollow, flat-fronted projectiles, capable of being charged with explosive or combustible compounds, may be fired through the new iron-plated vessels at much greater ranges than those at which the recent action was fought between the American vessels.

When my rifled $5\frac{1}{2}$-inch-bore gun was officially tried against the armour plates of the Trusty at the Nore (see *The Times* of May 28, 1860), every shot that hit the plates penetrated through them, and the shots that were picked up between the decks, after passing through both the iron plate and its timber backing, were found so little injured in the rear part that I have no doubt of being able to fire from my 7-inch guns hollow projectiles that will penetrate plates thicker than those of the Trusty.

Again, there is a mode of attacking the partially plated hull of the iron ship which ought not to be lost sight of. Official experiments made on board the Excellent have proved that my flat-fronted projectiles, after being fired through as much as 30 feet of water, retained great penetrating power. Iron ships are usually plated only to a limited depth, and flat-fronted projectiles, as they will go through water, are capable of inflicting great injury, both by damaging the propeller and by piercing the side of the ship below the water line.

These are points bearing so directly upon the question of what will be required henceforth in naval warfare that I think they call for careful consideration.

I remain, Sir, yours most obediently,

JOSEPH WHITWORTH.

Fenton's Hotel, April 4.

August 8th, 1862 *page 9*

THE BLOCKADE OF BERMUDA

TO THE EDITOR OF THE TIMES

Sir,—The reply of the Foreign Secretary to the merchants of Liverpool does not meet the case, as it does not allude to the practical blockade of the British ports of Bermuda by the Northern States, but simply recommends British merchants to "abstain" from a lawful trade for fear of wounding the feelings of the Northerners.

The new Foreign-office theory, that Might proves Right, may be diplomatic, but is hardly the thing for a Government Department so broadly to promulgate. However, my purpose more immediately is to ask—

First,—Is a British subject permitted or not to trade between any British port and another? If not, to what British ports is he permitted to trade? If trade to the Bermudas must "be refrained from," to please the Northerners, will trade to Jamaica or Demerara be allowed by them? Is the West Coast of Africa, with its suspicious gunpowder cargoes, tolerated? and will our Australian trade, like "Caesar's wife," be "above suspicion?"

Secondly,—Are British merchants in England to be unprotected in their legal dealings with other British merchants in British ports abroad because the Northerners may suspect that such lawful trade may possibly indirectly assist their adversaries?

Thirdly,—Why is it necessary for the Northern American Government to blockade these British ports? It can only be because their blockade of the Confederate ports is ineffective. Let them "sink, burn, and destroy" any vessel whatever found unlawfully running the blockade of those ports; but let it not be said that the Government of this great country will quietly permit British vessels containing British goods, and sailing between one British port and another, to be seized by the armed cruisers of a foreign Power in British waters on the simple suspicion that the cargo may indirectly find its way into their adversaries' country.

Will the Emperor of the French tolerate such interference with his flag when the trade is transferred to France and French bottoms, as is now being done to the great and lasting detriment of the trade of this country?

Surely these days of diminished exports, when the periodical returns of the Board of Trade are so anxiously scanned, are hardly the times for our Foreign Secretary to recommend our merchants to abstain from any lawful trade.

The great importance of this question will, I trust, be some excuse for this intrusion on your valuable space by

A BRITISH MANUFACTURING MERCHANT.
Liverpool, Aug. 6.

August 8th, 1862   *page 7*

MONEY-MARKET & CITY INTELLIGENCE

THURSDAY EVENING.

. . . The United States have now a currency of Government notes of the lowest denomination ever yet witnessed in the world—namely, one cent. of a dollar, or a half penny sterling. It is issued in the form of postage stamps, for the convenience of size, and from the fact of some idea of practical value being thus imparted to it; but that it is intended solely as a means of extending the inconvertible paper circulation is admitted, and in order to facilitate that end the covering of gum at the back is discontinued. The appliances for manufacturing these stamps are to be greatly increased to meet the new demand, though already "the contractor is turning them out by cartloads daily." They are not made a legal tender between individuals, any such provision being unnecessary, as from the hoarding of copper and silver there is no other form of small currency generally left; but they are a legal tender from and to the Government. The other denominations, besides those of a halfpenny, are severally equal to three halfpence, twopence halfpenny, one shilling, fifteen pence, and forty-five pence, and the amount likely to be put forth is therefore very considerable. After the American commercial panic in 1837 the various banks in Pennsylvania and other States issued notes as low as five cents., or twopence halfpenny, of which it was the fate of a considerable portion never to be redeemed; but to Mr. Chase, the present Secretary of the United States' Treasury, "the exclusive honour," according to the *New York World*, is now conceded "of being the first to issue paper money of the denomination of one cent."

The following relates to the novel practice, first introduced by the Pennsylvania Railway Company, of appropriating part of the shareholders' funds to promote a continuance of civil war:—

"Sir,—I observe in *The Times* of this morning that the Pennsylvania Railroad Company had offered to contribute $50,000 to provide for the bounties to volunteers. This is in clear violation of its charter, no such right having been delegated to the directors. A very large portion of the stock and bonds of this corporation is held in Europe. Innocent persons are therefore made to bear a part of the expense of the fratricidal war.

A STOCKHOLDER.

"August 7."

. . . .

August 25th, 1862   *page 10*

THE DISTRESS IN THE COTTON DISTRICTS

(FROM OUR OWN REPORTER.)

PRESTON, AUG. 23.

It is impossible, even if one had never heard of the Cotton Famine, to travel many miles through this district without being struck by the signs of the great calamity which has befallen it. The thick smoky curtain which ordinarily hangs between Heaven and earth over each centre of industry has been lifted up, there is an unaccustomed glare of sunlight and an atmosphere unusually bright and clear. On every side giant factories which

73

were the support of so many thousands stand mute and motionless, without a sign of life about them—their tall chimneys belch out no more long black clouds of smoke—only here and there a streamlet of thin vapour, lost almost as soon as it issues forth, speaks of "half-time" and wages reduced just short of starvation point. In the towns the evidences of the fast deepening stagnation are still more striking, though in Preston, which I selected for my first visit, they are not so apparent as in many places where the real distress is much less severe. Indeed, I must own that my first impression on walking through the streets was that the pictures which have been drawn of the state of the town were overcharged, and that the startling figures and facts which had been issued on official authority must be fallacious. I found Preston in a state of zealous preparation for the "Guild," a local festival of great antiquity which is celebrated every 20 years, and which the citizens after much deliberation have determined not to omit this year, notwithstanding all the discouraging circumstances of the times. With an army of painters and decorators at work, which gave the principal thoroughfare an air of Regent-street preparing for the season—many-coloured posters on every wall, announcing balls, concerts, operas, balloons, fireworks, and an endless round of pageants and amusements for high and low—the most ravishing ball dresses displayed in the shop windows, London ransacked for skilful hairdressers, and a special goods train just arrived with a varied cargo of fancy dresses in charge of that eminent *costumier*, Mr. Nathan,—with all these signs of festivity before one's eyes it was rather difficult to give credit to the official statistics which assure us that more than a quarter of the population of the town are dependent on charity for their daily bread and for the roof which covers them. I soon found, however, that this crust of apparent prosperity was very thin, and that it covered real destitution and suffering which the figures inadequately represent, and which, unfortunately, is but a type of the worse which remains to come. The corporation indeed refuse to despair of their commonwealth so far as to omit an ancient celebration which I believe is highly prized by the inhabitants of all ranks, and speculate perhaps on the benefit which the town may get out of the crowds of visitors who are sure to flock in from all parts of the country; but it would be a mistake for those at a distance, when they read the glowing accounts of the processions and the fêtes which are to come off ten days hence, to conclude that all the tales of distress which have reached them from this district are exaggerated.

With all these contradictory symptoms before my eyes, I made it my first business to diverge from the principal streets, and to endeavour to get a true idea of the condition of the people. Perhaps it will be better, therefore, to relate what I saw and heard on that point before describing the efforts which have been made to relieve the distress under which they are suffering. As I said, I began with Preston, because it was the town which was described as having received the severest blow from the stoppage of the supply of cotton. For this there are several causes. From the peculiar quality of the manufacture, which for the most part requires cotton of a very fine quality, which has hitherto been supplied almost entirely from one source—New Orleans—it suffered immediately from the first straitening of the supplies, and it is now close upon 12 months since the want of employment began to be felt. The great strike which took place here nine years ago, and the panic of 1857, which stopped many mills, wasted the resources of the operatives, and they had hardly had time to recover themselves when the present pressure came on. Of the total population of Preston, 82,900, it is calculated that 26,000 are in one way or other engaged in the cotton mills, and of these 12,460 are altogether out of employment, 5,697 are working half-time, 3,020 four days a-week, and 6,070 are at present working full time. To put it in a more striking form, there are now 10,553 persons receiving relief from the parish funds, of whom more than 8,000 are due to the present distress, and the Relief Committee has on its books 22,690 persons, some of whom receive relief from the parish, and some do not. Taking the two lists together, I believe it is under the mark to say that there are at least 23,000 in the town out of a population of 82,900 who live entirely on charity, and the number is daily increasing. But even this is not all—for I very soon found that the relief lists by no means measured the whole amount of privation and suffering, for the greater part of those working half-time are scarcely, if at all, better off than the absolute paupers. A large proportion of Indian cotton is now being used at the mills which still continue to run, but being unsuited to the machinery it is extremely difficult to work, and the hands can make hardly any wages with it.   "Half-time" is by no means synonymous with

75

half-wages. I was in not a few houses where a whole family depended on a pittance of 5s., 6s., or 8s. earned by one of its members, and where to all appearances the distress was as severe as if all of them had been totally unemployed. Fortunately the worst of such cases as these are included in the operations of the Relief Committee. The whole amount of wages lost to the operatives by the failure of employment is calculated at 13,000 livres a week—the place of which is supplied by a weekly dole, which last week amounted to a little over 1,000 livres; so that, in round numbers, each of the relieved population, including men, women, and children, is deprived of as many of the necessaries and comforts of life—to say nothing of saving and provision for the future—as can be purchased for something short of 10s. a-week. These general figures, though startling enough, but faintly express the actual privation which many poor creatures are suffering here. If I had confined my visits to the poorest quarter of the town—to places where good wages are spent recklessly on the belly and back, and where there is always more or less of poverty and no thinking of to-morrow—I might easily pile up cases of squalid misery hardly to be equalled in the most degraded dens of the Metropolis. For instance, in one court I found a poor woman with three children whose husband had three days' parish work and an extra relief of three shillings, in all six shillings a-week for the five. All their furniture was gone but a table and two chairs, and all five slept in one bed, which was placed in a dark hole with not a ray of light finding its way into it—such as we should hardly think too good to store coals in. All their clothes had been pawned, and most bitterly of all did the poor woman lament a good black suit of her husband which was "in" for 10s., and which they could never hope to redeem. Their earnings in good times had been about 25s. a-week. In the same court was another family of equal straits. Six people had to live on 8s. a-week, which the husband earned by working half-time; all were reduced to one bed, the other two having been long ago sold to keep the wolf from the door, and the whole family had just one sheet to lie on and a quilt to cover them. In another house I saw a sight which will be before my eyes for many a day to come. It was a little low stone-floored room, its only furniture a table, a stool, and a bed. On the bed was stretched a wretched object, I could not tell whether it was a man or a woman, worn to the bone—a very skeleton, in fact, her body covered with putrid sores, with not a rag on her,—literally naked but for the coarse sheet which was spread over her. The bed on which she lay was a rough brown sacking stuffed with a handful of straw. She had lain there I don't know how long; her husband had lain there before her, and died on the same bed. She was the mother of two girls, factory operatives, who earned or were relieved with a few shillings—I forget how many, for I own that I was too much shocked at what I saw to listen to figures. One can only hope, for the credit of the relieving officer, that this terrible case had escaped his notice, otherwise he would surely have strained or broken a rule, or had this miserable creature removed from the wretched den in which I found her. Even among a somewhat better class the suffering is hardly less extreme, and sad were the tales to which I had to listen of the gradual descent from comfort to utter destitution. In one little house, huddled all together, was a family of 11, all of whom had been 28 weeks out of work, and for 15 of these they had existed on something less than 1s. per head. The Relief Committee had just raised their pittance to 16s. for the 11. Before the bad times the family earnings had been about 3*l*. 15s., and they had had to part with nearly all their furniture. In a cellar, living with another family, I came upon a man and his wife and three children, who for weeks had been living on 6s. 6d. for the five. They had formerly lived in a house of their own, neatly furnished, but the landlord had turned them out when they did not pay their rent, and their furniture had absolutely all disappeared but a bed, a pan, and a kettle. Close by were a man and his wife with three girls and two boys, all over ten years of age, living on 10s. a-week. This family, too, had only one bed among them, and the children slept on the bare boards.

But perhaps the strongest illustrations of the distress actually chargeable on the present crisis are the cases of respectable men who have hitherto kept themselves in comfort, and endeavoured to provide for old age and infirmity. There was no difficulty in finding plenty of these. At one house I visited a young couple, not long married, who between them had earned over 2*l*. a week. They had both been out of work for some time, and when their savings were exhausted they had at last applied to the parish. Their present income was exactly 5s. 6d. a-week, out of which their rent was 2s. 7d., leaving them 3s. a-week for subsistence. Another young couple had 2s. a-week from the

Relief Committee; but, living with their parents, they had no rent to pay. In the next house there were four grown-up people living whose united incomes amounted to 9s., out of which they had to pay 2s. rent. A little further on I came on an overseer with a family of five children. His salary had been 30s. a-week, and though he had been out of work for more than a twelvemonth, he had managed to struggle on till about a fortnight ago, when, all his resources being exhausted, he had been compelled to apply for relief, and was now receiving, from one source or another, about 9s. a-week. An old woman and two daughters, both of them over 25 years of age—one employed half-time, the other receiving relief—had among them 4s. 6d. a-week. A highly respectable reed-hook-maker—whose wife cried bitterly as she told me her story—is earning, with the aid of one of his boys, 7s. a-week, which has to keep four of them, by dredging stones from the bed of the river. They had pawned all their clothes and much of their furniture before applying to the Relief Committee. I might go on for another column with cases of a similar character, but I have selected sufficient, I think, to show the common destitution in which all classes of operatives here, whatever may have been their previous position, are now plunged. So far as it is possible to get an average of the measure of relief—poor relief and Relief Committee combined—I should say that it could not be more than from 1s. 6d. to 1s. 8d. per head; and in very many cases which came under my own observation it did not amount to that; that is to say, the unemployed operatives and a large proportion of those on half time—on the most favourable representation of the state of things—are sustaining themselves and their families for about 1s. 6d. per head per week, and many of them, as we have seen, for less. A very small proportion of this is actual money; for the Relief Committee relieve wholly in kind—bread, soup, and coffee—and the guardians half in kind and half in money. But, whatever be the slender sum of ready money which finds its way into their pockets, they have to pay their rent out of it, varying according to the locality, from 1s. 6d. to 3s. 6d. a week, or, at least, they ought to pay it, but the owners of cottage property, especially those who are soft-hearted, are among the severest sufferers by the crisis. I have heard of one owner who has already lost 400*l.* in this way, and who is now losing regularly 20*l.* a-week by the inability of his tenants to pay their rents. As a general rule, I am glad to say there has been unusual forbearance shown by landlords, though I have heard of several cases where the poor creatures have been ruthlessly thrust into the street as soon as they began to run into arrear. To avoid this fate they will often pay the rent when they have not a morsel of food in the house, or will pawn their bedding, clothes, or furniture. With too many of them the season for these expedients is past. Most of their property is gone, the pawnbrokers' shops are full, and one of the largest pawnbrokers in the town told me to-day that it is a fortnight at least since he had any pledge of this sort offered at his shop. The articles which are now finding their way to him are the stock in trade of the small shopkeepers who begin to feel the pressure of the times, and especially of the 3s. rate which is now being levied with some threatenings of rigour. This is a class of the population very much to be pitied. Most of those who depend on the factory operatives have suffered severely—some are not doing a quarter of their accustomed business, and a few are already ruined altogether. I have been in two or three shops, which were really nothing but an array of empty cases—the mere ghosts of shops—no goods for sale of any sort—and shopkeepers living like their customers, from the parish or the Relief Committee. In one shop I cleared out the last remnants of the stock by purchasing a modest parcel of local sweetmeats for the swarms of children in the next court, and the woman who served me said it was the first sale she had made for three weeks. The children, by the way, so far as I have seen, for the most part continue to look healthy, though in many cases the poorness of their food, or the long continuance of meal diet, have shown themselves in scorbutic diseases. They are worst off in the matter of clothing, and many I saw moving about with nothing more than a thin cotton dress, and perhaps a petticoat, to cover them.

What I have described may not perhaps be actual starvation, but it only just stops short of it. A considerable proportion of the population of the town have managed to keep body and soul together on this fare for the last six or nine months. Numbers are descending into their condition daily, and as the resources of the provident classes are exhausted the distress must get wider. To-day two shopkeepers and a publican were taken on the list of the relief committee, which shows that the evil is gradually rising to the class above the operatives. The praises which have been bestowed on the men for their conduct at this trying time, so far as I have seen, is thoroughly deserved; they accept their misfortunes with resignation and bear them with fortitude. There has been a good deal of grumbling at the harshness and incivility of some of the guardians, and at the labour test—to which I shall have to refer hereafter—but with these exceptions, the men have borne themselves with wonderful cheerfulness. The loudest complainant I have heard is "Whistling Dick," a half-silly beggar who gets his living by whistling through the streets, and who, finding his harmony totally unremunerative at present, threatens to transfer himself to some other more liberal community. Besides him I have not seen a single beggar in the streets. Another fact which is very creditable to the men is that the police books show a decided decrease of crime. All the charges recorded are mostly petty offences committed by young lads, who are allowed to run wild about the street, no provision having yet been made either to employ them usefully or send them to school.

August 30th, 1862   *page 11*

AMERICAN PHOTOGRAPHS

The pencil of the artist was never more fancifully employed than when it delineated those battle scenes of the last century which delighted the Courts and decorated the palace walls of France and Germany. But it must be admitted nevertheless that the object of giving an idea of what "a battle is like," which is a legitimate and universal bit of curiosity among men and women in all ages, was then more successfully accomplished than it is likely to be by means of photographic processes, so far as we know of them at present. When we gaze on the acres of canvass in Versailles, Munich, Berlin, or Petersburg, covered with the semblance of masses of men and serried squares and lines of infantry, clouds of cavalry and smoke, we know that the figures, with a few exceptions of prominent individuals, whose verisimilitude is in proportion to the painter's skill, are purely imaginery, and that the wounded man in whom we take such an interest, or the dashing squadron leader heading his surge of horse against the rocky square, never existed at all in the world military, but, with the little drummer who is beating his *pas de charge* so manfully in the advance of his column, were picked up from the "models" of the day. The photographer who follows in the wake of modern armies must be content with conditions of repose, and with the still life which remains when the fighting is over, but whatever he represents from the field must be real, and the private soldier has just as good a likeness as the General. Barring faults of manipulation and artistic power, the likenesses must be like, and they must be real if the mechanism is of moderate goodness. When the artist essays to represent motion he bewilders the plate and makes chaos, and so far as we have yet gone, a photographic "charge" is an impossibility. Mr. Fenton was probably the first photographer who ever pitched his camera-stand under fire, but Mr. Simpson was out before him in the Crimea, and it is no disparagement to the former to say that the scenes in the trenches were much more interesting than the likenesses or groups or other works of the photographer, though, they were more ideal or less actual. It was considered something remarkable when Mr. Fenton succeeded in fixing on his plate the puff of smoke from a distant gun. After him, and perhaps with greater opportunity, certainly with greater success, came Mr. Beato, who has since been with the British armies in India and in China, reaping a golden harvest, whose reproductions of Oriental architecture were wonderfully good, but gave far less pleasure than the sketches of Mr. Lundgren, who was engaged for Her Majesty. The photographer, however, could multiply his copies as fast as he pleased, and every one could send home his image in jackboots, beard, dust, and topee for a few shillings. The artist could barely colour his drawings by working incessantly. The French had recognized photographers in attendance on their army in Italy, and for purposes of natural history, for architecture, and still-life their work is not to be excelled. America swarms with the members of the mighty tribe of cameristas, and the civil war has developed their business in the same way that it has given an impetus to the manufacturers of metallic air-tight coffins and embalmers of the dead. The young Volunteer rushes off at once to the studio when he puts on his uniform, and the soldier of a year's campaign sends home his likeness that the absent ones may see what changes have been produced in him by war's alarms. In every glade and by the roadsides of the camp may be seen all kinds of covered carts and portable sheds for the worker in metal acid, and sun-ray—

August 30th, 1862

Washington has burst out into signboards of ambrotypists and collodionists, and the "professors" of New York, Boston, and Philadelphia send their representatives to pick up whatever is left, and to follow the camps as well as they can. We have before us a collection of photographs by one of the best known of American photographers, Mr. Brady, of New York, which includes, however, not merely the war scenes to which we have alluded, but a number of interesting portraits of the most eminent Americans and of some strangers. First, there are two plates of the Monitor, one showing her deck, which seems raised a vast distance above the water, whereas it is only a few inches, and the cupola or revolving tower, with the shot-marks upon it from the Merrimac's guns. It is not too much to say that an Armstrong or a good solid shot gun would have destroyed such armour and such a fabric as the plate represents. There are but four marks on the armour, and those of the feeblest character. The other represents the crew on the deck in easy groups, which are creditable to the skill of the artist—a set of stout, brawny fellows, in no particular uniform, and rather unkempt—of whom a few have the air of the genuine "old salt." For guns and the like the lens is well adapted in experienced hands, and here we have a striking "picture of the effect caused by the bursting of a 100lb. shell" on board the Confederate gunboat Teazer, which was captured by the Federals, deck stove in, iron stanchions gone, a great crater in the hold, machinery torn into ribands, but at best the craft, with its engines exposed on deck, and frail scantling, was a perilous thing to put a gun into. Mr. Brady's artist went down to Richmond, and has sent us some views which are of interest, but generally the sun of Virginia was too powerful, and the appearance of snow is produced on most of the photographs, and an excessive whiteness of colour diminishes the effect. Groups of wounded out in the open sun at Savage's Station, on the railroad to Richmond, "the house where Washington wooed his Martha," burnt by the Federals when they abandoned the line of the Pamunkey, Virginian farmers' wooden houses; the balloon and its *modus operandi*, the Confederate works at Yorktown, the ruins of Hampton destroyed by Magruder with its venerable—for it was the oldest edifice of the sort in the States—church, batteries of artillery, horses and all, which would be a very curious subject of study to our Horse Guards, as they might get an idea of what the Federal cavalry are like by examining the appearance, seat, equipments, and horses of the field artillery, which are unquestionably the best part of the Federal army. These, and the like, are all very worthy of attention. It can be seen from them that the work executed by the Confederates at Yorktown was very slovenly, but that nothing that was ever seen of the most slovenly European soldiery can equal the utter want of military smartness in the Federal Artillery. Men with unbuttoned coats, and open collars, and all sorts of head gear are seated, with their overalls gathered half-way up the leg, in their saddles with an attempt to dress in line, which renders their short-comings more obvious. The most agreeable subject in the volume, perhaps, is one of a Confederate Lieutenant of the Washington family and name—for all the representatives of the *Pater Patriae* are and were Secessionists,—who was taken prisoner, sitting beside his college friend and relation, Captain Custis, of the United States' army, while a negro boy, barefooted, with hands clasped, is at the feet and between the knees of his master, with an expression of profound grief on his shining face. The Confederate, in his coarse gray uniform, sits up erect with a bull-dog, fighting face and head; the Federal, a fair-haired, thoughtful looking man, looks much more like a prisoner; the *teterrima causa belli*, who appears to think only of his master, is suggestive enough. We can see here that the houses in which the better sort of people live in this part of the old dominion would not content the humblest of our tenant-farmers or yeomen; that the Federal soldiery do not improve in appearance during the war; and that their attention to uniform is of the smallest, and we form some idea of the difficulties of fighting in such a country when we observe that every view is fringed by woods.

Turning to the volume of portraits, the eye is first arrested by Mr. Lincoln, sitting, in company with an ink-bottle, at a table, which does not conceal that foot which he is so often said by the papers "to put down" on various questions,—an odd, quaint face, sagacious notwithstanding the receding brow, and kindly despite the coarse, heavy-lipped mouth, but with such capillary arrangements that, in combination with the long-limbed, narrow body and great extremities, there is a gorilla expression produced by the *ensemble*. Next is Hannibal Hamlin, Vice-President, who is chiefly interesting on account of what he might become. Turn over and Mr. Stanton gives a sitting for his head alone, the lines of which do not stand comparison very well with the keen clear outline of Mr. Seward's features, next to it. Why did not Mr. Brady give the full face of Mr. Seward, so that one could see his eye? In other respects the likeness, though it does not convey that air of "cunning and conceit" which Prince Napoleon's attaché attributed in his *feuilleton* to the Secretary of State, is characteristic and true. Pass over Mr. Bates, and we come to Mr. Chase, who is standing with one hand outside his coat, over his breeches pocket, and the other on a plaster-of-Paris pedestal, looking as though he were waiting for some one to lend him a little money, and expecting it, too. He has one of the best heads among the Cabinet, though one cannot help remarking he has a defect in his eyes, and, oddly enough, so has General Butler, and so has Mr. Jefferson Davis. It is not too much to say that any stranger would be struck by the immense superiority of the heads and expression of Mr. Davis, of General Polk, of Beauregard, of "Stonewall" Jackson, and Lee to most of the Federal chiefs, or whom few are at all striking in any way. M'Clellan looks small, and anxious, and unhappy; Blenker stands like a soldier, and has the air of being one; and Burnside seems calm, and self-possessed, and capable; Halleck's head is intellectual, but the face is dreamy and the lower jaw feeble; Pope, a stout, florid, sanguine-looking man, is like a German bass-singer in fine condition; and there is no other to speak of, excepting perhaps Meagher and M'Dowell, in the list of soldiers worth looking at a second time, after we have passed Banks, the unhappy recipient of "Stonewall" Jackson's favours. The few naval men in the book contrast advantageously with many of the soldiers, but some of the best of the latter are not here. "Stonewall" Jackson's likeness is something like that of Ney—a remarkable head, but without the beetle-brows, shaggy and over-hanging the full eye, attributed to him. From the Confederate soldiers there is but the thickness of a cardboard to the Federal journalists, of whom the most remarkable thing is that they all seem to be above the age for liability to conscription. Literary men follow a group of the clergy, and the fine faces of Longfellow and Motley are among the best in the collection. Jefferson Davis, who comes after a batch of Federal politicians, is back to back with Jerritt Smith, and Mr. Stephens, the Vice-President of the Southern Confederacy, supports Mr. Charles Sumner. The portrait of Chief Justice Taney attracts one not merely on account of the air of the venerable old man, but because it is the likeness of the Judge who will, in all probability, prove the last that ever sat on the bench as head of the Supreme Court of the United States, and in whose person was signally demonstrated the complete worthlessness of that boasted palladium of the American Constitution when the storm arose and the sword was unsheathed by violent and unscrupulous men. *Place aux dames!* In the photograph of Mrs. Lincoln the loyalty and skill of Mr. Brady are as conspicuous as his gallantry in adapting the focus to the subject, but he has treated the wife of the President, who is, of course, the "first lady in the United States," much better than he has Miss Lane, who did the honours of the White House for President Buchanan, and who won such praise for her discharge of them. The women's portraits, which are almost at the end of the volume, are not many. Admitting many merits, and some very good specimens of the art in this collection, it does not appear from it that American photographers, among whom Mr. Brady occupies the highest place, have attained to that beauty of finish and fidelity which distinguish the better European artists, while they are immeasurably behind them in landscape. If one uses a magnifier to most of these subjects, it will be seen the paper is fluffy, and the photograph spoilt by a sort of dustlike covering, such as we were familiar with here some years ago. But the portraits are of lasting attractiveness, although we are too apt, when looking at them now, to forget that we are scanning the features of men who will be famous hereafter as actors in the greatest drama which the world has seen in these later ages.

The author of the following blazingly injudicious article was George Wingrove Cooke (1814-1865). Having passed simultaneously through Jesus College, Oxford, and the Middle Temple, he earned his living partly as a minor legal functionary (he worked for the Tithe Commutation Commission and the Enclosure Commission), partly as a voluminous author, chiefly of legal treatises. He wrote regularly for The Times, *and achieved some distinction as the paper's correspondent in China during the Second Opium War (1857); his dispatches were collected and published in book form, as were a subsequent set of reports from Algeria* (Conquest and Colonisation in North Africa, *1860). His qualifications for commenting on North American affairs are not apparent, but like Delane's other drudges, he was expected to be, or to pretend to be, omniscient.*

It is rarely that a man can be found to balance accurately mischief to another against advantage to himself. President LINCOLN is, as the world says, a good-tempered man, neither better nor worse than the mass of his kind—neither a fool nor a sage, neither a villain nor a saint, but a piece of that common useful clay out of which it delights the American democracy to make great Republican personages. Yet President LINCOLN has declared that from the 1st of January next to come every State that is in rebellion shall be in the eye of Mr. LINCOLN a Free State. After that date Mr. LINCOLN proposes to enact that every slave in a rebel State shall be for ever after free, and he promises that neither he, nor his army, nor his navy will do anything to repress any efforts which the negroes in such rebel States may make for the recovery of their freedom. This means, of course, that Mr. LINCOLN will, on the 1st of next January, do his best to excite a servile war in the States which he cannot occupy with his arms. He will run up the rivers in his gunboats; he will seek out the places which are left but slightly guarded, and where the women and children have been trusted to the fidelity of coloured domestics. He will appeal to the black blood of the African; he will whisper of the pleasures of spoil and of the gratification of yet fiercer instincts; and when blood begins to flow and shrieks come piercing through the darkness, Mr. LINCOLN will wait till the rising flames tell that all is consummated, and then he will rub his hands and think that revenge is sweet. This is what Mr. LINCOLN avows before the world that he is about to do. Now, we are in Europe thoroughly convinced that the death of slavery must follow as necessarily upon the success of the Confederates in this war as the dispersion of darkness occurs upon the rising of the sun; but sudden and forcible emancipation resulting from "the efforts the negroes may make for their actual freedom" can only be effected by massacre and utter destruction. Mr. LINCOLN avows, therefore, that he proposes to excite the negroes of the Southern plantations to murder the families of their masters while these are engaged in the war. The conception of such a crime is horrible. The employment of Indians sinks to a level with civilized warfare in comparison with it; the most detestable doctrines of MAZZINI are almost less atrocious; even Mr. LINCOLN'S own recent achievements of burning by gun-boats the defenceless villages on the Mississippi are dwarfed by this gigantic wickedness. The single thing to be said for it is that it is a wickedness that holds its head high and scorns hypocrisy. It does not pretend to attack slavery as slavery. It launches this threat of a servile rebellion as a means of war against certain States, and accompanies it with a declaration of general protection to all other slavery.

Where he has no power Mr. LINCOLN will set the negroes free; where he retains power he will consider them as slaves. "Come to me," he cries to the insurgent planters, "and I will preserve your rights as slaveholders; but set me still at defiance, and I will wrap myself in virtue and take the sword of freedom in my hand, and, instead of aiding you to oppress, I will champion the rights of humanity. Here are whips for you who are loyal; go forth and flog or sell your black chattels as you please. Here are torches and knives for employment against you who are disloyal; I will press them into every black hand, and teach their use." Little Delaware, with her 2,000 slaves, shall still be protected in her loyal tyranny. Maryland, with her 90,000 slaves, shall "freely accept or freely reject" any project for either gradual or immediate abolition; but if Mississippi and South Carolina, where the slaves rather outnumber the masters, do not repent, and receive from Mr. LINCOLN a licence to trade in human flesh, that human flesh shall be adopted by Mr. LINCOLN as the agent of his vengeance. The position is peculiar for a mere layman. Mr. LINCOLN, by this proclamation, constitutes himself a sort of moral American Pope. He claims to sell indulgences to his own votaries, and he offers them with full hands to all who will fall down and worship him. It is his to bind, and it is his to loose. His decree of emancipation is to go into remote States, where his temporal power cannot be made manifest, and where no stars and stripes are to be seen; and in those distant swamps he is, by a sort of Yankee excommunication, to lay the land under a slavery interdict.

What will the South think of this? The South will answer with a hiss of scorn. But what will the North think of it? What will Pennsylvania say—Pennsylvania, which is already unquiet under the loss of her best customers, and not easy under the absolute despotism of the present Government at Washington? What Boston may say or think is not, perhaps, of much consequence. But what will New York say? It would not answer the purpose of any of these cities to have the South made a howling wilderness. They want the handling of the millions which are produced by the labour of the black man. Pennsylvania desires to sell her manufactures in the South; New York wishes to be again broker, banker, and merchant to the South. This is what the Union means to these cities. They would rather have a live independent State to deal with than a dead dependency where nothing could be earnt. To these practical persons President LINCOLN would be, after his black revolution had succeeded, like a dogstealer who should present the anxious owner with the head of his favourite pointer. They want the useful creature alive. The South without its cotton and its sugar and its tobacco would be of small use to New York, or even to Philadelphia; and the South without the produce of its rice and cotton, and its sugar and tobacco, would be but a sorry gain, even if it could be obtained. If President LINCOLN wants such a conquest as this, the North is, perhaps, yet strong enough to conquer Hayti. A few fanatics, of course, will shout, but we cannot think that, except in utter desperation and vindictiveness, any real party in the North will applaud this nefarious resolution to light up a servile war in the distant homesteads of the South.

As a proof of what the leaders of the North, in their passion and their despair, would do if they could, this is a very sad document. As a proof of the hopelessness and recklessness which prompt their actions, it is a very instructive document. But it is not a formidable document. We gather from it that Mr. LINCOLN has lost all hope of preserving the Union, and is now willing to let any quack try his nostrum. As an act of policy it is, if possible, more contemptible than it is wicked. It may possibly produce some partial risings, for let any armed power publish an exhortation to the labouring class of any community to plunder and murder, and there will be some response. It might happen in London, or Paris, or New York. That Mr. LINCOLN's emancipation decrees will have any general effect bearing upon the issue of the war we do not, however, believe. The negroes have already abundantly discovered that the tender mercies of the Northerners are cruelties. The freedom which is associated with labour in the trenches, military discipline, and frank avowals of personal abhorrence momentarily repeated does not commend itself to the negro nature. General BUTLER could, if he pleased, tell strange stories of the ill success of his tamperings with the negroes about

New Orleans. We do not think that even now, when Mr. LIN-
COLN plays his last card, it will prove to be a trump. Powerful
malignity is a dreadful reality, but impotent malignity is apt to
be a very contemptible spectacle. Here is a would-be conqueror
and a would-be extirpator who is not quite safe in his seat of
government, who is reduced to such straits that he accepts a
defeat as a glorious escape, a capitulation of 8,000 men as an
unimportant event, a drawn battle as a glorious victory, and the
retreat of an invading army which retires laden with plunder and
rich in stores as a deliverance. Here is a President who has just,
against his will, supplied his antagonists with a hundred and
twenty guns and millions of stores, and who is trembling for the
very ground on which he stands. Yet, if we judged only by his
pompous proclamations, we should believe that he had a garrison
in every city of the South. This is more like a Chinaman beating
his two swords together to frighten his enemy than like an earnest man pressing on his cause in steadfastness and truth.

*Francis Lawley (1825-1901) ruined a promising political career by
gambling on horses, which in turn involved him in dubious activ-
ities on the Stock Exchange. He retired, disgraced, to America in
1854; however his contributions to* The Times *seem to have re-
habilitated him. At any rate he returned to England in 1865 and
became a writer on sport for the* Daily Telegraph. *Most of his Civil
War letters were forwarded to Printing House Square through the
French consulate at Richmond and the Paris office of* The Times,
*a circuitous route which sufficiently explains why they always
appeared in the paper so long after they were written. His reporting
is somewhat distorted by his pro-Southern bias and his close relationship to General Longstreet (thanks to whom, for example,
Lawley constantly over-rated Hood and under-rated Joe Johnston).
But he was hard-working, intelligent, and had an eye for the significant detail. He faithfully records the collapse of the South
though he does not entirely recognize the meaning of what he puts
on paper.*

THE SOUTHERN CONFEDERACY

FROM OUR SPECIAL CORRESPONDENT.

RICHMOND, Nov. 21.

... General Lee is, I believe, between 50 and 60 years of age, but wears his years well, and strikes you as the incarnation of health and endurance, as he rears his erect soldierlike form from his seat by the fireside to greet courteously the stranger. His manner is calm and stately, his presence impressive and imposing, his dark brown eyes remarkably direct and honest as they meet you fully and firmly, and inspire plenary confidence. The shape and type of the head a little resemble Garibaldi's, but the features are those of a much handsomer man. On the rare occasions when he smiles, and on still rarer occasions when he laughs heartily, disclosing a fine unbroken row of white, firm set teeth, the confidence and sympathy which he inspires are irresistible. A child thrown among a knot of strangers would be inevitably drawn to General Lee first in the company, and would run to claim his protection. The voice is fine and deep, but slightly monotonous in its tone. Altogether, the most winning attribute of the General is his unaffected childlike guilelessness. It is very rare that a man of his age, conversant with important events, and thrown to the surface of mighty convulsions, retains the impress of a simple, ingenuous nature to so eminent a degree. It is impossible to converse with him for ten minutes without per-ceiving how deeply he has meditated upon all the possible eventualities of the campaign in Virginia, and how sound and well-considered are the positions which he advances. It is obvious that the most entire and trusting confidence is placed in General Lee by his subordinate officers, whose respect and affection he seems thoroughly to have won. The General is still crippled in his hands from the effects of a fall which he sustained so long ago as the 30th of August. At dawn of that day he rode across the historical stream of Bull Run, and, observing a patch of herbage, he dismounted and allowed his horse to graze, recol-lecting that the animal had carried him the whole preceeding day almost without food. The General himself sat down on a stump. There was only a few cavalry pickets of Confederates between General Lee and the enemy. Suddenly a charge of a

90

large body of Yankee cavalry drove in the Confederate pickets, and came close up to the spot where General Lee was. The General ran forward to catch his horse, and, grasping at the rein as his horse sidled off, he fell heavily forward entangled in his cloak, upon both hands, and jarred the nerves of the arms right up to the shoulders. His horse was caught by one of his staff, and the Yankee cavalry, not knowing what a valuable prize was close at hand, fell back without approaching more nearly. The General rode throughout the whole of that eventful day, the 30th of August, but for many days and nights he suffered agonizing pain; and even now, on the 21st of November, he is far from having wholly recovered the full use of his hands; though not for one day or hour has he permitted himself to be absent from duty.

A similar abnegation of self is visible in every thought and act of General Lee. "If only I am permitted to finish the work I have on hand, I would be content to live on bread and beef for the rest of my life." "Occasionally we have only beef, occasionally only bread; but if we have both together, and salt is added to them, we think ourselves Sybarites." "Upon this occasion it was necessary to stop and procure food for some of the younger men." These are some of the characteristic utterances which struck me as they came from General Lee's lips. In reference to the last, it would seem as though the ordinary demands of human appetite were in him subordinated and subjected in presence of the imperious exactions required from his brain. In all the varied attributes which go to make up the commander-in-chief of a great army, it is certain that General Lee has no superior in the Confederacy, and it may fairly be doubted whether he has any equal.

General Lee has three sons in the army—the one a General, under General J. E. B. Stuart; the second a Colonel; the third, a lad of 18, who is a private attached to one of the batteries of General Jackson's corps. In reference to the last, General Lee told me a story which seemed to me, for the first and only time during many conversations, to have elicited from the narrator faint traces of emotion. Most certainly it was difficult to listen to the story without one's self experiencing such emotion. It appears that at the most critical moment of the Battle of Sharpsburg, when General Lee was ordering up every gun to meet the heavy masses of Federal artillery pressing on the centre, he observed a single gun harnessed and ready for action, the sole survivor of a battery which had been engaged earlier in the day, and had been roughly handled by the Federals. General Lee immediately ordered the gun to the front. As it passed to the front, coming close to the spot where General Lee was standing, he recognized in the postillion mounted on the leading horses his young son. The boy turned and smiled brightly on his father, exclaiming, "So I see that you are sending us in again." It is a pleasure to add that, although slightly wounded, the boy lived to come safely out of the terrible engagement.

At a distance of seven miles from General Lee's head-quarters, near the little village of Bunkerhill, were the head-quarters of the hero of heroes of this struggle, General "Stone-wall" Jackson. We had been taught to expect a morose, reserved, distant reception; we found the most genial, courteous, and forthcoming of companions. A bright, piercing, blue eye, a slightly aquiline nose, a thin, tall sinewy frame, "made all over of pin-wire," a great disregard of dress and appearance—these are the characteristics of General Jackson's exterior. There is also about him a very direct and honest look. The disappointing circumstance is, that his voice, which is rapid in its utterance, is weak and unimpressive. Passionately attached to the Valley of Virginia, which has for so long been the principal scene of his achievements, idolized by the inhabitants of Winchester and of the Valley, General Jackson has acquired such a fame in that entire neighbourhood that is sad to think what would happen if the one life round which such prestige clings should yield to a stray bullet or to the chance of disease. Sinewy and wiry as the General seems, it is impossible not to fancy that he is wearing himself terribly by his restless, sleepless activity, by his midnight marches, and by the asceticism of his life. The respect and consciousness of his presence, and what that presence means, exhibited by his staff, impressed me very strongly, and seemed to exceed the respect exhibited towards General Lee. He spoke a few hearty words of admiration of General Lee, saying that he never should wish to serve under an abler commander. But his heartiest and most enthusiastic utterances were in admiration of the Cathedral edifices of England, and notably of York Minster. He dwelt with great animation upon the vibration of the air produced by the deep notes of the organ in York Minster, and which he had never heard equalled elsewhere. It is rare to find in a Presbyterian such appreciation and admiration of Cathedral magnificence.

There are such endless stories about General Jackson that to repeat them would fill a volume. Stories of his being wrapt in prayer in the midst of a fierce engagement,—stories of the unaffected earnestness and piety of his life in his tent, and of his black servant saying that when his master, who invariably prays morning and evening, rises also in the middle of the night to pray, he knows that great and critical events are imminent. A most undemonstrative, reticent man, doubtless, in all that regards his vocation of a soldier. There is every reason to think that, when the war is over, General Jackson will be the very first man to bury himself in the deepest obscurity of private life. Throughout this war it has been the practice of General Jackson to throw himself, disregarding his own inferiority of numbers, upon large bodies of his enemy, and the day is ordinarily half-won by the suddenness and desperation of the attack. His usual policy then is to retire, upon which the correspondents of the Northern journals, who upon the day of General Jackson's onslaught have been half-frightened out of their lives, announce with their usual *fanfares* a great Federal victory, and joy and exultation are universal. In a few days, however, when the Federals have reached some spot where it suits General Jackson to attack them, he pounces upon them again, and frequently the very fame of his second approach drives his opponents to a precipitate retreat without fighting, if the ground admits of such a possibility. The upshot of nearly a year and a half of General Jackson's conduct of the war, frequently at the head of no more than a handful of men, is that no permanent foothold has been gained by the Federals in the Valley, and that, at will, General Jackson has run his opponents, sometimes including at once two or three Federal Generals of rank, out of the Valley. As there are many conflicting reports about the origin of the name "Stonewall," it may be interesting to repeat the true circumstances under which it was given. In the first battle of Manassas, on July 21, 1861, General Bee, of South Carolina (himself subsequently killed in the same action), observing his men flinching and wavering, called out to them to stand firm, exclaming, "Look at Jackson's men; they stand like a stone wall!" In his official report of the battle, General Beauregard employed the same expression in connexion with General Jackson's command, and the name has clung to General Jackson ever since. . . .

AMERICA AND THE LANCASHIRE DISTRESS

The following letter has been received at Manchester:—

"New York, Dec. 15. 1862.

"Gentlemen,—At a meeting of the citizens of New York, held in this month, a committee was appointed and denominated the 'International Relief Committee' for the purpose of collecting supplies of food and forwarding them to Liverpool, to be used for the relief of the suffering operatives of Lancashire and other parts of Great Britain. Copies of the appeal of that committee to the American people are herewith submitted for your perusal. In it you will find pointed out with sufficient clearness the objects of the movement, and the spirit in which they are sought to be accomplished. Both, we trust, will receive your ready approval.

"The contributions thus to be obtained are to be shipped freight free to the consignment of Messrs. Daniel James, of the firm of Phelps, James and Co. : Stephen B. Guion of the firm of Guion and Co.; Benjamin F. Babcock, of the firm of Benjamin F. Babcock and Co., Liverpool. These gentlemen are constituted a committee to receive the shipments; to procure, if possible, exemption from all the expenses of importation, and to deliver them to a committee of distribution well acquainted with the districts where the food is to be consumed, and with the wants of the poor operatives, and able to direct the supplies to those accessible points where they will accomplish the most good.

"We are advised by some of your numerous personal friends here that you not only possess those qualifications, but also that we shall find in you earnest advocates of the cause in which we are engaged and willing co-operators therein. We, therefore, have chosen you as a committee of distribution, and solicit your acceptance of the office and assumption of its duties. You also have authority in your discretion to add to your number.

"In the famine which desolated Ireland during the year 1847 the people of the United States contributed largely to the relief of the sufferers. On that occasion the British Government bore all the expense of introducing the contributions into the country, and the food was given to the comsumers without pecuniary cost or diminution.

94

"The vessels also which were laden with these supplies and carried them freight free were exempted from port charges and expenses of every kind. We are informed that the total amount thus added to that relief fund exceeded 40,000 livres. This precedent, it is to be hoped, Her Majesty's Ministers will now deem it expedient and just to follow.

"We solicit the exertion of your influence in aid of the committee in Liverpool in their efforts to secure exemption from import duties, dock and town dues, railway freight, and all other charges on vessels and cargo. We have taken the liberty to assure them that you would render them all the service in your power with the Government, local authorities, railway companies, and any other body or individual having the control of inland transportation.

"The ship George Greswold is receiving cargo here as fast as circumstances will permit, and will sail as soon as she can be filled with contributions to the Relief Fund. The ship Hope, partly freighted with contributions by the committee of the 'Produce Exchange' of this city, is about sailing for Liverpool. This committee acts in harmony and concert with the International Relief Committee. The objects of the two are identical, and the wish is that the shipments of both should flow in the same channel, and accomplish the same benevolent end.

"We are, Gentlemen, very respectfully,
"Your most obedient servants,
"JOHN C. GREEN, Chairman.
"JOHN TAYLOR JOHNSTON, Secretary.
"To Messrs. Thomas Feilden. W.S. Stell, Manchester;
Mr. Frank Crossley, Halifax. England."

January 23rd, 1863   *page 9*

THE SOUTHERN CONFEDERACY

(FROM OUR SPECIAL CORRESPONDENT.)

RICHMOND, DEC. 20, 1862.

... My last letter brought the narrative of events before Fredericksburg up to the night of Saturday, the 13th of December. It would be idle to pretend that upon that night the magnitude of the success which had been gained by the Confederates was fully gauged and comprehended by their Generals. It was hoped and

95

believed that Sunday, the 14th, would witness a renewal of the Federal attack; and the night of the 13th and the subsequent nights were busily employed by the Confederates in strengthening their fortifications and throwing up fresh earthworks on the Confederate centre and right. "If I had only thrown up these works before," exclaimed General Lee two or three days after the battle, "I should have saved many valuable lives." That a renewal of the Federal attack would have been most disastrous to the assailants it is now hardly necessary to state. It was felt by the Confederate Generals that after Saturday's experience no serious assault would again be directed against Marye's Heights, and ample provisions were made for meeting the heavy onslaught which it was expected would on the morrow be made against General Jackson's corps on the Confederate right. Never were the spirits of that General more ecstatic than during the fight on Saturday, and while his antagonists appeared to "mean business" on the morrow. But it must be confessed that, while the bulk of the Confederate army believed in the renewal of the battle on the 14th, there were not wanting Confederate Generals whose prescience told them that troops so roughly handled as the Yankees would be little apt to resume the offensive. Among others, on Saturday night, General Stuart hazarded the prediction that there would be no fresh attack by the Federals on the Confederate lines. A lingering wish to direct his Horse Artillery there and then against the enemy's flank was probably uppermost that night in the General's mind.

When Sunday, the 14th, came, it brought full confirmation of General Stuart's words. The day was clear and calm and warm as its predecessor, but totally devoid of haze or fog. The Yankees, on their left and centre, had passed the night in the plain, where darkness overtook them, without blankets, without fires, with only half-rations. The day wore away, and witnessed no Federal advance. There was heavy skirmishing between the pickets in front of General A. P. Hill's division, and occasionally the boom of a heavy piece of artillery, fired from one or the other side of the river, struck upon the ear, and sounded as a strange contrast to the incessant and continuous roar of the day before. On the night of the 14th prophecies that the Yankees had had enough of it, and would get back across the river as best they could, were more abundant, and when the morning of the 15th broke and still the Federals failed to advance, it became incontestable that the

Federal army was in a perilous strait, with a deep river and three pontoon bridges behind, and with a victorious and elated enemy and 300 pieces of artillery in front.

As the afternoon of the 15th advanced there was the same coquetting on the part of the Federals as to asking permission to bury their dead and carry off their wounded as had been displayed by them on the field of Sharpsburg. At Sharpsburg, as has been many times previously remarked, the ground on which the battle was fought was held by the Confederates. To have sent a flag of truce and asked permission to bury his dead would have seriously discredited General M'Clellan's repeated telegrams that he had gained a great victory. It became necessary, therefore, to have recourse to artifice, and a flag of truce was sent in by one of the inferior Federal Generals, which was subsequently disavowed and disclaimed, or perhaps was never recognized, by General M'Clellan himself. Such is believed here to have been the secret history of the Sharpsburg flag of truce. Something of the same kind was attempted on the afternoon of December 15. There was every disposition in the Confederate Generals to strain a point to alleviate the misery of the wounded Federals who had now lain three nights on the field; but General Lee's resolution that no flag of truce should be accepted unless sent by General Burnside to himself was final and inexorable. A flag sent in, as was believed, by the Federal General Birney was therefore rejected. Every possible effort was made by the Confederates to relieve the sufferings of those wounded men whom their companions had not carried off the field; but, as is usual on such occasions the individual cases of misery were terrible and heart-rending. Such a scene as a battle-field presents during the first night after a battle it would baffle any mortal pen to describe. In addition to the agonized cries for water, and to the groans of tortured and dying men, may be heard voices, constantly growing fainter and fainter, shouting out names and numbers of their regiments in the hope that some of their comrades may be within hearing, or that a party from their regiment may have been sent out to fetch in its wounded men. "Fourteenth Massachusetts!" "One Hundred and Fourth Pennsylvania!" "Forty-seventh North Carolina!" Such are some of the shouts which ring through the night air, and are never likely to be forgotten by those on whose ear they fall. In the end no flag of truce for burying the dead was on this occasion adjusted until the morning of Wednesday, the

17th of December, when the Federals sent over a large body of men to bury their numerous slain. The wounded were by permission carried off on the afternoon of Monday, the 15th.

But in the meantime, on the night of Monday, it was determined by the Federal Generals not to risk another day without putting the river between themselves and their victorious foe. A more favourable night for their purpose cannot be conceived. On the afternoon of Monday the wind began to rise, and by 7 in the evening and during the night it blew a hurricane from the south, so that all sound from the Federal army was carried away to the north in a direction contrary to the position occupied by the Confederates. At the same time there fell a deluge of rain. Great credit is certainly due to the Federal Generals for passing nearly 100,000 men and all their cannon in one night across three pontoon bridges without accident or confusion. If the purpose of the Federals had been penetrated, and the immense concentration of troops in the streets of Fredericksburg had been known to General Lee, no doubt a few shells thrown into the town might have caused considerable slaughter, and occasioned great confusion among the dense masses of the enemy. But when the morning of the 16th dawned great was the surprise of General Lee and of the Confederates to find that not one Yankee, save those who lay stiff and stark and a few wounded men in Fredericksburg, too badly injured to bear transportation across the river, remained on the southern side of the Rappahannock. There is a certain rhyme about the King of France and the manner in which he handled his 40,000 men which irresistibly recurred to the memory when it was found that General Burnside and his troops were all gone.

Gone, indeed, they were; but in what fashion? A glance at the long slope between the town of Fredericksburg and the foot of Marye's Heights gave the best idea of the magnitude of the toll which had been exacted for their passage of the Rappahannock. A ride along the whole length of the lines told also a sad tale of slaughter; but when the eye had once rested upon the fatal slope above mentioned the memory became fixed upon the spot; nor for 50 years to come will that scene ever fade from the memory of those who saw it. There, in every attitude of death, lying so close to each other that you might step from body to body, lay acres of the Federal dead. It seemed that most of the faces which lay nearest to Colonel Walton's artillery were of the well-known Milesian type. In one small garden, not more than half an acre in size, there were counted 151 corpses. I doubt whether in any battle-field of modern times the dead have ever lain so thick and close. By universal consent of those who have seen all the great battles of this war, nothing like it has ever been seen before. It is said that the morning after a victory always breaks upon naked corpses. It was not so in this case, but the sole reason was that the pickets of both armies swept the slope with their fire, and that any living thing which showed upon it was the target for a hundred bullets. But three or four mornings after the battle it was seen that the furtive hand which invariably glides into the pocket of victory had been busily at work, and naked corpses and others from which everything but their under clothing had been rifled were visible in abundance. So tremendous was the fire, chiefly emanating from Cobb's Brigade, posted in the lane at the foot of Marye's Heights, that even chickens in the gardens in front fell pierced by it. It was remarked by a Confederate General intimately acquainted with the Federal General Sumner, who commanded the Federal right, "Was there ever any other General but Sumner who would have got his men into a place in which not even chickens could live?" But the fire across the slope was fatal not only to men and chickens, but also to every other living thing. Horses by dozens were strewn along the hillside; and occasionally a dead cow or a dead hog lay close to the silent and too often fearfully torn and mutilated human bodies which everywhere met the view. Such a sight has rarely been seen by man. It is doubtful whether any living pen could do justice to its horrors; but it is certain that it would be easy to write more than any ordinary reader would care to read. It is known that during the nights of the 13th and 14th very many bodies were carried off and buried by the Federals; but when the party of Federals detailed to bury their comrades had completed their task it was found that under Marye's Heights they had buried 1,493 corpses, and 800 more on the Federal left. Computing that 3,000 Federals fell dead on the field, and adding six or seven times that number of wounded, you may gain an approximate estimate of the Federal loss on the 13th of December. To this must also be added upwards of a thousand prisoners taken by the Confederates, and all the stragglers and deserters who strayed away from the Federal army. It is incontestable that the 13th of December will be graven as deep in the annals of the great Republic as is the anniversary of Jena upon the hearts of the Prussian people.

It remains for me to give some account of the town of Fredericksburg, and the condition in which it was left by its ruthless invaders. Desolate it had appeared to me at the end of last month: how shall I describe its appearance now? The first impression of those who rode into its streets, and who had witnessed the *feu d'enfer* which the Federal guns had poured upon it for hours upon Thursday, the 11th of December, was surprise that more damage had not been done. But this is explained by the fact that the Federals confined themselves almost entirely to solid round shot, and that very few shells were discharged into the town. Nevertheless, a more pitiable devastation and destruction of property it would be difficult to conceive. Whole blocks of buildings have in many places been given to the flames. There is hardly a house through which at least one round-shot has not bored its way, and many are riddled through and through. The Baptist church is rent by a dozen great holes, while its neighbour, the Episcopalian church, has escaped with one. Scarcely a spot can be found on the face of the houses which look towards the river which is not pockmarked by bullets. Everywhere the houses have been plundered from cellar to garret; all smaller articles of furniture carried off, all larger ones wantonly smashed. Not a drawer or chest but was forced open and ransacked. The streets were sprinkled with the remains of costly furniture dragged out of the houses in the direction of the pontoons stretched across the river. Many of the inhabitants clung to the town, and sheltered themselves during the shelling in cellars and basements. Among others, it is stated that Mrs. Slaughter, the wife of the Mayor, returned two or three days after the bombardment to her house, which she found ransacked and gutted. A Federal officer offered a few words of explanation or apology, when she replied, pointing to half a dozen dead Federals lying within sight of her house, "I am repaid for all I have suffered by the sight of these." But there are sights more horrible than the devastation of property, and which, like the hillside below Marye's Heights, neither admit of nor invite description. It must be remembered that into the narrow limits of the town of Fredericksburg four-fifths of the Federal wounded were carried on the 13th and 14th of December. Hardly a house or shed but was converted into a hostpital; the churches and municipal buildings were crowded to bursting with dying and mangled men. Shutters and boards were laid down in gardens and yards, and upon them layer after layer of wounded men was stretched. Upon the night of the 13th the whole town was one continuous lazar-house; a few days later, when it was occupied by none except the dead, it became a continuous charnel-house. Death, nothing but death everywhere; great masses of bodies tossed out of the churches as the sufferers expired; layers of corpses stretched in the balconies of houses as though taking a *siesta*. In one yard a surgeon's block for operating was still standing, and, more appalling to look at even than the bodies of the dead, piles of arms and legs, amputated as soon as their owners had been carried off the field, were heaped in a corner. There were said to be houses literally crammed with the dead; but into them, horrified and aghast at what I saw, I could not look. . . .

Charles Mackay (1814-1889) was by courtesy a poet: he wrote the lyrics for innumerable songs, of which the best known was 'Cheer Boys Cheer'. A professional journalist, he had visited the United States in 1857 while editor of the Illustrated London News. *He was ill-suited to be the New York Correspondent of* The Times, *not only because, being a thoroughgoing defeatist, he told Delane and Morris, who were as defeatist as he, only what they wanted to hear, but also because he had none of the instincts of a reporter to go out and get a story. Instead he had the instincts of a columnist, an armchair commentator on events, which he had a genius for misinterpreting (as late as January 1865 he was still speculating about possible European recognition of the Confederacy). He had a bee in his bonnet about arbitrary arrests, which were freely sanctioned by Secretaries Seward and Stanton. At times he could write of very little else. His indignation was not wholly misplaced, but it was disproportionate, and certainly far exceeded that of most Americans. They remembered what he forgot, that the North was fighting for its life. They could make allowances. Mackay let his passion for individual liberties blind him to all other considerations. On the other hand, it must be remembered to his honour that he was never taken in by abolitionist cant. He knew, and repeatedly insisted, that the North was at least as racially bigoted as the South. Nor is he to be blamed for writing from his own point of view: he was hired to do just that. His dismissal in the spring of 1865 was an act of necessary injustice. As he himself commented, he had stood high in the favour of* The Times *'as long as Fortune seemed to smile on the cause of the Southern Confederacy'* (Through The Long Day, *ii, p. 395). When it became plain that the Confederacy was finished, Delane and Morris made Mackay the scapegoat for their own misjudgements. By getting a new New York correspondent they hoped to induce the world to overlook the errors of their leader writers.*

March 6th, 1863   *page 5*

THE CIVIL WAR IN AMERICA

(FROM OUR OWN CORRESPONDENT.)

NEW YORK, FEB. 17.

... The English student of Transatlantic public life is apt to become bewildered by the copious vocabulary of American party nomenclature. While in England Whig, Tory, and Radical, Free-trader and Protectionist, Liberal and Conservative, Obstructive and Destructive have been for five-and-twenty years almost the only party epithets that have obtained general currency and acceptation, America has employed a whole dictionary of phrases, invented by the exuberant humour, no less than by the equally exuberant hatred of contending factions. "Locofocos," "Hard Shells," "Soft Shells," "Dough-faces," "Knownothings," "Nigger worshippers," "Black Republicans," &c., have done duty, with such words as "Whigs," "Old-line Whigs," "Federalists," "Nullifiers," "Straight-out Democrats," and numerous other phrases, to designate the various divisions and subdivisions of parties. These were, however, the shibboleths and watchwords of a period of peace, and nearly all of them have disappeared. At the present time the political and Parliamentary belligerents of the North are separable into only two great bodies—the Democrats and the Republicans. But these lines do not, in reference to the war for the Union and the social and political *status* of the negro, make a clear demarcation. There are Democrats who love the Union more than they love liberty and happiness, or who imagine they do, and who even approve negro emancipation, provided the emancipated slaves are not allowed to

102

leave the South. On the other hand, there are Republicans who differ from the majority of their party on the question of slavery—who think that the President has done wrong in meddling with it, and who do not value the Union so highly as to look with complacency upon the ruin of the Northern people in the difficult, and it may be futile, attempt to restore it. Hence there are the divisions of "White Republicans" and "Black Republicans". The one is composed of Democrats and Republicans, who would not grant the negro any social position or political right whatever, and who maintain that Washington and Jefferson intended the Republic to be a Government of white men and of white men only. The other is composed of philanthropists, preachers, lecturers, and zealots, who proclaim that they would ruin and slay every white man, woman, and child in the South, rather than acknowledge that the negro was not a brother, and not as fully entitled as themselves to political equality; and who would obey—or say they would obey—a black President as implicitly as they would obey a white one, if, by the lawful agencies of that wondrous machine the ballot-box, Mr. Frederick Douglass, or any other whole or half-caste negro were nominated to the perilous position. The terms "Secessionists" and "Unionists" explain themselves, as do those of "Disunionists," "Peace Democrats," "War Democrats," and "Exterminators." Lately, however, three new words have obtained currency and fashion,—"Butternuts," "Copperheads," and "Woolly Heads." A "Butternut" is one who sympathizes with the South—one, in fact, who wears the uniform or livery of the Southern army, which is a brownish-gray colour, commonly the colour of the butternut, a species of walnut peculiar to America. The term "Copperhead" is employed by the Republicans to designate all persons, whether Republicans or Democrats, who are in favour of an armistice with the South, to be followed by a convention of the people to debate the terms of peace. The name is derived from that of a little venomous serpent very common in America—in the North as well as in the West and South,—which has a bright shining head of the colour of a new farthing. It haunts rocky places and stone walls, and its sting is supposed to be even more deadly than that of the rattlesnake. It is asserted that the word has a peculiar aptness not imagined by those who first applied it. The "rattlesnake" was the emblem of the State of South Carolina before it adopted the Palmetto. At certain seasons of the year, in the greatest heats of the summer, the rattlesnake becomes blind, and at such times, says popular tradition, it is always accompanied by the "copperhead," which acts towards it the part of a faithful friend in its calamity. Hence, say the Republicans and Exterminators, no term can be more appropriate for a venomous Northern man, who aids, comforts, and abets such a rattlesnake as South Carolina, than that of a Copperhead.

"Woolly Heads" is the new name given to the Negrophilists and Abolitionists by the Democrats. . . .

March 12th, 1863   *page 10*

LETTERS BY "HISTORICUS" ON
INTERNATIONAL LAW*

As the greater part of these letters lately appeared in our own columns, it is only necessary to notice them in general terms as a valuable contribution to the knowledge of a subject which has lately acquired a new and practical interest. The branch of international law which relates to the rights and obligations of belligerents towards neutrals had not unnaturally been neglected during the continuance of the longest maritime peace recorded in history. In the Russian war the superior force of the allies confined the enemy's fleets to their own harbours, and neutral traders were excluded from the Baltic ports of Russia, and at a later period from Odessa, by an effective blockade. For the purpose of conciliating France and of obviating collisions with the United States, the English Government for the first time waived the established claim of the following the goods of an enemy under a neutral flag. At the conferences of Paris the temporary concession was enlarged into a permanent relaxation of the laws of war among the nations of Europe. In return for the admission that the flag is henceforth to cover the goods, the Continental Powers abandoned in favour of England the right of employing privateers. The refusal of the United States to adopt the new arrangement has conferred a great and unexpected advantage on the Federal Government during the civil war. As

Letters by "Historicus" on Some Questions of International Law. Macmillan.

104

the American Courts have always adopted the English construction of maritime jurisprudence, the right of the Federal
cruisers to seize Confederate property in English merchant
vessels is unaffected by the European modification of belligerent
pretensions. As "Historicus" shows, the complaint of the owners
of the "Morning Star," that their ship had been overhauled by
the Tuscarora, was altogether groundless. Even under the regu-
lations of Paris, a ship may still be visited to search for contraband articles, or for the purpose of obtaining proof of an intention to violate a legal blockade. Although the Federal navy, in
a certain sense, commands the sea, the Confederate cruisers have
not failed to profit in their turn by the reserved right of seizing
hostile goods under a neutral flag. Yet, in the great majority of
instances, the Florida and Alabama have confined themselves to
the still more legitimate molestation of Federal vessels.

When the American war broke out, English traders and
jurists were almost startled by finding that, for the first during
many generations, their country occupied a neutral position. As
the maritime laws of war had been chiefly settled by decisions in
the courts of a Power which commanded the sea, it was suspected
that undue favour, formerly accorded to belligerents, might now
be found unduly burdensome to neutral commerce. An exaggerated form of the same belief produced, both on the Continent
and in America, fantastic hopes of disappointment to England
and extravagant versions both of history and of law. The experience of two years has, however, fully justified the wisdom and
judicial impartiality of Lord Stowell's decisions. From the
seizure of the passengers on the Trent to the latest capture of a
vessel at Charleston or Mobile, the rules which had been established by the English Courts of Admiralty, and deliberately
sanctioned by the great American jurists, have been found
adequate to the occasion. While sciolists and brawlers have
announced that neutral England had retracted the belligerent
claims of former times, the Government, with the full approbation of the country, has steadily abided by the ancient landmarks
of jurisprudence. Every argument which was advanced in support of the demand for the surrender of the prisoners from the
Trent was fortified by the authority of the judges and the
statesmen of half a century ago. "Historicus" comments with
merited contempt on the attempt of Mr. Sumner in the Federal
Senate to extract from the judicious act of reparation which had

averted an impending war a logical or legal triumph of doctrines which he represented as American, although they had been systematically repudiated by the American Courts.

A more culpable degree of ignorance and unfairness has been manifested by a French writer, who apparently believes that the destruction of English power is the final object and ruling principle of international law. On the occurrence of the Trent dispute M. Hautefeuille published an insidious pamphlet, ostensibly in favour of the surrender of the prisoners, which was hastily quoted as the testimony of a foreign jurist to the justice of the English demand. It was known that M. Hautefeuille had published a work of considerable pretension on the maritime law of nations, and it was at first assumed that in condemning the American outrage he relied on the reasons which influenced the advisers of the English Crown, and which ultimately prevailed over the reluctance of the American Government. An examination of his statement of the case, and of his arguments on the question in dispute, showed that the French writer only desired to procure the establishment of a precedent which might hereafter be quoted against England. After misrepresenting all the facts of the seizure, he endeavoured to prove, not that the passengers in the Trent were exempt from capture, but that neutral vessels under almost all conceivable circumstances ought to be secure against the interference of belligerent cruisers. In bad faith or in culpable ignorance he affected to condemn the American proceedings as deductions from an oppressive system introduced by England, and only renounced for purposes of temporary convenience. If there had been any doubt of the tendency of his argument, his motive would have been sufficiently illustrated by the more elaborate work in which he proposes the institution, during a time of profound peace, of an armed neutrality for the purpose of restraining the exercise of the maritime supremacy of England. "Historicus" has performed a public service in exposing with a vigorous severity the perversion of legal controversy to the objects of national animosity. He has clearly shown that M. Hautefeuille has founded his doctrines of international law neither on the principles which are generally acknowledged by the jurists nor on the sounder foundation of judicial decisions. His maxims are either vague inferences from an arbitrary moral code or generalizations from the provisions of particular treaties. It is difficult to imagine a more entire perversion of legal reasoning than the assumption that international conventions express the rules of public jurisprudence. As statutable enactments limit and vary the common law, special treaties operate in derogation of pre-existing relations. M. Hautefeuille has no hesitation in suppressing exceptional arrangements which were intended to have the force of declaratory interpretations. The treaty of England and Russia in 1801, which settled many disputed questions, is, as "Historicus" shows, systematically forgotten by M. Hautefeuille.

The argument of those letters which refer to the Confederate claim to recognition is fresh in the recollection of all readers who concern themselves with the discussion of similar questions. "Historicus" is fully justified in his opinion that the independence of the South is not yet so fully established as to authorize foreign recognition. In Greece and Belgium the Great Powers intervened to complete the separation, instead of simply taking notice of an accomplished result. The South American States were recognized only after Spain had virtually abandoned the task of reconquering their allegiance. The French acknowledgment of the independence of the American colonies led to an immediate declaration of war by England. As long as large Federal armies continue offensive operations on Southern soil, Europe cannot, without affording the United States a lawful cause of war, formally anticipate the result which is confidently foreseen. It is expedient that the difference between law and policy should be fully understood, and although an exhaustive treatise on international jurisprudence ought to be exempt from the influence of temporary complications, there is an obvious advantage in securing popular attention to sound doctrines by furnishing a scientific solution of questions which for the moment excite curiosity or anxiety.

THE CIVIL WAR IN AMERICA

(FROM OUR OWN CORRESPONDENT.)

WASHINGTON, Feb. 23.

New York exhibits no outward signs of the war and desolation that afflict the land. Washington, on the contrary, betrays them at every turn. The long straggling Avenues, planned in a spirit of magnificence, but so meanly executed, swarm with soldiers, camp followers, forage waggons, ambulances, and all the aids, instruments, and paraphernalia of strife. Thousands of young men, in gray-blue uniforms, swagger about the streets or lounge at the doors of the hotels, with the fresh jauntiness of the inexperience that has never yet confronted a foe; while mingled among them, at intervals painfully frequent, are to be seen the luckless veterans of the struggle—the men who can fight no more, the maimed and mutilated victims of "glory" and "patriotism," limping along on crutches, and turning their sunken eyes towards the by-passers with a piteous expression of countenance, as if to crave the sympathy of all who are still in the enjoyment of their limbs and faculties. The mud in all the main Avenues is ankle-deep, for there has been a heavy fall of snow, six inches thick, that only lay one day upon the ground before it began to yield to the fervid rays of a summer-like sun and the breath of a wind as warm, if not as balmy, as that of an English June. Through the rivers and lakes of slush pass and repass at all hours of the day and night immense droves of cattle, as many as 4,000 or 5,000 at a time, some going into Virginia for the use of the Army of the Potomac, and some destined for the consumption of the 60,000 men retained for the defence of the capital, together with an almost continuous procession of supply and forage waggons, each drawn by six mules, and driven by a negro or an Irish teamster, shouting and swearing as he goes. On any ordinary roads in England or in Europe, two mules would be amply sufficient for any vehicle of the kind, however heavily laden, but in the deep, greasy, tenacious mud of this region, six are none too many for the task they have to perform. Never, perhaps, in any city of the world was so much horse and mule flesh to be seen as in Washington at this moment, and such miserable horseflesh never before enriched a mob of contractors, or impoverished a nation. The soldiers are for the most part as rough and shaggy as the mules. Raw lads of 18 and 20 form the bulk of the army that defends Washington against the imminent aggression of General Lee. These youths revel and riot in their premature manhood, and exhibit their exuberant strength and insolence in drunken and other orgies that seem to have no limits but their purses. To inveigle the "greenbacks" out of their pockets and those of their officers a whole army of brazen courtesans and "painted Jezebels" has invaded the city, who ply their trade by advertisement in the newspapers and by public exhibition in the streets after a fashion so gross that it would shame even the Haymarket. The places where they have congregated have received the name new to American slang, and peculiar to Washington, of "Ranches," a word that in Texas signifies an enclosure for cattle. The "Ranches" of Madame This or That are as openly conducted as the hotels or boardinghouses, and the Provost Marshal and his officials make little or no effort to interfere with them. At every street, corner, and place of public resort are to be seen printed notices, warning simple-minded strangers against the multitudinous thieves who have congregated here from all parts of the world. In those "howling caravanserais" the leading hotels, where the utmost possible discomfort is paid for at the highest possible price, and where the bad cookery and the bad wine are only equalled by the bad accommodation and the bad attendance, are posted up at every angle of the vestibules, corridors, and reception rooms conspicuous warnings against the hotel thieves who have come hither from England and France, as well as from New York, to break into ladies' bedrooms at the dinner hour and decamp with their jewelry. Three days ago one of them succeeded in making off with the money and private papers of Mr. Ex-Secretary Cameron, while that unsuspecting diplomatist was quietly dining at Willard's. Another class of thieves, not so designated in polite society, but worthy of the name—the people who sell the Government rotten and unseaworthy steamboats for the conveyance of troops and stories; shoes for the army, that wear out in one day's march; and shoddy garments, nether and upper, that rot like blotting paper in a shower of rain; the "respectable" people who plunder under form of law and with the decent observances of trade, feed daily at Willard's and other public places, and make themselves conspicuous by the magnums of claret and champagne which they consume, and by the general loudness of their talk and behaviour. Then there are the "wire-pullers" and "log-rollers"; that is to say, men who have schemes before Congress, and who "engineer" their bills through both Houses by the vulgarest agencies of dinner and drink, as well as by other means not so visible to spectators, though perhaps more satisfactory to such members of the Legislature as are neither too honest nor too proud to be purchased. But the roguery and rascality of Washington are equalled by its misery. There are estimated to be no less than 40,000 sick, wounded, and mutilated soldiers within the district of Columbia, receiving such poor relief and consolation as circumstances will allow, not one twentieth part of whom will ever again be in a condition to fight the battles of the North. In addition to these are the negroes, or "contrabands" they are called in the slang which General Butler originated and made popular, who have escaped from Maryland and Virginia into the Federal lines, and are maintained by the Government at a heavy cost. Many of these poor creatures are able-bodied men, for whom no work is to be found even as teamsters—an occupation for which they are well fitted; but a large proportion are aged and infirm persons and young children. All of them are huddled together in wretched shanties at a remote corner of the town. Smallpox is making fearful havoc among them, and thence extending its ravages among the white population. Washington, though an immense city upon the map, is not sufficiently built up to accommodate the 250,000 people who have been drawn within its focus by the necessities of the war and the Government. Its drainage is so miserably defective that the wonder ought to be that it has not long ago been the theatre of pestilence as well as of war, and thus suffered the second as well as the first scourge of humanity.

Add to this that at the hotels accommodation is scarcely to be had; that travellers are often compelled to sleep six in a room; that everything to eat, drink, or wear is as dear as it is bad and some idea may be formed of the outward aspects of the national capital in this closing week of the 37th Congress. . . .

March 20th, 1863   *page 8*

SEVEN per CENT. COTTON LOAN of the CONFEDERATE STATES of AMERICA. FOR £3,000,000 sterling at 90 per cent.

110

The Bonds to bear interest at the rate of 7 per cent. per annum in sterling, from 1st March, 1863, payable half-yearly in London, Paris, Amsterdam, or Frankfurt.

The Bonds exchangeable for Cotton on application, at the option of the holder, or redeemable at par in sterling in 20 years, by half-yearly Agents for the Contractors in London.—Messrs. J. Henry Schröder and Co., 145, Leadenhall street.

This Loan has been contracted with Messrs. Emile Erlanger and Co., bankers of Paris, by the Government of the Confederate States of America, and is specially secured by an undertaking of the Government to deliver cotton to the holders of the bonds on application after 60 days' notice, on the footing aftermentioned.

The nature of the arrangement is fully set forth in Article IV. of the contract made with Messrs. E. Erlanger and Co., which is as follows:—

"Each bond shall at the option of the holder be convertible at its nominal amount into cotton at the rate of 6d. sterling for each pound of cotton, say 4,000 lbs. of cotton for each bond of £100 or 2,500f., and this at any time not later than six months after the ratification of a treaty of peace between the present belligerents. Notice of the intention of converting bonds into cotton has to be given to the representatives of the Government in Paris or London, and 60 days after such notice the cotton will be delivered:—if peace, at the ports of Charleston, Savannah, Mobile, or New Orleans; if war, at points in the interior of the country, within 10 miles of a railroad, or stream navigable to the ocean. The delivery will be made free of all charges and duties, excepting the existing export duty of one-eighth of one cent. per pound. The quality of the cotton to be the standard of New Orleans middling. If any cotton is of inferior quality, the difference in value shall be settled by two brokers, one to be appointed by the Government, the other by the bondholder; whenever these two brokers cannot agree on the value, an umpire is to be chosen, whose decision shall be final."

It is at the same time provided, that holders who do not convert their Bonds into cotton, shall be entitled to retain the Bonds, and receive interest at the rate of 7 per cent. per annum in sterling, payable half-yearly in London, Paris, Amsterdam, or Frankfurt, at the option of the holder, until repayment of the principal at par.

An Annual Sinking Fund of 5 per cent. is provided for, whereby $2\frac{1}{2}$ per cent. of the Bonds unredeemed by cotton shall

111

be drawn by lot half-yearly: the first drawing to take effect on the 1st March, 1864, and to be continued on the 1st September following, and on the 1st March and 1st September in every succeeding year, so as finally to extinguish the Loan in 20 years from the date of the first drawing.

The Bonds to be issued at 90 per cent., which is to be paid as follows:—

5 per cent. on Application,
10 ,, on Allotment,
10 ,, 1st May,
10 ,, 1st June,
10 ,, 1st July,
15 ,, 1st August,
15 ,, 1st September, less dividend 3½ per cent.,
15 ,, 1st October.
—
£90

Subscribers will have the option of paying the instalments in advance, on allotment, or on any of the above dates, under a discount of seven per cent per annum on such pre-payments; but, in default of due payment of the respective instalments, all previous payments will be liable to forfeiture.

(By payment, under discount, the price of the cotton is reduced to about 5¼d. per pound.)

After allotment, Scrip Certificates will be issued to bearer. These certificates, after payment of the last instalment will be exchanged for bonds to "Bearer" in sums of £100, £200, £500, £1,000 each, with Coupons attached, payable 1st March, 1st September, as stated above.

Arrangements have been made for the execution of the Bonds in Paris.

From the proceeds of the subscription the contractors and their agents are authorized to retain sufficient funds to pay the first two coupons.

The drawings for the operation of the sinking fund will be duly advertised previous to the half-yearly redemption.

An authenticated copy of the Act of Ratification of the Contract may be inspected either at the offices of Messrs. Freshfields and Newman, the solicitors to the contractors, or of Messrs. Crowder Maynard, and Co., solicitors to the agents of the contractors on London.

Applications for allotment to be addressed to Messrs. J. Henry Schröder and Co., 145, Leadenhall-street; and to the brokers, Messrs. Laurence, Son, and Pearce, Auction Mart, from whom forms of application may be obtained.

In the event of no allotment being made, the deposit will be immediately returned.

A public subscription is simultaneously opened in Liverpool, Paris, Amsterdam, and Frankfurt.

J. HENRY SCHRODER and Co., Agents to the Contractors.

No. 145, Leadenhall-street, March 19, 1863.

———

Cotton Loan of the Confederate States of America.

Form of Application to be forwarded to Messrs. J. Henry Schröder and Co., after payment of the preliminary deposit to the bankers.

No.—.

To Messrs. J. Henry Schöder and Co., agents for the contractors of the Cotton Loan of the Confederate States of America.

Gentlemen,—Having paid to Messrs. Jones Loyd and Co. the sum of £—, —hereby request you will allot £—of the Cotton Loan of the Confederate States of America, and — hereby agree to accept the same, or any smaller amount that may be allotted to — , and to pay the further sum of £10 per cent. on the same when allotted.

Gentlemen, your obedient servant,

....Signature.

....Address in full.

....Date.

July 28th, 1863   **page 12**

THE RIOTS IN NEW YORK

(FROM OUR OWN CORRESPONDENT.)

NEW YORK, JULY 14.

... The readers of this correspondence have been from time to time informed that the working classes were not only disgusted with the war and all relating to it; that they did not sympathize with or take any interest in the abolition of slavery, except to condemn it; that they looked upon the negroes with mistrust and dislike; that they felt the burden of the war in the enhancement of the price of food and clothing, and of every article of comfort and necessity; and that, above all, they were opposed to the principle of a conscription and had banded themselves into secret societies to resist it. All these motives of action came into play yesterday, and were intensified by the sympathy and support of the women, who turned out into the streets in immense numbers to incite their sons, brothers, fathers, husbands, or lovers to the work of destruction. The lists of those who were draughted in the Ninth District were published in the evening papers on Saturday, and repeated in the Sunday journals. This publication was the only notice of their doom that the unfortunates had received; and all day on Sunday the lists were studied by excited groups of working men, gathered at street corners, at church or chapel doors, and at the less tranquil resorts of lager-bier saloons, grog-shops, and hotel bars. The verbal opposition to the draught was loud and universal. It was declared to be illegal, unfair in its mode of operation, as exempting from personal service the man who was rich enough to pay 300 dollars, and as an assumption of power on the part of the Federal Government which could not be submitted to in a country that still claimed to be free. It was alleged in one of the Sunday journals that no less a person than Mr. Horatio Seymour, Governor of the State, had declared his opinion that the act of Congress was unconstitutional and could not be enforced; and that its legality would be tested before the recognised tribunals of New York.

This statement, which ought to have allayed the agitation of the people, produced a contrary effect. Early in the day gangs of workmen went from workshop to workshop to call upon their fellows to leave their labour and proceed to the building in the Third-avenue where the formalities of the draught were to be resumed. By eleven o'clock some thousands of persons had collected. They commenced by throwing stones at the windows. They next rushed into the office, seized the wheel by which the lots were drawn and broke it into fragments, got hold of the enrolment lists and tore them into shreds,—thus rendering the prosecution of the draught impossible until a new enrolment had been completed—assaulted and severely ill-treated the functionaries employed, and were debating what was next to be done, when a man suddenly appeared on the platform with a pail of turpentine, which he deliberately poured upon the floor. A lucifer match was immediately applied. The turpentine blazed up furiously, and in less than half an hour afterwards the whole edifice was in a blaze from the basement to the roof. The firemen arrived to extinguish the conflagration. They were received by the mob with loud cheers; but were not permitted to throw water on the flames. The fire spread rapidly until eight contiguous houses were enveloped in one common destruction. The crowd assisted the terrified inmates to escape; but otherwise manifested a stern resolution to suffer no interference with their vengeance. Their next business was to tear up the iron of the street railways, to prevent the passage of cars with troops or police to the rescue, and to provide themselves with weapons. This done, they cut the telegraphic wires in all directions, and broke up into several separate mobs, each bent on its own purpose, or going wherever chance conducted it. Of course, such a riot became the holyday of all the rowdies, blackguards, and thieves of this city, who, scenting plunder as the crow scents carrion, turned out in large numbers to swell the volume and disgrace the character of the crowd. Hitherto no blood had been shed. A detachment of the Provost Guard that had been hastily sent from the Park Barracks, to prevent further destruction, if they could not restore order, arrived at Forty-first-street, in the very heart and focus of the riot, and found their further progress impeded by a dense mass of people, supposed to amount to 5,000 or 6,000, who received them with shouts and yells of execration, and pelted them with stones and brickbats. Thus hemmed in and surrounded, and in danger of being torn to pieces, they fired a deadly volley into the crowd, and about 20 people fell mortally wounded. No one knows whether or not they received orders to fire, or whether the fatal discharge was the unpremeditated and unauthorized act of their own fear; but the consequence, as might have been expected, was only to add to the fury of the multitude. The Provost Guard no sooner fired than it retreated, pursued by the crowd. The men threw away their firearms to facilitate their escape, and these being picked up by their pursuers seemed to suggest to the mob that in a future conflict with the troops it would be necessary that they should have muskets and rifles. Several soldiers and policemen—it is not yet known how many—were killed, and the crowd, growing larger and more furious as it rolled, invaded an armoury on the Second-avenue, belonging to Mr. Opdyke, the Mayor of New York, where a large store of arms and ammunition for which this gentleman and his brother had contracted to supply the Government was known to exist. It was defended for a short time by the servants and workpeople of Mr. Opdyke. But all resistance was in vain. The people overflowed into the building like an advancing sea, and in a few minutes the musketry and ammunition were seized and distributed among the insurgents. Whatever was not of a nature to be made available as a weapon was destroyed. This done the torch was applied to every corner of the edifice, which in a short time was in such a blaze as would have defied all the efforts of all the firemen of New York to extinguish. While this scene was being enacted another body of rioters, who had chased an obnoxious soldier or policeman into a large stone house at the corner of Lexington-avenue, surrounded the building, and demanded that he should be given up. The cry was raised that the house belonged to a "shoddy contractor," who had made a fortune out of the war. The allegation, true or false, was fatal to the house.

The mob burst into it, tore down the pictures from the walls, cut them to pieces with their knives, or dug holes in them with railroad iron, demolished a large and costly pianoforte, threw the fragments out of the windows, took the books from the library and set fire to them in the street, broke open pantry and larder, wine cellar and plate chest, closet and wardrobe, and carried off every portable article of value and the wearing apparel of the male and female members of the household as trophies of their achievement. Finally they set fire to the building; and, watching the progress of the flames until they were quite assured that the work of destruction would be complete, marched off to commit new outrages. The next place that received a visit was the splendid house of Mr. Opdyke, the Mayor, in the Fifth-avenue, a gentleman particularly noted for the fervour of his war sentiments, the richness of his contracts, and the vehemence of his Black Republicanism, or philanthropic love for the negroes. Cries were raised to gut and fire the house, and in one minute more the thing would have been done, had it not been for the opportune presence and judicious speech of one of the city judges, Mr. Barnard, who endeavoured to calm the fury of the mob. Having obtained a hearing, from a doorstep, he bade them remember that Mr. Opdyke was the legally elected chief magistrate of the city, and, as such, entitled to their respect and obedience. He entreated them not to sully their just cause by acts of violence. He declared that, in his opinion, as a lawyer and judge, the Conscription Act was illegal and unconstitutional; and added that, if any citizen, taken from his home in pursuance of that Act, applied by his counsel for a writ of *habeas corpus* before him, he would grant the writ, and bring the question to a test in the State and city of New York. This restored the crowd to good humour, and with three cheers for the judge they proceeded on their way, leaving Mr. Opdyke's mansion unmolested.

But, although opposition to the draught was the main motive that impelled the people to these lawless deeds, another passion took possession of them as the day wore on. In their hatred of the war and the draught which had grown out of it, they remembered that Mr. Lincoln by his Proclamation of Emancipation had so embittered the South as to render a restoration of the Union impossible. Hatred of the war and hatred of the negro, whom they supposed to be the cause of it, were equally strong in their minds. No negro could venture into the crowd without insult or danger. One unfortunate man of colour, being hooted and pelted with brickbats and brought to bay by a furious gang of assailants, drew a revolver from his breast and shot the foremost man dead. He was immediately pursued by a mob of hundreds of excited ruffians, seized, thrown to the ground, beaten on the head with clubs and pieces of iron, stamped and spat upon, and next, after every shred of clothing had been stripped from his back, hung, stark naked from a lamp-post, and pelted with stones and mud by an assemblage of juvenile ruffians, from the age of 12 upwards. After dangling for a few minutes all the available combustible rubbish of the neighbourhood was piled under his feet and set fire to, the maniac crowd dancing around in a frenzy of blood and horror. In another part of the city a second negro met a similar fate; and toward 6 in the evening a body of several thousand persons, breathing vengeance against that unhappy race—most of whom this day in New York would have been glad to exchange the peril of liberty in the North for the security of Southern slavery and protection—marched up to a large building, called the "Coloured Orphan Home," an institution, as its name implies, devoted to the maintenance and education of orphan negro children. Giving the inmates an hour to escape, they declared their intention to set fire to the building, which intention they ruthlessly carried into execution at the appointed time. One life only appears to have been lost,—that of a poor negro child, who was accidentally trampled to death in the rush of the inmates to escape destruction. Amid scenes like these, the local authorities being almost, if not entirely, powerless to resist the progress of the insurgents, the night darkened down upon a city that would have been doomed to destruction if the mob had had as much leadership as it had ferocity.

But leadership was wanting. The vast mass was in spontaneous combustion. Its actions were neither planned nor directed. If they had been, there was nothing to prevent it from seizing every arsenal and armoury in the city, and providing arms and ammunition for 100,000 men. Fortunately the local authority had sufficient presence of mind to despatch troops to the most vulnerable of these stores of mischief. At 11 o'clock at night, the sky—covered by a dense hot mist, as hot almost as a vapour-bath—was lit up by the lurid glare of a dozen fires in different parts of the town, and 40,000 or 50,000 rioters were in undisturbed possession of the streets. There is no knowing what might have happened before daybreak if it had not been for the sudden downfall of a drenching rain-storm that cleared the thoroughfares in a few minutes. The rain continued for several hours,—a better conservator of the public peace than ten thousand soldiers might have proved in fine weather.

This morning the riots were resumed at daybreak. The lower part of the town towards Wall-street and the Exchange was but little affected; but up beyond Grace Church and Union-square the whole region lying between those points and the Central Park was at the mercy of the crowd. It was asserted that by some means the people had managed to obtain possession of several pieces of artillery; that all the omnibuses and cars plying up Broadway and the railroad avenues were seized as soon as they came within the lines of the insurgents, and that the carriages were converted into barricades and the horses impressed for the service of artillery. But the statement does not appear to have been true. The mob, however, had abundance of small arms, and when these were wanting made up for the deficiency by bludgeons, clubs, brick-bats, and fragments of iron rail. The rioters still entertaining a feeling of vengeance against Mayor Opdyke, a gentleman who has made himself conspicuous, not alone for his uncompromising and unconditional support of the Emancipation policy of the Government, but also for his assertion that war has its "noble side," betook themselves about 11 in the morning to his mansion, in Fifth-avenue, and manifested a disposition to devote it to the fate which it yesterday escaped at the intercession of Judge Barnard. Today the neighbours formed themselves into a guard for its protection, and were sufficiently powerful to save it from the crowd of small boys and young men who wished to commit it to the flames, with all its luxurious furniture and trappings. The house of the postmaster of New York, Mr. Wakeman, was less fortunate, and, after having been plundered of its contents, was burnt to the ground. The houses of scores of other persons who by their action in the war and their support of the Government had rendered themselves obnoxious to the working-classes have shared a similar fate. The offices of the *Tribune* newspaper have been barricaded during the day with piles of wet printing paper and all the banks in Wall-street and the neighbourhood have been closely guarded. The leading citizens have enrolled themselves into a special constabulary to assist in the restoration of order; but as yet the crowd is all but undisputed master of the situation, and no one knows what the night may bring forth. Governor Seymour, having been summoned by telegraph from Long Branch, a watering-place on the coast of New Jersey, whither he had gone last week for health and recreation, arrived in the forenoon, and, after a hasty consultation with the civic authorities at the City-hall, appeared at the bacony and addressed a crowd of about 12,000 persons. His speech was temperate and judicious. He denounced the rioters, but at the same time declared his belief that the State authorities were able to preserve or restore order without the aid of the Federal Government, and added that he had sent a special messenger to the President on Saturday last to urge upon him the expediency of countermanding the draught, at least until time had been allowed to bring authoritatively before the Courts the constitutionality of the Act of Congress upon which it was founded, and by which alone it was justified. To this message he had received no reply. Great confidence seems to be generally entertained in the wisdom of Governor Seymour in bringing this unhappy business to a safe issue, though he is greatly hampered by some injudicious and timid fools in high station in the city, who clamour for the establishment of martial law as the only possible means of preventing anarchy. . . .

The night passed over more quietly than was anticipated. An announcement made in the evening, as if by authority, that the Federal Government had consented to forego the draught throughout the whole State of New York tended to allay the agitation. It did not, however, completely satisfy the mob. Too many thieves and assassins had mingled themselves in its proceedings to accept any promise on the part of the Government as a warrant for their laying down their arms, and these persons kept the city in terror until daybreak. It is this morning announced that 5,000 troops are in position to quell all further disturbance, and that the Militia regiments ordered to the relief of Pennsylvania at the first alarm in that State, consequent upon the late Confederate invasion, are on their way home and expected during the day. The principal merchants, bankers, and other householders have formed themselves into an armed special constabulary, and guard all the principal posts of danger. Business is almost wholly suspended, but there is a general impression that the worst is over, and that New York will be saved the primary disgrace of further mob law, as well as the secondary disgrace of being indebted to the Federal Government for the restoration of order. It seems to be conceded on all hands that the draught must be abandoned. The contagion of opposition has communicated itself to other towns and cities in the North. There have been riots in Hartford, in Connecticut, and even sober Boston, where negrophilism reigns triumphant and supreme, has seen in its streets since yesterday a mob of upwards of a thousand people, declaring against the draught, pronouncing it to be unconstitutional and oppressive, and expressing their determination to resist it. A few fanatics of the press in this city persist in urging the Government to maintain the conscription. If the Government be unwise enough to follow their counsel, the indications are that it will speedily have a new civil war on its hands, in addition to what it technically calls the "rebellion" of the South.

Antonio Carlo Napoleone Gallenga (1810-1895) was much the most exotic of The Times's *correspondents in this period. Born in Parma, he was from an early age an Italian liberal and nationalist, which naturally entailed a choice between prison and exile. He went to New York in 1836 and England in 1839, earning his living as a professor of modern languages. But he continued to be active in Italian politics, and was a deputy in the Piedmontese and Italian parliaments from 1859 to 1864. He reported the Risorgimento and the Danish War for* The Times, *and was a leader-writer from 1866 to 1873. In 1863 he was sent out to report on affairs in the North, especially in the western states, with stern instructions from Morris to report nothing but* facts *(trebly underlined). He returned to England at the beginning of December.*

August 8th, 1863   *page 9*

AMERICAN AFFAIRS

(FROM OUR SPECIAL CORRESPONDENT.)

NEWPORT, RHODE ISLAND, JULY 24.

JULY 25.

... I found Newport in song and dance as I arrived here the other day. The big hotel, Ocean-house, was swarming with fair ladies dressed in the pink of fashion, with all the colours of the wing of a gaudy butterfly. Wealth and luxury reign supreme among these people. Yet the season is a very dull one, up to this time of the year. The first year after the outbreak of the war, in 1861, was also marked by the same want of social enjoyment. The Americans were at that time stunned by the first blow of their calamity, and the affair of Bull Run had laid the country in sackcloth and ashes. They rallied in the following year, and Newport last summer was more crowded and noisier than usual. The company was none of the best, however. A set of new men came up, contractors, smugglers, and other political blacklegs, men to whom the ill wind of the war has blown all sorts of good, and who fattened on the common sufferings, like those Monatti of the Milan pestilence described by Manzoni, who had the care of the dead, and enriched themselves with the spoils of the dying. This year these ghouls have not made their appearance, and the best class of citizens, who have found for them the new appellation of "shoddy" gents, are delighted at their riddance of such company. Lee's invasion of Pennsylvania, and the riots at New York, are, naturally enough, keeping a great many of the holiday folk from their darling haunts. For my own part I should be glad

121

to hear that the Americans are in no humour for amusement, but people assure me that I only come too early, and that Newport will be quite full in August and September. There is good reason, indeed, why such places should be sad and desolate. Throughout New England you scarcely enter a door without being aware that you are in the house of mourning. Whatever part the Irish, German, and other hirelings may have borne in this war, I must bear witness that the best classes of Americans have bravely come forth for their country. I know of scarcely a family more than one member of which has not been or is not in the ranks of the army. The youths maimed and crippled I meet on the high road certainly do not for the most part belong to the immigrant rabble of which the Northern regiments are said to consist; and even the present conscription is now in many splendid instances most promptly and cheerfully complied with by the wealthy people, who could easily purchase exemption, but who prefer to set a good example by the sacrifice of themselves. This justice, I think, I owe to the Americans.

August 18th, 1863   *page 7*

THE SOUTHERN CONFEDERACY

THE BATTLES OF GETTYSBURG

(FROM OUR SPECIAL CORRESPONDENT.)

.   .   .

HEADQUARTERS OF GENERAL LONGSTREET, NEAR GETTYSBURG, July 1.

After camping near the top of the South Mountain (which, as I have in previous letters explained, is the continuation from Harper's Ferry northwards of the Blue Ridge of Virginia), we proceeded this morning slowly on our road towards Gettysburg. Before us (by "us" I mean the corps of General Longstreet) was the corps of General A.P. Hill; to our left, descending from York towards Gettysburg, was the corps of General Ewell. As we neared the mouth of the mountain gorge, the loud boom of guns between us and the little town of Gettysburg proclaimed that the Federals, who were generally believed to be much nearer to Washington, had advanced thus far to meet us. Undoubtedly, the

122

near proximity of the Federal army to Gettysburg was a surprise to Generals Lee and Longstreet. Before either of these Generals were aware of the fact, General A. P. Hill, coming from the west, and General Ewell descending from the north, were hotly engaged with the enemy, and destined, in the preliminary struggle of the 1st of July, to meet, as it proved, with a triumphant success.

The country in the immediate neighbourhood of Gettysburg, remarkably English in its general aspect, is not unlike many portions of Surrey, especially reminding the spectator of the gently swelling banks densely clothed with trees which are found between the towns of Dorking and Reigate. About four miles west of Gettysburg one of General A. P. Hill's divisions, commanded by General Heth, came upon a strong picket of Federals, thrown out by the 1st corps of their army, under the command of General Reynolds. To the north of the town, the divisions of Generals Rodes and Early, both belonging to General Ewell's corps, found themselves face to face with the 11th corps of the Federal army, which, as the reader will remember, attained at Chancellorsville unenviable notoriety, as comprising within its ranks the "Flying Dutchman," of whose flight it will be long before Carl Schurz, the German orator and Federal General, hears the last. Instinctively, and against the wish of General Lee, between the three Confederate divisions indicated, and the two corps of the Federal army, a hotly contested battle arose. The divisions of Generals Rodes and Early were fortunate in lighting upon the 11th corps and experiencing a resistance which, though it compared favourably with the memories of Chancellorsville, was ill calculated to stem the fiery attack of Stonewall Jackson's veterans. Again the Germans broke and fled, but their swift retreat was not bloodless and unharmed, as it had been through the thickets and copsewood of Chancellorsville. Thickly and heavily shot and shell and musket balls fell with damaging accuracy upon their shrieking ranks, and it is the belief of many that if General Ewell, after driving his enemy for four miles and through the town of Gettysburg, had not, by superior orders, stayed the pursuit within the town itself, his victorious troops would have camped on the night of the 1st of July upon the top of that ridge which upon the two subsequent days all the desperate efforts of the Confederates were inadequate to storm. For the division of General Heth, opposed to

General Reynolds and the First Corps of the Federals, a fiercer conflict was in store. Standing firmly on his ground, General Reynolds met the Confederate attack unflinchingly, and it was not until bayonets were on the eve of crossing that several of his regiments, and notably the 24th Michigan and two regiments from New York and Pennsylvania (the latter said never to have been in action before), broke into sullen retreat, leaving about half their number dead and wounded on the ground. The retreat once commenced knew neither pause nor stay until the town of Gettysburg was gained and passed. Among its victims was numbered General Reynolds, one of the most active of the Federal Generals, who yielded his life upon the best contested field which, in the opinion of competent judges, the "Grand Army of the Potomac" had hitherto known. General A. P. Hill, no inexperienced witness, bore willing testimony to the gallantry with which the Federals fought.

If the events of the two following days had not eclipsed the notice taken of the first day's struggle, much more would be said and thought of a Ligny which, though inexpensive to the Confederates, cost the Federals not less than 10,000 in killed, wounded, and missing. The large mass of Yankee prisoners, between 5,000 and 6,000 in number, the headlong retreat to which in the end their troops were driven, the apparently fortuitous occupation by their army of a strong ridge in the rear of Gettysburg, conspired to induce the belief that little more was wanted than a vigorous onslaught on the morrow to drive the Federals from the heights and open the way without let or hinderance to Baltimore or Washington. But even on the night of the triumphant First of July warning voices indicating distrust and apprehension in regard to the strength of the enemy's position were not inaudible. Among others General Longstreet shook his head gravely over the advantages conferred by this position, and thoughts of turning it by flanking were undoubtedly uppermost in his mind and General Lee's. The gallant though premature achievement of the troops of Generals Ewell and Hill, the memories of Bull Run, Manassas, Richmond, Fredericksburg, and Chancellorsville, the impracticability of turning either Federal flank, the impatience of General Hood and his fine division, lightly engaged at Fredericksburg, and absent at Chancellorsville, combined to inspire the leading Confederate Generals with an undue contempt for their enemy, although he was fighting on his own soil, with his back to the wall, and in a position which for strength and eligibility for defence has not been surpassed during 27 months of warfare. It was deemed desirable not even to wait until one of the finest divisions of General Longstreet's corps—the division of General Pickett—had joined the main body. Hope reigned triumphant in every Confederate breast; delay was likely to afford the Federals, whose activity with the spade has been repeatedly and marvellously manifested, time and opportunity for intrenching themselved *ad libitum*. A cry for immediate battle louder and more peremptory than ever ascended from the Highlanders of Claverhouse or Montrose swelled the gale—timid and hesitating counsels were impatiently discarded; and, as it appeared to me, the mature and cautious wisdom of General Lee had no choice but to float with the current, and to trust the enthusiasm of his troops to carry him triumphantly on the morrow over the heights which frowned darkly and menacingly in our front.

JULY. 2.

There is no reason to think that the admirable position to which on the evening of the 1st the two shattered corps of the Federals fell back, and in which they joined themselves to the rest of the Northern army, was deliberately selected, or that the firm and successful stand which, thanks to the positon, General Meade was there enabled to make was the result of anything but that which in human affairs we are accustomed to call accident. Just beyond the town of Gettysburg runs a horseshoe ridge of low uniform hills, seemingly from two to three miles in length, terminating at both ends in a steep sugarloaf peak, which thoroughly protected either flank. On the Federal right and centre the hill was almost entirely bare of trees; on the Federal left their batteries were planted, under the shelter of forest—the sugarloaf peaks at both ends of the line were densely clothed with timber. To attempt to march round these sugarloaf pinnacles would have exposed the Confederates to the danger of weakening their front so greatly as to make it easy for the Federals to advance and cut off the flanking force. There was nothing for it but either to attack the Federals right in front, or shrink back into the gorge of the South Mountain, from which we had just emerged, and there to await an attack, or to sidle off the whole Confederate army with its enormous transportation trains towards our right flank in the direction of the Potomac, with our rear clinging to the South Mountain range. Each of these three courses was hazardous. To the second, which might otherwise have been the safest, the great objection was that General Ewell's Corps could not be got within the mountain gorge the single road of which was already occupied by the two Corps of Longstreet and A. P. Hill. In my judgment, the least objectionable course of the three, so far as design, though not so far as time of execution is concerned, was selected by General Lee.

His plan of battle was to attack the Federal left through General Longstreet's agency, while Generals A. P. Hill and Ewell pressed heavily on the enemy's centre and right, with instructions to advance their whole line should Longstreet's attack meet with any success. Two-thirds of the day wore away in making preparations for this general attack, in getting the battalions of artillery into position, and disposing the troops, which had been on the tramp for the two previous days, for the onslaught. It may be noticed that the expression, "battalions of artillery," is, unless I am mistaken, peculiar to this continent. A battalion of artillery signifies the aggregation or lumping together of three or four batteries into one body. Nominally, each battalion should consist of 20 guns; in practice, the number varies from 12 to 20, or upwards.

I know not whether I am mistaken, but it struck me that both General Lee and Longstreet yielded reluctantly, and *contre-coeur* to the policy of pressing forward at once to this day's attack. Undoubtedly, General Longstreet would have preferred to wait for General Pickett, who would have joined him on the evening of the 2d. General Lee struck me as more anxious and ruffled than I had ever seen him before, though it required close observation to detect it. When any check or failure is experienced there spring to the surface so many "ifs," any one of which would have secured a different result, that on any occasion like this it would fill columns of this journal to give expression to them in language. Only in one solitary surmise shall I venture on this occasion to indulge. My impression is, that if no attack had been made on the 2d of July, and that if on the 3d General Pickett's division had been thrown upon the Federals in support of the divisions of Hood and M'Laws the heights would have been carried and held, although at considerable cost. As it was, neither upon the 2d nor the 3d was the attacking force of General Longstreet large enough to reap the fruits of that victory which on both days they gained, but could not realize. It will hardly be requisite to state to any military leader that it was not in the fiery onset which led up to the Federal guns that the Confederates suffered such loss, it was when they had to leave the Federal works, which had already been carried, and to retire broken and shattered across the slope. To say that the attack of the 2d would have been far more likely to succeed if delayed until the 3d is nothing else than the repetition of my previous opinion, that Hill's and Ewell's engagement of the 1st was premature, and, although glorious in itself, was productive of the first and only failure to attain marked success which, during nearly 12 months of observation of General Lee's army, it has been my fortune to record.

It was not till 4 in the afternoon that the battle commenced. Upon the extreme Confederate right advanced General Hood and the Texans, who would follow his tall form up to Gehenna's gates, and the day's disasters commenced by a wound which he at once received, shattering his left arm below the elbow and forcing him from the field. His division fell to the command of the senior Brigadier-General, Robertson, who swiftly shared General Hood's fate, and resigned the command to General Law. On Hood's left advanced, hardly with sufficient promptitude, the division of General M'Laws. Observing some delay in their advance, General Longstreet threw himself at the head of Wofford's brigade, and led them under such a fire as has rarely been witnessed right up the slope. Repressing the disposition of his men to cheer him as he took his place at their head by the brief exclamation of "Cheer less, men, and fight more," General Longstreet, mounted upon the same charger which he has ridden in a score of battlefields, without either horse or rider, both recklessly and constantly exposed, encountering even a scratch, plunged into the thickest of the fight. There are in all wars undemonstrative, unselfish, and natural men, whose worth is chiefly known to their soldiers, who seldom attract and care nothing for public applause, but on whom in the direst stress of critical battle the sternest and most hazardous *rôle* devolves. To this order belongs General Longstreet—a man fighting not for praise, or civil or social distinction, with a repugnance to those self-seeking politicians (a class happily almost unknown to England) who manipulate for their own advancement the reputation of such Generals as condescend to become their creatures.

Few, indeed, among the Generals of Lee's army are such self-seekers—least self-seeking of all Generals Lee and Longstreet themselves. It was natural that one of the Federal prisoners brought back in this very charge by Wofford's Brigade should, upon learning that the big man who led the advance was none other than General Longstreet, have exclaimed, "No wonder we are thrashed upon every field; there is not in the whole of our army a Lieutenant-General who would have risked his life in such a charge." Against the first position of the Federals the advance of Longstreet's two divisions was completely sucessful; against the second and stronger position he had not men enough to essay seriously upon this day to prevail.

Meanwhile on the Confederate centre and left Generals Hill and Ewell mingled in fierce conflict with their sternly-resisting enemy. Vain indeed would be the attempt to portray in language the scene which the Cemetery-hill, held by the Federal centre, and the lines of their right wing, lying immediately behind Gettysburg, presented to the spectator. If it had not been reserved for me to listen next day to a still more awful din, I should have fancied that no such scene had ever before saluted mortal eye or ear. A thick canopy of smoke, constantly rent by bright darting flashes of flame, cast its dense pall over the struggling, bleeding thousands who toiled and died in its centre, while out of the opaque gloom, as though from the bowels of the earth, one deep prolonged bellowing roar never ceased to issue. Through the deepening twilight and on far into the night the fierce struggle continued, until, in the gloom, the dazzling parabolas of flame, bursting into sparkling jets and coruscations as the shells cracked and exploded, made a ghastly pyrotechnic display. It was not until late in the night that it was learnt that the divisions of Rodes and Early had at one time actually carried a part of the Cemetery hill, and had sent down a peremptory entreaty for support to Generals Pinder and Anderson of A. P. Hill's corps. But General Pinder lay at the moment desperately wounded. The request was, for some unknown reason, unheeded by General Anderson. Rodes and Early fell back to their old positions, and the only advantage gained by the Confederates consisted in the carrying by General Longstreet of the first position of the Federals upon the extreme right of the Confederate line.

JULY 3.

Between the first and second positions originally held by the

Federal left intervened a large bare sloping meadow, nearly a mile in width. Across this Valley of the Shadow of Death the Confederates' advance, committed this morning to the divisions of Generals Pickett and Pettigrew, had no option but to proceed, swept by the concentrated fire of the countless Federal guns, and exposed when nearing those guns to hailstorms of musketry bullets. The distance was too great to advance at the double; it was necessary to move slowly and deliberately, that, as the men approached the batteries, there might be some dash left for the final onslaught. Early in the morning General Longstreet's line stood thus:—On the extreme right the division of General Hood, commanded by General Law; next to him the division of M'Laws—these two divisions being by General Longstreet held in hand to launch against the Federals should success attend the onward movement to their left. Next to M'Laws came the *spes gregis* of the moment—the division of General Pickett, supported and assisted on its left by the far larger division of General Pettigrew, belonging to A. P. Hill's corps, and ordinarily commanded by General Heth, who received a singular wound on the first day. He was struck in the centre of his forehead by a Minié bullet, which laid bare the bone and then glided off. He attributes his escape to the fact that he was wearing a Yankee hat which was too large for him, and in front of the forehead he had inserted a thick wad of paper, which was strong enough in its resistance to the bullet to save the General's life. It should be noticed that most of Pettigrew's division consisted of men who had never been seriously engaged before. They have recently been drawn from North Carolina, where for months and months they have been engaged in watching the fantastic menaces of Generals Hunter and Foster, and others in the neighbourhood of Newbern—menaces which must have caused the Federal Government untold millions of dollars, and which have been productive of no good to them beyond the larceny of a few negroes and the sack and pillage of sundry houses of non-combatants. It would have been easy to secure the only material advantage sought by the Federals on that coast—the suppression of the shad and herring fisheries in Pamlico and Albemarle Sounds—by the presence in those waters of a few sloops of war.

The division of General Pickett, shorn of two of its brigades, lately left in the vicinity of Suffolk, but likely, I believe, shortly to join Lee's army, did not in number much exceed 4,000 men. The strong division of Pettigrew, which in its engagement of the 1st, against General Reynolds, sustained inconsiderable loss, numbered, with the addition of Willcox's Brigade, temporarily attached to it, about 10,000 men. It was naturally desirable before their attack was delivered that a heavy cannonade from the Confederate batteries should, as far as possible, exhaust and perhaps silence some of the Federal guns. Accordingly, under the instructions of Colonl Walton, Chief of Artillery to General Longstreet, and Colonel Walker, Chief of Artillery to General A. P. Hill, battalions of artillery, numbering in all 140 guns, were got into position, while similar arrangements were made by General Ewell on the left, so that in all upon the Confederate side alone there must have been a concert of about 200 guns. It can hardly be doubted that their thunder was echoed back from a similar number of pieces on the Federal side, and to the reader's imagination must it be left to conczive the diapason of 400 guns. The thundering roar of all the accumulated battles ever fought upon earth rolled into one volume could hardly have rent the skies with fiecer or more unearthly resonance and din. Far back into the mountains the reverberations rolling from hillside to hillside startled strange and unmusical echoes. Vast cumuli of cloud, such as would have shrouded 10,000 Homeric goddesses, had they cared in these days of villainous saltpetre to mingle in the *melée,* floated over the strife; horses, the suffering and tortured ministers of man's fury and wrath, lay thickly dead or horribly mutilated upon the ground; constantly from out of the white pall of vapour issued wounded and mangled men, and rumours that this or that General was killed, that this or that regiment was reduced to a corporal's guard, traceable to no authentic source, neither believed nor disbelieved by the listeners, rose as it were out of the ground, until the spectator, a prey to that whimsical caprice which at moments of fierce and absorbing excitement seizes on men's minds, found himself wandering in thought to strange and far-off scenes, to happy valleys which had never seen war, and vaguely speculating how their echoes would awake and respond to such a thunderous din.

Precisely at 1 o'clock, responsive to the warning summons of two signal guns, the 110 pieces in the Confederate centre and right opened fire; nor were their voices hushed until 40 minutes after 2. Then came General Pickett's turn, and nobly did he spring to the head of his undaunted men, and marshal them to the attack. With long floating locks, with a seeming recklessness, which is, perhaps, partly assumed, but which stamps him of the Murat type, General Pickett, of more demonstrative courage than other Generals, but not less unflinching than his own sword, seemed as he advanced to lead his men into the very jaws of death. Slowly emerging into the open ground, with shells (singularly ineffective, as it seemed to me, considering the apparently murderous precision with which they all burst) cracking and snapping over them at every stride, General Pickett's men seemed to take hours to surmount the mile of interval which divided them from the Federal batteries. At length their destination is reached; with a wild yell they spring into the Yankee earthworks; astride of each Federal gun rides a Confederate soldier; the group around General Longstreet congratulates him that the advance is a complete success, and for a few moments breath is drawn more freely. But the quick eye of General Longstreet discerns that Pettigrew's division, upon whose almost simultaneous advance depends the retention by Pickett of the captured guns, is in confusion. Upon their left Pettigrew's men, when close up to the Yankee batteries, perceive a large column of Federals descending the hill to flank them. Retaining that fatal habit of thinking for themselves which is so pernicious to a soldier, the Confederates first halted, then got into confusion, then broke and fell back. The frightful damage from grape and canister which, shrinking at this perilous moment, they could not but sustain, was compared by an eyewitness of both scenes to the punishment inflicted on the Federals from the heights of Fredericksburg in December last. In vain did General Longstreet send Major Latrobe to General Pettigrew, shortly before the latter's troops broke, urging him in military language "to refuse his left"—that is, to meet the flanking column by a line thrown obliquely out to meet it. Major Latrobe's horse was shot as he sped on his message, and on foot he could not get up to General Pettigrew in sufficient time to instruct and guide him. When Pettigrew and his men fell back, the flanking column of Yankees, meeting with no resistance, swept round until they approached and overlapped Pickett. Then and not till then he commenced to give way. "Hide, blushing glory, hide" the cost of that retreat. Out of a division of 4,300 men he brought out, in the first instance, about 1,500, though I believe that another 1,000 straggled in the next day. His three Brigadier-Generals lay dead or desperately wounded upon the field; out of all his field-officers only one major came out unwounded; 11 out of the 13 colours which he carried into action were lost. Since the commencement of this war I know of no division on either side which has ever made so resolute an advance, or been so rudely and murderously handled. Long will the 3d of July be remembered in anguished Virginia, from which State almost all Pickett's division was drawn. General Pickett and his staff, all of whom miraculously escaped, were torn by grief at the loss of friends known for a lifetime, but doubly and trebly endeared by the common perils and sufferings of these last two years.

But if at an earlier stage of this letter I fancied that less than his usual calmness was visible in General Lee's face, all trace of cloud and anxiety passed away in this hour of our deepest gloom. Riding from knot to knot of the stragglers, with kind, firm, calm words encouraging the disheartened, rallying every man who could carry a musket or was only slightly wounded, he infused confidence and spirit into his men at the moment which of all others is most trying to volunteers. General Willcox, riding up to him with tears in his eyes, exclaimed, "General, I have tried to rally my men, but as yet they will not stand." General Lee responded, "Never mind, General; the fault is all mine. All that you have to do is to help me to remedy it so far as you can." If any testimony to the affection and confidence inspired by General Lee were wanting, it might be found in the cheers issuing from the interior of ambulances as they passed him, bearing their ghastly load of wounded to the rear. This scene was witnessed by Colonel Fremantle, of the Coldstream Guards, who has returned to England, leaving behind him many a friend in the Confederate army, which he has accompanied for the last three weeks.

After the repulse of General Pickett's division the struggle was virtually over. It is true that on the extreme Confederate left General Johnson, of Ewell's corps, captured a hill which would have been important had complete success attended Longstreet's attack. As it was, both armies, fearfully exhausted by their losses, fell back on the night of the 3d, to commence on both sides preparations for retreat on the 4th; the initiative in retreating, as was subsequently believed, having been taken by General Meade. The incidents of the day's battles—the struggles of individual companies, which, to borrow Napoleon's expression, "belong rather to the biography of a regiment than to the history of an army," would fill a volume. Suffice it to say, that while the particulars of the Confederate loss being more known to me are given in more detail, there is abundant evidence that the Federals, with their heavy columns of troops massed behind their batteries, and fearfully exposed to artillery fire, suffered a loss as unprecedented as was the valour which, for the first time in its existence, the Grand Army of the Potomac on this occasion displayed.

JULY 4.

A steady downpour of rain from a low brooding leaden sky—a day in keeping with the fortunes of the nation whose once joyous national holiday, the 80th since the acknowledgment by England of its independence, was rolling gloomily and unobserved away; the sight in every grove and almost under every tree of burying parties, sometimes with tears of convulsive and agonized grief, rendering the last sad offices to the fallen, depressed every heart; nor was the prospect of a night march in such weather, known to be imminent so soon as darkness should fall, calculated to cheer or elevate the spirits. All day long, while the big guns on either side frowned at each other in angry silence, General Ewell's enormous train, swollen to vast bulk by the plunder in horses and wagons which on their first incursion into Pennsylvania he had abundantly collected, was filing off behind the Confederate centre and right, and pushing into a pass of the South Mountains (not the same as we had traversed when advancing from Chambersburg), which leads obliquely to Hagerstown. Towards evening the wagon train of A. P. Hill's corps, which occupied the centre, followed Ewell; and it was not till long after midnight that the train of Longstreet's corps got under weigh. From 7 in the evening till 3 in the morning we lay silent and moody upon the soaking muddy ground, clinging to the log fire which the damp and chilly night made most acceptable, deluged by frequent dashes of heavy rain, watching General Longstreet as, in deep thought, he walked ceaselessly backward and forward like a sailor on his quarterdeck. Presently we were joined by General Lee. It cannot be pretended that the spirits of the party, under circumstances which would have drawn heavily on the resources of Mark Tapley, were as radiant as usual, but even to this night came an end at last. It was a strange scene to witness. The thick gloom, the heavy rain, the all-pervading sea of glutinous slimy mud, and through it knee deep, sometimes barefooted, sometimes with trousers turned up above the knee, tramping file after file of men, while along the roadside the bright camp fires, stretching for thousands of yards, dazzled and bewildered the rider's eyesight, as he tried to steer his way through droves of oxen goaded with much shouting fiercely forward, among flocks of terrified sheep, and through the interstices of mile after mile of wagons, and caissons, and guns, and attendant camp-followers.

At length, on the morning of the 5th, the rain stopped, though only for a short season—a halt was permitted—food and absence of rain exercised their restorative influence, but as we set forward again in the afternoon the pertinacious downpour was resumed. Another wretched night, passed half on the march, half in a saturated wheat field, another long day's march, and on the night of the 6th we reached the little town of Hagerstown, distant about five miles from the Potomac.

Nassau William Senior (1790-1864) was a leading economist and, in tandem with Edwin Chadwick, the principal architect of the New Poor Law of 1834. In his later years he took to keeping a journal of his conversations with the distinguished men he met on his frequent continental holidays, and circulated it freely among his friends. Occasionally (as in the letter below) he printed extracts, though it was not until after his death that the greater part of it was published in book form.

August 31st, 1863   *page 7*

THE CONFEDERATE STEAMERS

TO THE EDITOR OF THE TIMES.

Sir,—I read to-day with great pleasure your remarks on the vessels now building, or rather built, in British yards for the use of the Confederates. You have argued with force and with truth that to let them go forth to prey on Federal commerce will be an offence against international law, and also against the spirit, and probably against the words, when correctly interpreted, of our municipal law. You have shown that it is our duty and our interest to prevent this offence from being committed, and not to let it take place and lament over it when it has become irremediable.

For if these vessels once get out—nay, even if only one of them gets out, and receives a Confederate commission, we shall then have no right to arrest her, and the Federals, as we know from experience, will have no power.

And this is a matter not of months, perhaps not of days, not even of hours. I am not informed what is the state of preparation of the ship in the Clyde, but I am told that those in the Mersey are ready. An acquaintance of mine passed last week the Florida hovering in the Irish Channel for the purpose of joining and arming them.

It appears to me, however, that you have omitted one, and that a very important, motive for the immediate interference of our Government, and that is the effect which its torpidity will produce on the feelings and conduct of the Federals.

I have conversed during the last month with Americans of both parties. On one subject only are they unanimous, and that is that the escape of these vessels will produce the evil which we have exercised so much forbearance and endured such sufferings to prevent—a war with the North.

They all believe that, whatever be the wish of the Northern Government, the indignation and rage of the Northern people will force it to declare war. This is the expectation of my Federal friends, who look on a war against us with horror, and of my Confederate friends, who exult in its approach. This is the object for which, in their utmost penury, they are spending hundreds of thousands on these ships. The ravages of the Alabama and the Florida do not seriously injure the military force of the Federals, but they enrage them. The Confederates have always looked to foreign support. They long hoped that want of cotton would lead the English Government to attack the Federals. A few months ago I had a conversation on this subject with a distinguished Federal statesman (Mr. Dayton, the Federal Minister in Paris), a man of great talents, knowledge, and calmness. I thought it so important that I made a note of it. That note I append to this letter. I should, of course, have asked Mr. Dayton's permission to do so, if the matter were less urgent. But he may be absent from Paris. Four or five days might pass before I could obtain that permission, and four or five days hence all may be over.

I throw myself, therefore, on his mercy, and hope that he

135

will allow my wish to contribute to the aversion of so tremendous a misfortune as a war between England and the United States to be a sufficent apology for the publication of a private conversation.

    I have the honour to be, Sir, your obedient servant,

NASSAU W. SENIOR.

Kensington, May 28th.

———

"Paris, May 2, 1863.

"I called on Mr. Dayton, the Federal Minister. I said to him that during the last five weeks I had conversed with many persons of iolitical eminence on American affairs; that I found fears that the conduct towards us of the Federal Government would lead to war universal, and an opinion that it was intended to produce war prevalent; and that I thought it desirable that he should know the opinions, as to that conduct, of persons of political eminence, not merely impartial, but favourable to the cause of the Federals. He answered that he should be grateful for the information. I then related to him the substance of several conversations with persons belonging to different political parties.

    " 'I recognize,' he answered, 'in all that you have told me *The Times.* I believe that it is useless for a Northern American to state any facts, to contradict any falsehoods, or to use any arguments in England or in France. You all of you, French as well as English, take all your opinions, all your premisses, and all your conclusions blindly from *The Times.* I have known men treat *The Times* sometimes with contempt, sometimes with indignation, describe it as the unscrupulous organ of the English aristocracy, and laugh at those under its influence, and immediately afterwards talk to me pure *Times.* The Government of the United States would be frantic if it did not do everything and submit to everything in order to avoid a war with you.'

    " 'That,' I answered, 'is precisely what they say, and the inference which they draw from your conduct is that you are frantic. If, they say, the President and his advisers wish for a war with England they are mad. If they do not wish for it, and yet do all that they can to bring it on, then also they are mad. Take the appointment of Captain Wilkes.'

    " 'I do not know,' he answered, 'what are the rules of our

service. Captain Wilkes is the most popular man in our navy. He may have had claims which could not be refused.'

" 'Captain Wilkes's popularity,' I answered 'for having done all that he could to bring on a war with us, is a proof of the madness of the people. An English officer who had so acted would have disgusted everybody. What, then, do you think of Mr. Cassius Clay, and of the motives which led his Government first to publish his despatches, and afterwards to employ him?'

" 'You gave us,' he answered, 'great provocation, by assisting the rebels. The Alabama is manned by English sailors.'

" 'And is not your blockading fleet,' I answered, 'manned by English sailors? Can you tell me how to prevent a sailor from taking service where he likes?'

" 'You ought to have exerted,' he replied, 'greater vigilance to prevent her sailing. You ought not to have thrown on Mr. Adams the onus of proving her destination. When you complained during the Crimean war that we were building vessels for the Emperor of Russia, we did not throw on your Minister the burden of proof. We examined ourselves, ascertained that it was so, and stopped the ships.'

" 'I admit,' he continued, 'that it is difficult to prevent the people who are the greatest manufacturers of military supplies in the world from supplying belligerents with arms. But, if you cannot, as you say that you cannot, prevent Nassau from being a base of operations to the Confederate armies, you should use the utmost toleration of our efforts to prevent this. If your sympathies are with those who are endeavouring to ruin us, you should not parade them. If you think that you will gain in the rupture of the Union you are mistaken. Do you suppose that the Confederates sympathize with you, except so far as they believe that you hate us?'

" 'No.' I said, 'I have no doubt that the Confederates hate us as much as you do. An honest neutral is always hated by both the belligerents,—but they have the merit of keeping their secret better. If we knew all that they think and feel, we probably should feel towards them as you seem to be trying to make us feel towards you.'

" 'Well,' he said, 'I do not believe, with your French friends, that our public men are mad. I do not believe, therefore, that they wish for war. Nor do I believe that yours do so. But each party is excited; each party is—whether voluntarily or not—doing great mischief to the other. I see no remedy but patience, and an earnest attempt to repress the evil passions of the educated mobs in your country and of the uneducated mobs in mine. Of one thing I am certain,—that if you think that any interference on your part will stop the war you are wrong. Not England, and France, and Russia,—not all Europe could influence us.'

" 'Not,' I answered, 'by persuasion?'

" 'Not,' he replied, 'by force. What the South wants is food, and that you cannot give her. She has arms enough, but she is starving, and she will be starved out.'

" 'My expectation of peace between you and us,' he continued, 'depends much on the manner in which you deal with the ironsides which the Confederates are now building in England and Scotland. You excuse yourselves for not having stopped the Alabama on the ground that she was not obviously a ship of war. These ships are so. No merchant vessel is plated. We maintain they are intended for the Confederates—intended to prey upon the commerce of the Federals, your friends. How can we prove it except by the facts which are already as obvious as they can be made? For what other purpose can they be intended? The builders alone have the documents by which the innocent destination of the ships can be shown. You should call on the builders to produce them. If they refuse you may safely assume that they are intended to attack us. I do not ask you to confiscate them, or even to stop their progress, but merely to detain them until the builders prove, which they can do in a day, the innocence of their destination. In the Crimean war we did much more. We actually stopped the progress of the Alexandra on the suspicion that she was intended for the Russians. Not an axe or a hammer was allowed to be lifted in her. We found our laws, as you have found yours, insufficient. We amended them. You merely fold your arms, and allow proceedings opposed to your own municipal laws, and to international law, to good feeling and to good faith, to go on, because your municipal law has not sufficient detective power. Then give it that power. You are not, as we are, bound by a constitution. Your Parliament is omnipotent. If it is not skilful enough to invent a law which shall enable such atrocities to be detected and prevented, let it copy the law which we passed for that purpose, and which was sufficient. If you refuse to do this, and, in consequence of your negligence, or of your self-inflicted impotence, these ironsides escape and plunder us, the American people, irritated enough already, will be ungovernable. You have seen enough of them to know that their resentment is not under the control of their interests. They will really become as mad as your French friends call them. They will be quite ready to ruin themselves in order to ruin you.' "

October 5th, 1863   *page 7*

THE WESTERN STATES

(FROM OUR SPECIAL CORRESPONDENT.)

ST. LOUIS, MISSOURI, Sept. 19.

It takes some time to conceive a distinct idea of the extent to which confusion reigns in the State of Missouri. There is a vast conspiracy on the part of the whole press and of the whole society of America to rob a disinterested observer of the blessed light of truth. Every party man must needs pin you down to his own political faith. He wishes you to "embrace a decided course," to "proceed upon a consistent system," as if you were an actor, instead of a spectator—as if your object were to sway the destinies of the country as a ruler, or even simply as a voter, while your task is simply to listen to all each party has got to say, and to draw, or rather to enable a reader to draw, from their conflicting evidence such conclusions as in all fairness and in perfect indifference may be come to. "A plague o' both your houses!" The State of Missouri was intended by Nature to be one of the richest and happiest regions of the Union. To its inexhaustible agricultural resources it adds boundless mineral wealth, and its climate is more favourable to every variety of product than that of the territories lying to the north or south of it. Well, at this moment Missouri is little better than a vast field for the worst kind of marauding enterprise. The papers are full of guerilla outrages; reports of deeds of murder, robbery, and arson fill up their daily columns, yet most people assure me the disorder is far greater than the press can represent it, far greater than man would believe or could conceive it. If you take the version of the Republicans, the malefactors are, of course, merely the friends and partisans of the Democrats; if you listen to these

139

latter, all the mischief is the work of the "bloody-minded" Radicals. The Western counties on the borders of Kansas are the scene of incessant raids; parties intent upon mutual destruction are perpetually crossing the Missouri River. It is in the power of every ragamuffin to raise companies and regiments. Every thief and cut-throat exercises the right of private warfare. The other day it was Jim Lane, self-styled a general, and actually a senator of the United States, a man who travels with an "executioner" at his heels, who assembled the Kansas boys at Paola, and projected an inroad into Missouri. Jim Lane is more ready with his tongue than with his hand, however, and the Paola *leveedes boneliers* turned out, to use an elegant American expression, a "perfect fizzle." But on the night of the 14th to 15th inst. a raid was made into Buchanan county by Kansas boys from over the river, and the house of Major M'Roberts, with those of some of his neighbours, was robbed and burnt. That county and all the others on the North-West "have been for the last three months theatres of murders, nightly house-burnings, indiscriminate robbery, and lawless violence of the most desperate character." A man named Jennison, a petty livery stable-keeper in Kansas, is raising a regiment on the borders, which is to march on Missouri, as its leader proclaims, "with the revolver in one hand and the torch in the other," to" carry the flag, kill with the sabre, and hang with the gallows."

I dare say there is more vain bragging than settled purpose among these loathsome ruffians. Men are valued for their "energy" in these Western countries; but their energy is often little more than mere big talk and intolerable swagger and bluster. But if the leaders are mere wind bags, their followers are earnest thieves, and the work of all these "bushwackers," "jayhawkers," and "red legs" is not likely to come to an end before those once flourishing Western counties are utterly laid waste and depopulated.

Guerillas are no less active in the eastern parts of the State, though they are only to be met with in little squads, and their outrages partake more of the character of common highway robbery. The country within two or three miles of St. Louis even is not safe from their depredations. I gave you a few words the other day respecting the burning, on Sunday the 13th, of four steamers on the levee, or quay, of this city. I am told that the deed is traced to some members of an extensive conspiracy, who had plotted the destruction not merely of those vessels, but of the whole town, by fire.

Such are the outward results of the heaving of the masses under the influence of political agitation. What politicians may be quarrelling about in Missouri is not quite clear at first glance. They all profess themselves "Unionists," and all agree that slavery, at least in their own State, must come to an end. To that effect an ordinance was voted by the Legislature in July last, providing that emancipation shall be completed before July, 1870. The ultra-Republicans, or Radicals, however, are unwilling to acquiesce in that decision, and are clamouring for absolute, immediate, and violent abolition. The brigand bands which are ravaging the country are therefore, either partisans of these fanatics, whose avowed object it is to free the negro wherever they fall in with him, or the supporters of the slaveowner and of the pro-slavery politician acting in self-defence. The ranting Radicals seem likely to carry the day by mere blustering vehemence: they have organized a "Committee of Public Safety;" they put no limits to their abuse of General Schofield, and of most of the other military authorities, whom they charge with lukewarmness in the public service, and a leaning towards the slave-holding interest, and are especially savage against Hamilton R. Gamble, who was appointed provisional Governor of the State at the time of the Convention of February, 1861. They protest that they must have a Governor springing from regular popular election, and not a Presidential nominee, whose moderation they characterize as disloyalty and treason.

The nominees and representatives of the Washington Government, and the central Administration itself, are looked upon as little better than Copperheads by the ultra-Republican Abolitionists, and are loudly denounced as such. The action of these constituted authorities is hampered and thwarted at every step. Their efforts to organize and mobilize so-called "provisional" militia regiments, to be marched to the protection of the Southern frontier, are being frustrated by these Radical agitators, who represent the enrolment of the militia under such circumstances as an illegal measure. Incited by their suggestions, the 11th East Missouri Militia, who were embarked on board the steamer D. R. Hamilton, bound to New Madrid, cut themselves adrift from their moorings the night before last, and drifted down the stream for about a mile, when they landed and scattered themselves, or "skedaddled," about the country. The Colonel and Lieutenant-Colonel were not yet on board, and the other officers, mere recruits, like their refractory privates, never dreamed of offering any resistance. Some of the ill-advised fugitives have since been arrested, and others have voluntarily surrendered themselves to the authorities. The dispersion of this one regiment has, however, induced the authorities to abandon their scheme of the enrolment of a provisional militia altogether, and the other regiments have been dismissed, to the great relief of the British Consul, Mr. Edward Wilkins, by whose strenuous exertions many Irish and English subjects had to be struck off from the rolls, into which they had been carelessly, or perhaps somewhat wilfully, entered as citizens. . . .

It is, perhaps, necessary to point out that the following extract, the only version of the Gettysburg Address printed by The Times *during the Civil War, is badly mangled: it leaves out about a quarter of Lincoln's short speech.*

December 3rd, 1863   **page 12**

LATEST INTELLIGENCE

[A portion of the following appeared in our Second Edition of yesterday:—]

AMERICA

(By Electric and International Telegraph.)

Per the Edinburgh, *via* Queenstown, Dec. 2.)

NEW YORK, Nov. 21, 11 A.M.
The consecration of the Gettysburg battle-field as a national cemetery took place on Thursday. President Lincoln, Mr. Seward, the Hon. Edward Everett, and Governor Seymour were present. Mr. Lincoln delivered the dedicatory address, in which he said:—

"Four score and seven years ago our fathers brought forth upon this continent a new nation conceived in liberty, and dedicated to the propositon that all men were created equal. Now we are engaged in a great civil war, testing whether the nation, or any nation so conceived and so dedicated, can long endure. We are met upon a great battlefield of that war. We are met to dedicate a portion of it as the final resting-place of those who here gave their lives that that nation might live, and to resolve that the dead shall not have died in vain—that the nation shall, under God, have a new birth of freedom, and that the government of the people by the people, and for the people, shall not perish from the earth."

Mr. Everett made a long speech recapitulating the events of the campaign which terminated with the battle of Gettysburg.

Gold, 153.

The Edinburgh takes out $500,000 in specie.

December 4th, 1863   *page 9*

THE CIVIL WAR IN AMERICA

(FROM OUR OWN CORRESPONDENT.)

NEW YORK, Nov. 20.

... The papers of to-day are almost entirely filled up by two speeches delivered by two orators as unlike each other as it might well be possible for this Western world to produce—Mr. Everett's inaugural oration at Gettysburg, and Mr. Beecher's "Impressions of the feeling in Europe with respect to the American War," spoken at the Brooklyn Academy of Music.

The inauguration of the cemetery at Gettysburg was an imposing ceremony, only rendered somewhat flat by the nature of Mr. Everett's lecture, and ludicrous by some of the luckless sallies of that poor President Lincoln, who seems determined to play in this great American Union the part of the famous Governor of the Isle of Barataria. Honest old Abe arrived at Gettysburg on Wednesday evening, and after supper was serenaded by the band of the 5th New York Artillery. There was a loud call for the President. He appeared, and was loudly cheered, when he opened his mouth and said:—

"I appear before you, fellow-citizens, merely to thank you for this compliment. The inference is a very fair one that you would hear me for a little while at least were I to commence to make a speech. I do not appear before you for the purpose of doing so, and for several substantial reasons. The most substantial of these is that I have no speech to make. (Laughter.) In my position it is somewhat important that I should not say any foolish things. (A Voice,—'If you can help it.') It very often happens that the only way to help it is to say nothing at all. (Laughter.) Believing that it is my present condition this evening, I must beg of you to excuse me from addressing you further."

Mr. Seward soon afterwards spoke rather more to the purpose, urging that the cause of the war was slavery, and that the war would end in the removal of its cause. He had hoped to see slavery die by the fates of war. The after-supper speeches of Wednesday, however, were hardly to be looked upon as a prelude of the great sayings and doings of the ensuing day. Yesterday the proceedings were opened by the Rev. Mr. Stockton with a long and impressive prayer, followed up by the dedicatory address by the President, got up in a somewhat different style from his extempore effusion of the eve, when at last the time came for the orator of the day to open his MS.

The Hon. Edward Everett is a lady's orator. I remember conversing with fair enthusiasts who sat under that gentleman's pulpit on his *début* as a Unitarian minister in Boston, and who had not, after many years, recovered from their rapture at the "solemn, handsome, inspired countenance," the "stately bearing," the "deep, mellow voice" of the youthful preacher, and especially at the "graceful wave of the dazzling white hand," as it followed the cadence of his well-rounded periods. On all occasions where words are wanted—not thoughts—where feelings are to be tickled—not roused—nothing can be more refreshing or pleasing than to hear and see Mr. Everett. Here, however, mere rhetoric was out of place, and whatever effect the lecture may have had on the feminine part of the audience, which mustered rather strong on the spot, there is no doubt that it reads tame beyond belief, and is such a performance as would scarcely win the prize for composition over the common run of undergraduates. Mr. Everett begins by high-sounding allusions to Athens and Marathon; he gives a very minute description, or say circumstantial and more than technical report, of the three great battle-days of July, 1863; then launches forth into an inquiry into the causes of the war, proving that "the kettle began it," that the rebels are rebels, and rebellion the most hideous crime man can be guilty of when it aims at the overturn of the best of all possible Governments. He added that division had always been the bane of all communities, but that the wounds inflicted by political dissensions soon healed, and the very scars were effaced by time, and instanced the case of England, the wars of the Roses, the rebellion and revolution, and those of Germany, Italy, France, &c. Anything more dull and commonplace, anything less calculated to call forth deep or lively or lasting emotions, it would not be easy by the most fastidious taste, the most un-wearied industry, and the most consummate scholarship without a soul to it to produce. Mr. Ward Beecher's address was something different. It is not his first appearance before a Brooklyn audience since the popular preacher got home; but he was awfully sea-sick during his voyage, and his qualmish efforts to speak before his full recovery must not be taken into account. Last evening he was in the vein, and being addressed by a brother preacher, Mr. Storrs, who praised him for "having literally taken the British lion by the ears, and drawing it with so dexterous a gentleness, and so wise a firmness, that the Royal beast roared in approbation of the treatment," Mr. Beecher answered, modestly enough, that, "he put no immoderate esti-mate on his services," though "he believed he did some good wherever he spoke. The object of his speech was to point out to his countrymen which classes and parties of the English public were in favour of the Northern cause and which were against it. He was sure of the middle and lower classes—of the heart of the English people;" "the upper-class, as they are called, are on the side of the South." The reasons by which these latter are actuated are "commercial interest and rivalry therein, class power and fear of contagion of American ideas; the fact that the Americans are too large and strong a nation." For the rest, the cause of the Union numbered many friends in England among the members of the Government—the Queen and the late Prince Consort first and foremost,—many organs of the Press, and a number of worthy and influential persons, of whom he gave the names in the midst of the applause of his delighted audience. Mr. Beecher's style of eloquence is now familiar to most people in England, and needs no remark on my part. Only it seems that he last evening addressed his audience with a kind of home feeling, and that the certainty of success bore him up so as to render his triumph more brilliant than any achieved by him on former occasions. . . .

LATEST INTELLIGENCE

THE SINKING OF THE ALABAMA

(FROM OUR OWN CORRESPONDENT.)

LIVERPOOL, SUNDAY EVENING.
The following telegram has been received at the Liverpool Underwriters' Room from Lloyd's agent at Cherbourg:—
"CHERBOURG, SUNDAY, 12 10 P.M.
"The Alabama left this morning, and is now engaged with the Kearsage. A brisk cannonade is heard.

"1 40 P.M.
"The Kearsage has just sunk the Alabama. An English yacht has saved the crew."

We are informed by a gentleman connected with the firm of Messrs. Saunders and Otley, who saw Captain Semmes at Cherbourg yesterday, that the Alabama was to go out to fight the Kearsage to-day, and with this intention Captain Semmes confided to this gentleman his journals and other documents connected with the cruises of the Alabama.

(BY ELECTRIC AND INTERNATIONAL TELEGRAPH.)

TO THE EDITOR OF THE TIMES.

Sir,—Herewith I send you a copy of my log respecting the engagement between the Confederate steamer Alabama and the Federal steamer Kearsage:—
"Sunday, June 19th, 9 a.m.—Got up steam and proceeded out of Cherbourg harbour.
"10 30.—Observed the Alabama steaming out of the harbour towards the Federal steamer Kearsage:—
"The Alabama commenced firing with her starboard battery, the distance between the contending vessels being about one mile. The Kearsage immediately replied with her starboard guns; a very sharp, spirited firing was then kept up, shot sometimes being varied by shells. In manoeuvring both vessels made seven complete circles at a distance of from a quarter to half a mile.

firing, the Alabama making head sail, and shaping her course for the land, distant about nine miles.

"At 12 30 observed the Alabama to be disabled and in a sinking state. We immediately made towards her, and on passing the Kearsage were requested to assist in saving the Alabama's crew.

"At 12 50, when within a distance of 200 yards, the Alabama sunk. We then lowered our two boats, and, with the assistance of the Alabama's whale boat and a dingy, succeeded in saving about 40 men, including Captain Semmes and 13 officers. At 1 p.m. we steered for Southampton."

I may state that, before leaving, the Kearsage was apparently much disabled. The Alabama's loss, so far as at present ascertained, in killed and wounded, &c., was as follows,—viz., one officer and one man drowned, six men killed, and one officer and 16 men wounded. Captain Semmes received a slight wound in the right hand.

The Kearsage's boats were, after some delay, lowered, and, with the assistance of a French pilot boat, succeeded in picking up the remaining survivors.

JOHN LANCASTER.
Steam Yacht Deerhound, off Cowes, June 19th.

July 29th, 1864   *page 12*

LATEST INTELLIGENCE

·   ·   ·

AMERICA

[The following appeared in our Second Edition of yesterday:—]
QUEENSTOWN, WEDNESDAY.

The Inman steamer City of Baltimore, from New York on the 16th inst., has arrived.

The following narrative of the appearance of the Confederates before Washington, and their subsequent retreat, is dated the 14th inst., and was written in the city itself:—

"The investment of the northern defences of Washington by the enemy, for the first time in the progress of this war, commenced early last Monday morning. That brief time, however, has been filled with so much hope and fear, and anxiety and excitement, that its sudden end is hailed all the more gratefully. On Sunday last, after defeating the forces of General Wallace at Monocacy-bridge, the enemy sent a column of troops down the Washington and Frederick turnpike. It entered Rockville on Sunday morning, and appropriated all supplies that it could lay its hands on, and then moved on towards Washington. Five miles from Georgetown, and two miles beyond the fortifications, it drove in our pickets one mile on Sunday night. At daybreak on Monday morning skirmishing commenced within rifle-shot of Fort Pennsylvania, three miles from Georgetown. The fort startled the citizens of Georgetown by opening its heavy guns. Skirmishing lasted all day and into the night, the enemy not seeming in large enough force to advance their line. Simultaneously with the appearance of this force another division of troops appeared on the Seventh-street-road, four miles from the city, directly north, and immediately in front of Forts Stevenson and De Russey. Here they seemed in larger force, and in skirmishing with invalid regiments and militia our forces got the worst of it. At times the rebels were within 200 yards of the forts, and their sharpshooters picked off a good many who stuck their heads above the parapets.

"By Monday noon the enemy had a strong skirmishing line, and some 60 killed and wounded; but at dusk the veteran troops came up and advanced to the front, when fighting became severe for skirmishing. The rebels began to use artillery, and Forts Slocum and De Russey opened in reply with their heavy guns.

"The fight, which was seen by hundreds of spectators on the Seventh-street-road, was very exciting to novices. The country was well situate to see all the firing of infantry and heavy fort artillery, while burning residences, barns, and other buildings, which had been fired by both parties to get better range of each other, lighted up the fields and woods that skirt just outside the outer line of fortifications.

"At noon intelligence of the cutting of all telegraphic and railroad lines between Baltimore and Washington came to hand, and added, it was thought then, something as to the enemy's full design. Washington became isolated, and so remained 36 hours. Tuesday afternoon Pennsylvania-avenue was crowded with troops marching in all directions, while an incessant flood of extras from newspaper offices announcing that Fort Lincoln, situate on the Baltimore turnpike, 10 miles north-east of the capital, had been attacked, wrought up the excitement to the highest pitch yet reached during the invasion. In the meanwhile skirmishing continued all Tuesday afternoon all along the lines, without anything new being developed in the enemy's lines; and so Tuesday wore into night, and, notwithstanding published rumours of the advance of the rebel force on the south side of the Potomac, a perfect feeling of security prevailed, for it was then doubted if the rebels intended an assault, and if they did our forces would prove too much for them.

"During the early part of the night their line was strong as usual, stretching from the railroad this side of Bladensburg to Fort Pennsylvania, two miles from the Potomac. The city now being perfectly isolated, many of the places of business were closed, and provisions reached 'panic' prices.

"Flour rose in price $10 per barrel, and citizens found great difficulty in providing for their families when suddenly ordered into the ranks. Tuesday afternoon no one was allowed to go to the front without a pass, and rumour was glib enough. There was but little excitement except among the militia. It was well understood all was in readiness by our forces to attack on Wednesday morning.

"But daybreak came, and behold the skirmish line and pickets had vanished, and the enemy was gone.

"Ruined fields, smouldering houses, and his dead and wounded were all left behind; a most sickening memento of his visit.

"Cavalry followed in pursuit, and the enemy were found to be retreating towards Fredericksburg. A small battery had remained near Bladensburg, firing at the railroad train long after the main line had retreated. Thus commenced and thus ended the rebel invasion of the district of Columbia and investment of Washington.

"The enemy's troops came nearer the city than they ever have before. At several points in their lines the city could be plainly seen, and objects of special interest designated, while from some of the public buildings skirmishing could be seen with the aid of a common opera-glass. The rebel head-quarters were at Silver Springs, in the residence of F. P. Blair, sen. This was about the only house spared from the flames in the Seventh-street-road. Postmaster-General Blair's residence, adjoining it, was burnt, with all its contents. Early and Breckenridge were two days at Blair's house, and it was through the influence of Breckenridge that it did not share the fate of his son's.

"The President and Secretary Stanton showed their anxiety in the situation by being present at the wharf where the steamers were unloading troops, and hastening them to the front, while the former, in company with General Halleck, was at the front a good deal of the time. All three were in Fort Stevens, when several were killed near them.

"Various opinions prevail as to the real intention of the enemy. Many insist that a feint was made on this city to cover the retreat of the larger force towards the Potomac, laden with plunder, while others declare that a general attack was premeditated and miscarried. Our forces are pursuing the retreating foe and the city has settled down into quietness, after enjoying the most tremendous sensation in its history during the war.

"The railroad and telegraph lines are being rapidly put in repair. The former was only slightly damaged. During the most critical period all the forts were connected with the department by telegraph, the entire force of the American telegraph officers being detailed as operators. In this way troops could be centred on any weak part of the line. The country adjoining the city on the north, which a week ago was blooming with bountiful harvests, is now a barren waste. The enemy destroyed everything, even cutting down orchards, firing haystacks, &c. The destruction of property is very large. Our entire loss during the investment was between 400 and 500, including a good many officers." . . .

November 22nd, 1864 *page 6*

. . . Mr. LINCOLN has, no doubt, been, as everybody foresaw he would be, elected President. The question which concerns us now is not so much how he came to this second elevation as what influence that elevation is likely to have on our own relations with the United States. On this point we see no reason for alarm; nay, it may probably be that we are safer in the hands of Mr. LINCOLN than we should be in those of any one else. As regards foreign States, ourselves in particular, we may reasonably believe

150

that he has sown his wild oats; he has gone through the course of defying and insulting England, which is the traditional way of obtaining the Irish vote, and we may not unreasonably hope that he is unlikely to repeat the experiment. Ever since he found himself firmly established in his office, and the first effervesence of national feeling had begun to subside, we have had no great reason to complain of the conduct of Mr. LINCOLN towards England. His tone has been less exacting, his language has been less offensive, and due allowance being made for the immense difficulties of his situation, we could have parted with Mr. LINCOLN, had such been the pleasure of the American people, without any vestige of ill-will or ill-feeling. He has done as regards this country what the necessities of his situation demanded from him, and he has done no more. A new President might possibly feel called upon for a demonstration of more hostile spirit. It is an ordeal through which all American politicians must pass, and we may deem ourselves fortunate in having to deal with one who has passed through it already.

Though, however, we have no reason as impartial lookers-on to complain of the re-election of a Chief Magistrate with whom we have, at any rate, contrived during the last four years to keep up friendly relations, the case is very different with regard to the nation which has thus re-elected him for its chief. The case of the Democratic minority is soon stated. Even while the election was yet pending, while an arbitrary or unpopular act might lose much valuable support and embitter much lukewarm opposition, they were denied the franchise which the Constitution gives them by the Generals of the PRESIDENT, and the denial was supported in words and in writing by the President himself. What fate have they to expect when the election is decided? What right will be held sacred when this right of election, on which all others rest, is boldly and advisedly set at naught by the very candidate who is seeking for the suffrages which he violates? henceforth we may consider the Democratic party as expelled from the arena of practical politics, and destined to purchase either an ignominious impunity by inaction and submission, or to suffer all the miseries that tyrants can inflict or martyrs can endure. We can regard the reappointment of Mr. LINCOLN as little less than an abdication by the American people of the right of self-government, as an avowed step towards the subversion of a popular Government, which may still exist in

151

form, but which in substance is gone. We would not be supposed to insinuate that it is the destiny of Mr. LINCOLN to be the real founder of the dynasty to which he has taken so long a step; whatever be his merits, his warmest admirers themselves can scarcely contend that he is made of Imperial stuff. His hand has shaken the tree, but we yet await the man who is to gather the fruit. Future historians will probably date from the second presidency of Mr. LINCOLN the period when the American Constitution was thoroughly abrogated, and had entered on that transition stage, so well known to the students of history, through which Republics pass on their way from democracy to tyranny.

December 12th, 1864 *pages 8-9*

The whole history of the American subscription for the relief of the Lancashire operatives is told in an elaborate Report which now lies before us. The idea was first broached in November, 1862, and the accounts of the "International Relief Committee" were finally closed in the summer of the present year. The interval embraces the darkest period of the Cotton Famine, for, as we learn from the returns published on Saturday, the *maximum* of pauperism was reached in the first week of December, 1862, when 274,860 persons were relieved by the guardians, and the *minimum* was touched in the fourth week of August last, when the number had fallen to 78,730. The real amount contributed in this country to mitigate the effects of this overwhelming calamity will never be known, but whatever it may be, the efforts made in the United States for the same benevolent object, at a time when the resources of the country were severely taxed by the war, will ever deserve to be remembered with gratitude. The actual sum collected by the International Relief Committee in money or money's worth appears to have been about $140,000, but to this must be added nearly $30,000 received from the "Produce Exchange Committee" of New York, more than $60,000 from the Philadelphia Committee, and the cost of provisions, &c., sent through various channels to Ireland, and estimated at above $100,000. Altogether "the relief sent to the United Kingdom in 1863" is stated at nearly $350,000, exceeding by about $100,000 the aggregate of the American subsidy during the Irish famine of 1847-8. This is a munificent donation from the wealthy classes of one country to the suffering poor of another, and it is but justice to add that the manner in which it was offered was such as to enhance its value. In the public appeals made by the New York Committees to their countrymen two motives, and two only, are put forward—the contrast between the wants of Lancashire and the abundant harvest of America, and the fact that the former were chiefly due to the American war. In the letter forwarded to the gentlemen in Liverpool who were to superintend the distribution of the consignments, "all semblance of a political bearing" is emphatically disclaimed, and sentiments of humanity are mingled with the expression of sincere goodwill towards Great Britain. We need hardly say that the gift was received in the same spirit. Lord DERBY moved that the cordial thanks of the Central Relief Committee should be given to the donors. The Government, as well as the railway companies, did all in their power to facilitate the transmission of the bounty to its 183 destinations without charge or diminution of any kind, and the great manufacturing towns vied with each other in their glowing addresses of welcome. It was a generous deed, and it was generously received.

It would have been too much to expect that every individual should exhibit the same good taste and abstinence from all that could mar the grace of the benefaction. There is a curious passage in the original letter of Messrs. GRISWOLD to the New York Chamber of Commerce, placing a new ship at their disposal, which betrays a curious sense of restraint in the indulgence of their friendly feelings. After urging that a cargo of food should be sent "to our suffering friends abroad," they proceed thus:—"We say *friends* because these people have shown a forbearance and consideration for the North which some in higher positions have not evinced. This donation should be intended not only as a relief to her suffering subjects, but as a token of our respect for the QUEEN and her friendship for the United States. *We are of the belief that her regard of the opinions and her firmness in adhering to the advice of her excellent husband, Prince Albert, alone prevented a rupture between Great Britain and this country.*" Another most liberal contributor, who sent no less than $7,000 to purchase 1,000 barrels of flour, could not help resting the claims of the operatives on the ground that they "will not join the clamour of interested leaders," but understand "the value of our unity as a nation, and refuse to part with their birth-right in this land of promise." "I can assure you," says Mr. STELL, one of the selected consignees. "that every attempt that has been made to induce them to pass resolutions in favour of the Rebels has *signally* failed, which has presented a *strong contrast* to the course pursued by the middle and privileged classes, who have acted as if they were enemies to peace, progress, and freedom."

We have not scrupled to give publicity to these expressions, because they are part of the Report, and will go forth to the American people, but we hasten to assure our "friends" on the other side of the Atlantic—meaning thereby all those, privileged or unprivileged, whether of the upper, middle, or lower classes, who retain an affection towards the old country—that we in no degree resent them. It is absolutely impossible that a nation in the sad position of the Federal States should understand the attitude of neutrality. We should probably not understand it ourselves if a third part of the United Kingdom should assert its independence, and though a great deal may be said about the different nature of secession under a Monarchy and under a Republic, the pain of dismemberment may be assumed to be about equal. It was perfectly natural that the citizens of the North, hearing that the British aristocracy looked coldly on their cause, and firmly believing in the paramount influence of that Order, should owe it a grudge, and turn for sympathy to the "working men," who, as they were also told, were all Northerners to the backbone. How they came to identify the private inclinations of HER MAJESTY with those of this class we cannot explain; still less can we accept the theory of our Constitution implied in the allusion to them; but the alleged desire of some party in this country for war with the United States has been from the first a pure fabrication. No such desire ever existed on the part of any social or political section whatever, and the only fear has been that we might be forced into war, against our will, by some such act as the seizure of the Florida in the harbour of Bahia. Those who can see nothing but selfishness and jealousy in our so-called partiality for the Confederates would do well to compare it with the feeling manifested in the case of Denmark. England had nothing to gain or lose by the severance of the Duchies from the Danish Monarchy, yet such was the indignation excited by the unscrupulous aggressions of Germany that at one time an armed intervention was imminent, and nothing but the hesitation of France prevented it. England has suffered untold loss by the blockade of the Southern States, and by a mere recognition of their independence might have turned the scale in their favour and established a balance of power in North America; and yet, though France would have stood by us, hardly anyone has seriously advocated breaking the blockade, ineffective as it sometimes was, and very few were prepared for recognition. Let Northerners ask themselves calmly how they would have been tempted to act under like circumstances, and whether they could have resisted the temptation.

Though the aspirations of the Liverpool Chamber of Commerce have not been realized, and no "signal national deliverance" has arisen for the desolated continent of America, our own share in its misfortunes has, happily, been lightened. Though some 100,000 persons in the cotton districts are still in receipt of relief from the poor rates, the worst of the crisis is long since passed, and we have ceased to depend on the cotton-growing States of the South. Perhaps the exaggeration is pardonable, but it is rather beyond the truth to say that even in the winter of 1862 "very many actually perished from starvation, or the diseases induced by it;" or, again, that "tens of thousands were saved from the horrors of starvation" by the timely succour of America. Things never came to that pass, but the distress was bad enough, and assistance from all quarters most welcome. It is greatly to the credit of the International Relief Committee that they scrupulously applied the funds at their disposal to their proper objects, and absolutely refused to appropriate any portion of them "in aid of emigration." Such a course, as they justly observe, "might have subjected them to reproach from the British Government, as well as from those who were not averse to finding occasion for the ascription of dishonourable motives, even in a work of the purest philanthropy." To their wise discretion in this delicate matter it is due that their mission of mercy, instead of leaving bitter reminiscences behind it, has really tended to cement the bonds of union between the two great Anglo-Saxon communities.

December 21st, 1864

Mr. GIDEON WELLES, the Secretary of the Federal Navy, is undoubtedly entitled to claim credit for the exertions of his Department during the great Civil War. He falls into the exaggeration characteristic of his countrymen when he ascribes to the American Marine achievements without parallel or precedent in any naval history; for good Admirals have lived before FARRAGUT, though they did not go into battle with ironclads, and great naval expeditions have been undertaken, though the means were adapted to the age and the occasion. But if we look impartially at the work which devolved suddenly upon the American Admiralty four years ago, at the resources which then existed for its performance, and at the manner in which it has been actually performed, we must admit that the tone of gratulation pervading the Secretary's Report is by no means without justification.

In the month of March, 1861, when Mr. WELLES entered upon his duties as head of the Naval Department, the Navy of the United States contained but 76 vessels of all descriptions available for service. It now contains 671, a large proportion of which are vessels newly constructed, on the principles suggested by modern warfare. In this powerful fleet there are no fewer than 71 ironclads, and 559 ships out of the 671 are propelled by steam. At the commencement of the war the Government had but 7,600 seamen in its pay, and of these only 207 were in the home ports. In the present month the number of men borne on the Estimates is 51,000, while during the present year, though 26 vessels have been lost to the Federals by shipwreck, battle, or capture, the *Navy List* still shows an increase of 83 vessels over the fleet of 1863. Nor has this provision for the exigencies of the war been upon any excessive scale. The blockade maintained by the Federals extends over a coast line of 3,500 miles, and this service, at any rate, is really unprecedented in magnitude. The "squadrons" maintained on the several stations occupied by the fleet deserve the epithet of "immense," which Mr. LINCOLN gave them. The Mississippi itself is divided into ten naval districts, each under a separate command, and the incidents of the war have taught us how skilfully and serviceably the Navy has co-operated with the Army even in the interior of the continent. The whole war, in fact, on the Federal side has been half a naval war, and the gunboats of the Union have enabled its land forces

156

to attempt and execute what would otherwise have been impracticable enterprises. In the face of so much success it would be invidious to insist upon failures; but we cannot forget that all the chief seaports of the Confederacy, with the exception of New Orleans, are still in Confederate hands, that the formidable Navy of the Federals had no enemy to deal with, and that the depredations on American commerce, which Mr. WELLES charges so bitterly to the account of British malice, were due only to the temporary inability of the Northerners to keep the police of the sea.

If Mr. LINCOLN's statistics are correctly reported, we may say something more of the Federal Navy, and admit that it has been economically raised and thriftly maintained. The PRESIDENT's Message gives the entire cost of the Navy from the beginning of the war to the present time as less than 50,000,000*l*., which would represent an annual expenditure of some 12,000,000*l*. only—a charge hardly exceeding our own. But there is either some mistake in these figures or the Federal Navy Estimates must be increasing at an enormous rate, for Mr. WELLES now informs us particularly that the charge for the approaching year will be upwards of 22,000,000*l*., or nearly double the average of former years. Still, even that sum appears moderate in comparison with the prodigious expenditure upon the Army, especially if we recollect that the American Estimate includes the cost of the ordnance stores, which in our own Estimates are separately provided for. Mr. WELLES, however, contemplates spending no less than 11,000,000*l*. in the construction, repair, and equipment of vessels during the coming year.

It will not have escaped the notice of attentive readers that at the moment when we are urged in this country to abandon or curtail our Government establishments for the maintenance of the Navy, the head of the Navy Department in America is strenuously insisting on the absolute necessity of such establishments. What Mr. GIDEON WELLES said in previous years he says over again now, and reiterates more eagerly than ever his conviction that the Federals must have such yards and arsenals as would place the Government above the necessity of depending on contracts with private builders. He has argued this question, indeed, not only on the score of exigency, but on that of economy; asserting that it would be cheaper as well as better for the country to manufacture for itself the vessels and machinery which it is now compelled to buy. We have remarked on former occasions that these opinions are to be received, perhaps, with some qualification as proceeding from the pen of an official; but it was impossible not to perceive, from the more detailed statements given in some of his previous Reports, that the service and the Treasury were really suffering together from the system which has been recommended for our own adoption.

The instruction which we might otherwise derive from the experience of the Americans in marine armour and projectiles is materially diminished by the circumstances under which the chief Reports have been made. The great trial of the Federal ironclads took place in the attack upon Charleston, and the failure of that attack was attended with so much quarrelling and recrimination among the officers concerned as almost to invalidate the accounts received of the engagement. The Admiral in command reported disparagingly of the Monitors and their performances; other officers differed entirely from him in their estimates of facts, and the Federal Government was disposed to reject reports tending to depreciate the new Navy of the nation, and to give corresponding encouragement to the Confederates. These contests led all parties to speak with so much personal feeling on the subject that it is natural to suspect their statements of bias, and we feel unable to say whether the model on which the Federals have constructed an iron fleet is or is not successful. We do, however, know that the Monitors are, at any rate, unfit for sea service, and that Admiral FARRAGUT has persisted, hitherto with impunity, in hoisting his flag on board a wooden frigate.

It should not be forgotten in looking at the expenditure of the Americans upon their Navy that they have hitherto been exempted from the charge for the non-effective service by which our own Estimates are necessarily swelled. Our effective Navy costs us at present only 8,700,000*l.*, to which 1,400,000*l.* must be added for half-pay and pensions. But it is obvious that no Navy can be actively employed without creating claimants entitled to this consideration, and Mr. WELLES is already obliged to introduce the item into his accounts. The "pension roll," he tells us, comprised at the date of his report 769 invalids and 840 widows and orphans. Whether these are provided for in the "miscellaneous" vote, or whether the "pension fund" suffices to defray the charge, we do not know, but the fund in question seems to be rapidly increasing. It is constituted from a moiety of all the prize property forthcoming from the war, an amount rendered very considerable by the incidents of the blockade. No fewer than 324 vessels were captured during the past year, and the whole number of prizes since the beginning of the war amounts to 1,379. Half of the proceeds go to the captors, half to the pension fund; so that if the fund is judiciously preserved, the American Estimates will be lightened of some of their burden.

The extreme acrimony displayed by Mr. GIDEON WELLES in his remarks upon the Confederate cruisers is doubtless due in some measure to the susceptibilites of his Department; but it may be usefully contrasted with the moderation and candour observable in the language of President LINCOLN himself. Mr. WELLES must know full well that our Government could not have done more than it did to prevent the sailing of these vessels. The question of right itself was legally debatable, and even if it had not been, the means of evasion were so numerous that the efforts of any authorities might have been defeated. The real source of the mischief was the inefficiency, or rather the pre-occupation, of that Navy over which Mr. WELLES presides. For some time the Federals had more than enough to do in giving a character of efficiency to the prodigious blockade which they had undertaken, and in the interval a couple of Southern cruisers ranged the seas uncontrolled. The event might have been unavoidable, but its consequences should not be laid thus unjustly at our door.

January 5th, 1865   *page 6*

General SHERMAN'S campaign in Georgia will undoubtedly rank hereafter with the most memorable operations of modern war. His principal enterprise, it is true, proved unexpectedly easy and practicable, but that only reflects credit on the discernment which could forecast the result, and it must also be added that no slight portion of this remarkable success is due to the military skill with which the great march was planned and conducted. It should be remembered in estimating the tactics employed that SHERMAN really commenced his advance, not from Atlanta, but from Chattanooga, and the resistance which he encountered between those two points, when compared with the impunity which has attended his subsequent operation, appears to show that the strategy of

General JOHNSTON, the commander originally opposed to him, deserved more approval than it obtained. From Chattanooga to Atlanta the distance is only 93 miles; but in traversing this distance the Federal General consumed upwards of ten weeks, and lost, it is said, nearly 40,000 men. From Atlanta to Savannah the distance is about 250 miles; and yet SHERMAN has now marched from the former city to the latter in 23 days without any loss worth recording. Of course, the chief explanation of this difference is that in the first portion of the campaign the advance of the Federal army was obstinately contested, while in the latter portion it was unopposed; but SHERMAN owes his security in great part to his own foresight and science.

On the 12th of November General SHERMAN, finding himself in the predicament which has been often described, quitted Atlanta upon his extra-ordinary march to the coast. His stay in the captured city was useless, his pursuit of HOOD, who was interposed between the Federals and their original base at Chattanooga, was unavailing, and his evacuation of Georgia altogether would have been a confession of practical discomfiture. Under these circumstances he determined to march onwards, to leave his adversary behind him, to commit the defence of Tennessee to one of his lieutenants, and to seek a solution of his own difficulty in a new and adventurous enterprise. As he lay with his army in Atlanta he touched two railroads which ran from that town in an easterly direction to the Savannah River, traversing in their course the whole breadth of Georgia. One of these, called the Georgia Railroad, struck its eastern course at once and ran straight to Augusta. The other, known as the Georgia Central, ran at first south and south-east, till it touched the town of Macon, but from that point it took up its eastern course in a line almost parallel to the Georgia Railroad, and went on to Savannah. Between these two lines a junction was effected at a short distance from their eastern termini by a line running south from Augusta on the Georgia line, and striking the Georgia Central at a town called Millen. There is no other junction between them, but a second cross-line with this object has been commenced at Gordon, about 25 miles east of Macon on the Georgia Central, from which point a line runs north through Milledgeville, the State capital, to Eatonton, distant only some 20 or 30 miles from the Georgia line. If these points are borne in mind, SHERMAN's dispositions will be readily understood.

160

The Federal General resolved to move in two columns by these two lines, partly, probably, with the view of destroying the railroads in his march, and partly because his march would thus be conducted through the most populous and productive districts of the State. The right column, under his own command, took the southernmost route, along the Georgia Central; the left column, under SLOCUM, followed the Georgia Railroad. The rendezvous for the two columns was given at Milledgeville, being the point where the two routes make the nearest approach to each other. This was the first great stage of the projected march. From Milledgeville the united columns were to advance to Millen, the point of junction of the Augusta and Savannah lines, and about equidistant from these towns. This would complete the second stage of the expedition, and then, at Millen, General SHERMAN would develop the ultimate object of his enterprise. From Atlanta to Milledgeville the distance is about 95 miles; from Milledgeville to Millen, 74; from Millen to either Augusta or Savannah, about 79. Two rivers, running almost parallel to each other and to the Savannah River, the Ocmulgee and the Oconee, had to be crossed in the march.

The first object of the Federal Commander was to deceive the enemy, and thus secure himself from molestation by concealing his route and design. With this view he skilfully availed himself of a strong force of cavalry under General KILPATRICK, which he employed in pressing the enemy and driving him from the line of march. Thus, at first, he induced the Confederates to believe that he was aiming at Macon, but when, on the seventh day of his march, he arrived within 25 miles of that town, where the Southern Generals had posted themselves, he suddenly turned to the north, left Macon behind him, crossed the Ocmulgee, and struck the Georgia Central again at Griswoldville, only ten or twelve miles from Gordon, and therefore close to the rendezvous at Milledgeville. Here SLOCUM, who, as having a shorter distance to traverse, had left Atlanta two days later, was found true to his time. He seems to have experienced little or no opposition on his march, and on the 22d of November the right and left columns of the army were united at Milledgeville, on the Oconee, having achieved the first state of the expedition with complete success.

Some little resistance was offered by the Confederates to the passage of the Oconee, but it was of no avail, and the army advanced to Millen, its left wing being still under SLOCUM, and its right under SHERMAN. In eight days more Millen was reached according to the plan, little more than a fortnight having been consumed in the whole march. At Millen the strategy of the Federal General was called into play. Hitherto he had evaded opposition by deluding his adversary, but he was also greatly assisted by the weakness of the Confederate force in the field. The army which he had outwitted at Macon consisted only of WHEELER'S cavalry and a few battalions of militia, and though a small force might doubtless have succeeded in impeding or harassing his march it could have done little more. But Augusta and Savannah contained considerable garrisons, and if these could be combined and thrown across SHERMAN'S route they might have given him serious trouble, and, perhaps, caused the miscarriage of his enterprise. The object of that enterprise, we are now assured, was always Savannah, but at Millen the Federal Commander manoeuvred so cleverly that neither at Savannah nor Augusta could it be divined where the blow would fall, until, after a day or two's suspense, he suddenly headed his forces and advanced by rapid marches on Savannah. As he has not even yet captured that city, it may be conceived how his difficulties would have been increased by a battle at Millen and the reinforcement of the garrison in Savannah by the troops from Augusta.

It thus appears that though there was no army in Georgia competent to encounter SHERMAN on equal terms, there were forces sufficient to have given him considerable trouble had he not evaded them by his skilful dispositions. He deserves, too, no slight credit for his acute appreciation of the work before him. It is remarkable that the New York journals, in giving descriptions of this famous march, introduce their readers to the statistics, geographical configuration, and natural features of Georgia, exactly as if it were a foreign country unknown to American citizens, and it speaks well for SHERMAN'S discernment and resolution that he could plunge into such a region with unwavering confidence. At the same time the circumstances were strongly in his favour. He had left far behind him the only army capable of opposing his movements, and he took with him the army which had already marched from Chattanooga to Atlanta and was familiarized with such expeditions. He traversed the richest parts of Georgia, and escaped the swampy and thinly settled districts of the South. Still the great fact that after marching nearly 100 miles from Chatanooga to Atlanta, he should then have marched 250 more, and brought his army, after all, in good condition and efficiency to the seacoast, is a testimony to professional qualities of no common order.

February 10th, 1865 page 9

CANADA AND THE UNITED STATES

In the present unsatisfactory position of affairs between Canada and the United States the official correspondence that has grown out of the act of violence known as the raid on St. Albans, a town in the State of Vermont, by a band of Southerners, and on the proposed termination of the long-existing convention between England and America as to the employment of armed vessels on the frontier lakes, will be read with interest. Of the outrage committed at St. Albans these despatches contain the first official account. It does not materially differ from the reports published at the time in the American and Canadian journals. The facts themselves may be very briefly stated, but the feeling they excited was soon inflamed on both sides by the orders of General Dix, commanding at New York, and the failure of justice in the case of the raiders when their liability to be given up to the Federal authorities was tried before Judge Coursol at Montreal. The outrage was committed on the 19th of October last, when a party of men from 20 to 30 in number, well armed, entered the town, or rather village, of St. Albans, in Vermont, robbed the three banks in the place of $200,000, stole horses enough to mount all the party, fired on a crowd of unarmed citizens, wounding three men, one mortally, and setting fire to one of the hotels. The whole transaction occupied only three-quarters of an hour, and the band immediately started for Canada, where 13 of the marauders were arrested and confined at St. John's. As soon as the outrage was reported to the Canadian authorities they did everything in their power to arrest the perpetrators, and Mr. Seward, on the 21st of October, expressed to Mr. Burnley, of our Legation at Washington, his "sincere satisfaction" with their proceedings. Mr. Seward regarded the outrage as a deliberate attempt to embroil the Governments of England and the United States, and involve them in a border war. But he rejoices that the officers and agents on both sides of the frontier had acted together in good faith, and with due respect on each side for the lawful rights and authorities of the other. This, he adds, "is in entire conformity with the wishes of the United States." It should be added that a great proportion of the stolen money was found on the persons of the raiders captured, and was taken possession of by the Canadian police. Lord Lyons, when the transaction occurred, appears to have been at New York, but immediately returned to Washington. The legal proceedings in the cases of the prisoners were not very rapidly despatched, and early in November Mr. Seward speaks rather angrily of the requisitions for the offenders whose crimes were committed on Lake Erie and for the burglars and murderers who invaded Vermont remaining unanswered. In fact, the latter were discharged by Judge Coursol on a supposed technical defect in the instrument under which they were tried, released from custody, and the money restored to them. They were thus discharged on December 14, and a new chase began. The moment the intelligence of their release reached New York, General Dix issued his celebrated order, and the public feeling on both sides the St. Lawrence became unfortunately irritated. At this crisis this part of the correspondence terminates, as at the date of the last despatch the fugitives had not been recaptured; but the instructions of Her Majesty's Government to Lord Monck on the facts of the case had been received. The Governor-General of Canada had been directed "to be guided by the decision of the proper legal authorities in the province whether the persons in custody ought or ought not be be delivered up under the Treaty of Extradition. If that decision shall have been that they ought, Her Majesty's Government would entirely approve Lord Monck's acting on this decision. But if, on the contrary, the decision shall have been that they ought not, Her Majesty's Government consider that the opinion of Lord Monck's legal advisers should be taken, whether, upon the evidence, and other information in the possession of the Canadian Government, these persons may not properly be put upon their trial on a charge of misprision and violation of the Royal prerogative, by levying war from Her Majesty's dominions against a friendly Power."

The telegrams are so much in advance of official correspondence that, even to comprehend the bearing of the present despatches, it is necessary to add, unofficially, that the fugitives were recaptured, some on the British side of the St. Lawrence, and some in the State of New Hampshire, by the Americans themselves. Those in the custody of the Canadian authorities have been again put on their trial, and the leader, at least, is to be surrendered.

A second part of this correspondence refers to the Convention of 1817, regulating the naval armaments of both nations on the Lakes. It is terminable on a notice of six months, and Mr. Seward makes the seizure of two American steamers on Lake Erie by "rebels from the Canadian shore" the reason for suggesting that the Convention should be suspended or terminated. The subject is first directly mentioned in a communication to Lord Russell on the 30th of September last. Mr. F. W. Seward, as Acting-Secretary of the Washington Department of State, says that, "Owing to the recent hostile and piratical proceedings on the Lakes lying between the United States and Her Majesty's possessions, it has been deemed necessary for the present to increase the observing Forces of the United States on those Lakes; that the arrangement is temporary, and will be discontinued as soon as circumstances permit, and that the vessels to be employed on this service are to be under instructions to respect British rights in all cases." On the 24th of October Mr. Seward himself adds to the seizure of the steamers the incursion into Vermont as an additional argument for defensive measures on the frontier, and states that two steamers have been chartered for service, one on Lake Erie, the other on Lake Ontario. This does not seem to exceed the force allowed by the Convention of 1817, which permits "one vessel not exceeding 100 tons burden and armed with one 18-pounder cannon to each," to cruise on each of the larger Lakes. But Mr. Seward urges the British Government to stronger measures of repression on the Canadian side now, that "would prove a rock of safety for both countries hereafter."

THE EVACUATION OF RICHMOND

(FROM OUR SPECIAL SOUTHERN CORRESPONDENT.)

NEW YORK, APRIL 11.

... Upon the afternoon of Saturday, the 1st of April, Richmond, long familiar with the sights and and sounds of war, wore its usual look of unconscious security, and there were but few persons acquainted with the fact that Sheridan, with some 6,000 or 8,000 cavalry, supported by Warren's corps of infantry and artillery, was at work upon General Lee's right, that he was opposed only by a handful of Confederate cavalry, and that momentous events were probably at hand. It should be mentioned that for some days prior to the opening of April Grant had been massing troops on his extreme left, near Hatcher's Run, and that Lee had been compelled to mass correspondingly on his own extreme right. But, in addition to massing on his left, Grant had withdrawn all his troops, save two small divisions, from the north of James River and from the Bermuda Hundred lines, and had placed them opposite to General A. P. Hill's corps, at a spot where, in the immediate neighbourhood of Petersburg, it was known that the Confederate lines were weakly manned. It was not until Saturday, the 1st, that General Lee discovered that General Ord and his troops had been withdrawn from the north side, and that he set to work also to bring General Longstreet and most of his men across the river to the south side. My impression is that before Longstreet had taken position near Petersburg, the Federal attack of Sunday morning, conducted by Generals Wright and Ord, had been successfully delivered. Be that as it may, at 5 upon the morning of Sunday, the 2d, the Federals swept forward in a fine broad front, and ran fairly over A. P. Hill's weak lines of defence. Onward, right onward, the Federals eagerly pressed, until they got into the immediate neighbourhood of General Lee's head-quarters. I believe that in one or two spots the Confederates, and especially Mahone and Gordon, succeeded in re-establishing their lines, but the fact remained that a broad belt of the Confederate earthworks, including four or five important forts, was in Grant's possession, and General Lee immediately saw that the evacuation of

166

Petersburg, and consequently of Richmond, was inevitable. He telegraphed at once to Richmond, desiring that everything necessary for its instant evacuation should be done (your readers will have gathered that the first steps towards its evacuation were taken two months ago), and announcing that the enemy would probably enter and take possession the following morning at daybreak. Upon the arrival of General Lee's despatch in Richmond President Davis was occupying his accustomed seat during morning service in the Church of St. Paul's, in which church, served by the same clergyman, the Prince of Wales attended divine service upon the occasion of his visit to Richmond, and the President was surrounded by a congregation, of which the fairer portion was, as usual, arrayed with an elegance which has long been an unfailing source of wonder to those who reflect upon Richmond's four years of blockade. Suddenly the sexton, approaching President Davis, handed to him a paper, which was slowly perused. Rising from his seat with singular gravity and deliberation, Mr. Davis left the church, and immediately afterwards several prominent citizens were by the same sexton summoned to follow him. It will be believed that the excitement among those who remained was at its highest, but it was remarked by sly observers that the excellent clergyman, who has endeared himself to his congregation by four years of brave and hearty sympathy with their trials, did not omit to make the usual collection—possibly with the design of impressing upon his congregation that nothing unusual had happened, possibly to give credit to a currency from which all felt that every semblance of value was passing away. The congregation was not slow to disperse, and quickly from mouth to mouth flew the sad tidings that in a few hours Richmond's long and gallant resistance would be over. The scene that followed baffles description. During the long afternoon and throughout the feverish night, on horseback, in every description of cart, carriage, and vehicle, in every hurried train that left the city, on canal barges, skiffs, and boats, the exodus of officials and prominent citizens was unintermitted. About 8 in the evening President Davis, accompanied by all the members of his Cabinet, except General Breckenridge, started by an express train for Danville, with a view to await further tidings there, and thence to proceed and form, if possible, the nucleus of a fresh Government at Charlotte, in North Carolina. Up to the hour of their departure from Richmond I can testify that Mr.

167

April 25th, 1865

Davis and the three most prominent members of his Cabinet went undauntedly forth to meet the future, not without hope that General Lee would be able to hold together a substantial remnant of his army, and to effect a junction with General Johnston. That hope, your readers are aware, has been disappointed, nor shall I now attempt to gauge the future history of those 10 or 11 vast provinces which are still in heart as rebellious as ever, but of which the organized resistance seems for the moment beaten down.

It will be believed that during that memorable night there was no sleep in Richmond. In front of every Government bureau, of every auditor's office, around the Capitol, and upon each side of Capitol-square, the glare of vast piles of burning papers turned night into day. As the night wore away the tramp of Kershaw's division and of Custis Lee's local Militia was heard in the streets, and it was felt that as the last men were now withdrawn from the north side there was no longer anything to interpose between Richmond and the enemy. As the first streak of dawn heralded the approach of day, several tremendous explosions seemed to shake every building in Richmond to its foundations. As I walked up between 5 and 6 in the morning of Monday, the 3d, to catch the early train upon the Fredericksburg Railroad, a vast column of dense black smoke shot into the air, a huge, rumbling, earthquake-like reverberation rent the ground, and the store of gunpowder garnered in the city magazine passed out of existence. As the eye ranged backwards along the James River, several bright jets of flame in the region of Pearl and Cary streets augured the breaking forth of that terrible conflagration which subsequently swept across the heart of the city. As the train moved off from the Fredericksburg depôt about 6 o'clock I parted with Mr. Conolly, the member for Donegal, who had passed a month in Richmond, and was upon this eventful morning still undecided whether to follow General Lee's army or to strike northwards like myself. About half an hour after my departure General Breckenridge, one of the last passengers who traversed the already blazing railroad bridge over the James River, started to rejoin his collegues. About two hours after my eyes rested for the last time upon the dingy old Capitol under whose shadow I have passed so many hours, the Stars and Stripes floated in triumph from its rebellious roof. The scene which upon that Monday morning greeted the incoming Federals will

168

not soon, I imagine, be obliterated from their memory. Upon the edge of the roaring crackling flames, larcenous negroes, crazy Irishwomen, in a word, all the dangerous classes of Richmond (many of them infuriated and made reckless by whisky, of which hundreds of barrels had been emptied into the streets), danced, and dived into cellars and into the open and undefended doors of warehouses, plying their search after plunder, with the howls of demoniacs. Thousands of hogsheads of tobacco, and among them, I believe, the warehouses which contained the French tobacco, which has so long been a subject of diplomatic discussion between Mr. Seward, Mr. Benjamin, and the Emperor's Government, added to the volume of the flames. Never might Prospero's words, "Hell is empty, and all the devils are here," have been more appositely spoken. It was a scene unparalled, I believe, even among the ghastly revelations of this war.

April 27th, 1865   *page 7*

LATEST INTELLIGENCE

AMERICA

ASSASSINATION OF PRESIDENT LINCOLN

OFFICIAL REPORT

The following official telegram from Mr. Secretary Stanton has been received by the United States' Legation in London:—

(*Via* GREENCASTLE, *per* NOVA SCOTIAN.)
"Sir,—It has become my distressing duty to announce to you that last night his Excellency Abraham Lincoln, President of the United States, was assassinated, about the hour of half-past 10 o'clock, in his private box at Ford's Theatre, in the city. The President about 8 o'clock accompanied Mrs. Lincoln to the theatre. Another lady and gentleman were with them in the box. About half-past 10, during a pause in the performance, the assassin entered the box, the door of which was unguarded, hastily approached the President from behind, and discharged a pistol at his head. The bullet entered the back of his head and

169

penetrated nearly through. The assassin then leaped from the box upon the stage, brandishing a large knife or dagger, and ex-claiming '*Sic semper tyrannis!*' and escaped in the rear of the theatre. Immediately upon the discharge the President fell to the floor insensible, and continued in that state until 20 minutes past 7 o'clock this morning, when he breathed his last. About the same time the murder was being committed at the theatre another assassin presented himself at the door of Mr. Seward's residence, gained admission by representing he had a prescription from Mr. Seward's physician which he was directed to see administered, and hurried up to the third story chamber, where Mr. Seward was lying. He here discovered Mr. Frederick Seward, struck him over the head, inflicting several wounds, and fracturing the skull in two places, inflicting, it is feared, mortal wounds. He then rushed into the room where Mr. Seward was in bed, attended by a young daughter and a male nurse. The male attendant was stabbed through the lungs, and it is believed will die. The assassin then struck Mr. Seward with a knife or dagger twice in the throat and twice in the face, inflicting terrible wounds. By this time Major Seward, eldest son of the Secretary, and another attendant reached the room, and rushed to the rescue of the Secretary; they were also wounded in the conflict, and the assassin escaped. No artery or important blood-vessel was severed by any of the wounds inflicted upon him, but he was for a long time insensible from the loss of blood. Some hope of his possible recovery is entertained. Immediately upon the death of the President notice was given to Vice-President Johnson, who happened to be in the city, and upon whom the office of President now devolves. He will take the office and assume the functions of President to-day. The murderer of the President has been discovered, and evidence obtained that these horrible crimes were committed in execution of a conspiracy deliberately planned and set on foot by rebels under pretence of avenging the South and aiding the rebel cause; but it is hoped that the im-mediate perpetrators will be caught. The feeling occasioned by these atrocious crimes is so great, sudden, and overwhelming that I cannot at present do more than communicate them to you. At the earliest moment yesterday the late President called a Cabinet meeting, at which General Grant was present. He was more cheerful and happy than I had ever seen him, rejoiced at the near prospect of firm and durable peace at home and abroad, manifested in a marked degree the kindness and humanity of his disposition, and the tender and forgiving spirit that so eminently distinguished him. Public notice had been given that he and General Grant would be present at the theatre, and the opportunity of adding the Lieutenant-General to the number of victims to be murdered was no doubt seized for the fitting occasion of executing the plans that appear to have been in preparation for some weeks, but General Grant was compelled to be absent, and thus escaped the designs upon him. It is needless for me to say anything in regard of the influence which this atrocious murder of the President may exercise upon the affairs of this country; but I will only add that, horrible as are the atrocities that have been resorted to by the enemies of the country, they are not likely in any degree to impair the public spirit or postpone the complete and final overthrow of the rebellion. In profound grief for the events which it has become my duty to communicate to you, I have the honour to be

"Very respectfully, your obedient servant.
EDWIN M. STANTON."

[A portion of the following appeared in our Third Edition of yesterday:—]

(BY BRITISH AND IRISH MAGNETIC TELEGRAPH.)

(FROM OUR OWN CORRESPONDENT.)

(PER THE NOVA SCOTIAN, *via* GREENCASTLE, APRIL 26.)

NEW YORK, APRIL 15th, 11 A.M.
. . . An actor named J. Wilkes Booth, together with his horse, has disappeared from his home, and is supposed to be the assassin of the President. A letter found in his trunk makes it evident that the assassination was planned previous to the 4th of March, but was not carried into effect owing to the faintheartedness of the accomplice, who is supposed to have made the attack upon Mr. Seward.

The calamity has excited intense indignation and horror in this city.

Business is almost wholly suspended. . . .

(REUTER'S TELEGRAMS.)

(PER THE NOVA SCOTIAN.)

NEW YORK, APRIL 15, 1 P.M.

... Andrew Johnson was sworn in as President by Chief Justice Chase at 11 o'clock this morning. Secretary M'Culloch, Attorney-General Speed, and others were present.

Johnson said, "The duties are at present mine. I shall perform them. The consequences are with God. Gentlemen, I shall lean upon you. I feel I shall need your support. I am deeply impressed with the solemnity of the occasion and the responsibility of the duties of the office I am assuming."

Johnson appeared remarkably well, and his manner created a very favourable impression.

The whole of New York is draped in black, and there is general mourning throughout the country....

.   .   .

(REUER'S TELEGRAMS.)

FRANCE

PARIS, APRIL 26.

All the Paris evening journals express a feeling of horror at the assassination of President Lincoln.

ASSASSINATION OF PRESIDENT LINCOLN

THE HOUSE OF COMMONS AND THE NEWS FROM AMERICA.

On receiving the melancholy intelligence of the lamentable occurrences in the United States, the Members of Parliament assembled, consisting of gentlemen of all parties, immediately signed the following address of sympathy to theresident American Minister, and to whom it was presented at 6 o'clock yesterday evening:—

"We, the undersigned, members of the British House of Commons, have learnt with the deepest horror and regret that the President of the United States of America has been deprived of life by an act of violence; and we desire to express our sympathy on the sad event with the American Minister now in

London, as well as to declare our hope and confidence in the future of that great country, which we trust will continue to be associated with enlightened freedom and peaceful relations with this and every other country.

"London, April 26th."

_____

The intelligence of the assassination of President Lincoln and of the attempt to assassinate Mr. Seward caused a most extraordinary sensation in the city yesterday. Towards noon the news became known, and it spread rapidly from mouth to mouth in all directions. At first many were incredulous as to the truth of the rumour, and some believed it to have been set afloat for purposes in connexion with the Stock-Exchange. The house of Peabody and Co., American bankers, in Broad-street, had received early intelligence of the assassination, and from there the news was carried to the Bank of England, whence it quickly radiated in a thousand directions. Meanwhile it was being wafted far and wide by the second editions of the morning papers, and was supplemented later in the day by the publication of additional particulars. Shortly after 12 o'clock it was communicated to the Lord Mayor while he was sitting in the Justice-room of the Mansion-house, and about the same time "the star-spangled banner" was hoisted half-mast high over the American Consulate at the corner of Grace-church-street. The same flag had but a few days before floated in triumph from the same place on the entry of the Federals into Richmond, and still later on the surrender of General Lee. Between 1 and 2 o'clock the third edition of _The Times_, containing a circumstantial narrative of the affair, made its appearance in the city, and became immediately in extraordinary demand. A newsvendor in the Royal Exchange was selling it at half-a-crown a copy, and by half-past 3 o'clock it could not be had there for money. The excitement caused by the intelligence was manifest in the public streets, and the event was the theme of conversation everywhere. The revival of the affair of the Road-hill murder, which in the earlier part of the day had created a profound sensation, sank into insignificance in comparison with the interest and astonishment excited by the news of the tragedy at Washington. A photographer in Cornhill, "taking time by the forelock," exhibited _cartes_ of the deceased President in his window, inscribed "the late Mr. Lincoln," and accompanied by an account of the assassination cut from the second edition of a contemporary. Throughout the remainder of the evening papers were sold in unexampled numbers, and often at double and treble the ordinary price, all evincing the universal interest felt in the astounding intelligence.

LIVERPOOL, APRIL 26.
The reading of the telegram announcing the assassination of President Lincoln produced a general expression of horror and disgust on the Liverpool Exchange to-day. At first it was alleged that the assassin was a Confederate, but the Southern men indignantly repudiated the imputation, and some of them who had known Booth positively asserted that he was an abolitionist of the Johnston and Butler school, and had been known to be mad for some months. The flags on the Townhall and Exchange-buildings were hoisted half-mast, and in the course of the day a proposal to hold separate meetings of the Northern and Southern men for the purpose of expressing their abhorrence at the crime met with general acquiescence. The effect of the news on 'Change was a rise in cotton and the Confederate Loan, and a decline in Federal securities.

MANCHESTER, APRIL 26.
Such a state of excitement as was produced by the news of President Lincoln's assassination this morning was never witnessed here before. On the Exchange and everywhere the general expression was one of reprobation and horror that such a crime should have been committed. The news put a stop to all business, and the day has passed away in mere talk and excitement.

BIRMINGHAM, WEDNESDAY EVENING.
The news of the assassination of the President of the United States has produced a profound sensation here, and as much of sympathy, consternation, and dismay as can be conceived; in fact, as to all of these feelings, second only to one other calamity which might have afflicted this nation and the world. It was a little past 12 o'clock when the first telegram was received here announcing this sad occurrence. Like all other bad news this spread rapidly, and in less than half an hour the Exchange, where the telegrams were posted, was thronged with persons in whose faces were depicted an expression of the deepest anxiety. Very many were reluctant to believe the news, and in a state of

feverish and eager desire clung to the hope that the telegram was some stock-jobbing trick or fraud for some sinister purpose; and in these times when so much is done for the sake of creating a sensation, or for some more unworthy end, it is no wonder that even the public should at length have been taught to be cautious, and be reluctant to swallow the highly-spiced dishes set before it.

Nearly three hours passed away without the receipt of any confirmation of the first telegram, and hope was reviving when the full details of the appalling tragic occurrences just perpetrated at Washington came to hand. There was no face in which grief was not depicted, no sentiment uttered but that of abhorrence at these foul crimes. Of the truth of that the American people may rest assured, so far as this town is concerned, for although there has always been a strong feeling of sympathy here for the Southerners, and never more so than during the last hours of the gigantic efforts of the noble-hearted Lee and his valiant soldiers, there is nothing but destestation at the foul murder with which this fratricidal war has been crowned.

The Mayor was absent in London when this afflicting news was received, but his worship was immediately telegraphed to by Mr. Alderman Hawkes, with the view of some immediate expression in reference to this untoward event by the people of the town.

The following very handsome recantation of The Times's *repeated vilification of Abraham Lincoln was written, at Delane's suggestion, by H.A. Woodham, one of his principal leader-writers. Woodham was a Fellow of Jesus College, Cambridge, and edited Tertullian. He was also a genial epicurean, and an industrious journalist. According to the* History of the Times, *he wrote 221 leading articles in 1861, 'a representative year'.*

April 29th, 1865   page 8

If anything could mitigate the distress of the American people in their present affliction, it might surely be the sympathy which is expressed by the people of this country. We are not using the language of hyperbole in describing the manifestation of feeling as unexampled. Nothing like it has been witnessed in our generation, for we except of course those domestic visitations in which the affliction of a Sovereign is naturally the affliction of the nation. But President LINCOLN was only the chief of a foreign State, and of a State with which we were not unfrequently in diplomatic or political collison. He might have been regarded as not much more to us than the head of any friendly Government, and yet his end has already stirred the feelings of the public to their uttermost depths. It has been said that the Papal Aggression created a more universal excitement among us than had been produced by any political event for a whole generation, but that excitement was of gradual and tidy growth. At first the news fell flat upon the public mind, and was treated with unconcern. It was not till later in the day that the resentment of the nation found a voice. But now a space of twenty-four hours has sufficed not only to fill the country with grief and indignation, but to evoke almost unprecedented expressions of feeling from constituted bodies. It was but on Wednesday that the intelligence of the murder reached us, and on Thursday the Houses of Lords and Commons, the Corporation of the city of London, and the people of our chief manufacturing towns in public meeting assembled had recorded their sentiments or expressed their views. In the House of Lords the absence of precedent for such a manifestation was actually made the subject of remark.

That much of this extraordinary feeling is due to the tragical character of the event and the horror with which the crime is regarded is doubtless true, nor need we dissemble the fact that the loss which the Americans have sustained is also thought our own loss in so far as one valuable guarantee for the amity of the two nations may have been thus removed. But, upon the whole, it is neither the possible embarrassment of international relations nor the infamous wickedness of the act itself which has determined public feeling. The preponderating sentiment is sincere and genuine sympathy—sorrow for the chief of a great people struck down by an assassin, and sympathy for that people in the trouble which at a crisis of their destinies such a catastrophe must bring. ABRAHAM LINCOLN was as little of a tyrant as any man who ever lived. He could have been a tyrant had he pleased, but he never uttered so much as an ill-natured speech. The Civil War was attended by all war's own horrors in too many instances, but there was no cruelty at Washington or New York—hardly any prolonged or unaccountable severity. In the whole of this sanguinary strife, notwithstanding the exasperation of popular feeling, there has been no political bloodthirstiness. Fanatical speakers have given vent to their passions on the platform, but violence never went beyond words. If the people of the Seceding States were rebels, as the people of the North chose to consider them, never was rebellion, except on the field of battle, more gently handled. The North put forth its whole strength and exerted its whole energies to conquer the insurrection and subdue the insurgents, but, on the single condition of reunion, it would promptly have made peace with them again. At first, the South might have had almost its will even in the matter of slavery, and to the very last, even up to the meeting of President LINCOLN with the Southern Commissioners in Hampton Roads, he was ready with amnesty, oblivion, and liberal consideration for incidental difficulties. At any moment the rebellion itself and all its terrible cost would have been forgiven, and the South might have had its venture for independence at no charge but that of the war itself.

A melancholy interest will now attach to the ceremony of inauguration on the 6th of last March, and those who incline superstitiously to the notion of prognostics or coincidences will probably think with some emotion of the brief and even mournful speech in which the re-elected PRESIDENT characterized the occasion. The grave and despondent tone of his short address was so strongly contrasted with the usual oratory of his countrymen as to create remark at the time, and it seemed as if some insight into the future impressed him with misgivings unknown to others. Except, indeed, for such forecast or presentiment, there was nothing to suggest distrust. The dreadful storm by which the eve of the inauguration had been signalized, and which frightened the members of Congress from their seats in the dim gray of the dawn, had given way to fairer weather, and a streak of light in the sky enlivened the day. We read now, with a strange kind of sensation, of the popularity and security which the PRESIDENT enjoyed, and which enabled him to drive unprotected and in an open carriage through the streets of the capital. At the time, the fact seemed hardly worth recording, but we were reminded that four years before it had not been so, and that when in 1861 ABRAHAM LINCOLN first took office his appearance in public was thought not unattended with risk. With still deeper interest may we observe that on this last occasion, when all around the PRESIDENT seemed so depressed, his life did, perhaps, hang by a thread. It appears not improbable that the crime just perpetrated was originally plotted for the day of inauguration. The mail of that time informed us that a man was actually arrested at Washington on suspicion of such a design, and it is now said that papers belonging to the assassin show that before the 4th of March the conspiracy had really been matured.

In all America there was, perhaps, not one man who less deserved to be the victim of this revolution than he who has just fallen. He did nothing to aggravate the quarrel; short of conceding the independence demanded by the South, he did every thing to prevent or abbreviate it. He recognized it as his one great duty to preserve the Union, and, whatever opinions may be entertained in this country about the war and its policy, nobody can say such a principle was otherwise than becoming in the PRESIDENT of the Republic. He was doubtless glad at last to see slavery perish, but his personal opinions on that subject were not permitted to influence the policy of the Government while there was a chance of escaping the extremities of strife. His homely kindness of feeling, his plain sense, and his instinctive aversion from violence combined to keep him in a course of clemency and to incline him to conciliation whenever it might be practicable. He was hardly a representative Republican so much as a representative American. He did not express the extreme opinions even of his own party. He did worship the union, but next to that he put peace.

These are the feelings which have prompted our present manifestations, and if the Americans set as much store by our English opinions as they are said to do they may console themselves with the assurance that no incident in the history of a foreign State could have excited more universal or more genuine sensation. The addresses which they will receive from us are expressions of sincere and unaffected sympathy. In its political aspect the event is momentous enough, but of that at the moment we do not desire to take heed. We trust that the counsels of the Republic may be guided by a spirit like that of its late chief, but by our present proceedings we design only to put on record and communicate to Americans a feeling which can differ only in intensity from that of Americans themselves.

FURTHER READING

Dictionary of National Biography Articles on Delane, Russell, Mackay and Lawley. It is unfortunate that several of the chief figures on *The Times*—above all Mowbray Morris—do not appear in the D. N. B.
Dictionary of American Biography Article on Bancroft Davis
History of the Times, vol. ii, London, 1939

Adams, E.D., *Great Britain and the American Civil War*, New York, 1924
Adams, Henry, *The Education of Henry Adams*, Boston, 1918
Atkins, J.B., *Life of Sir William Howard Russell*, London, 1911
Brodrick, G.C., *Memories and Impressions*, London, 1882
Catton, Bruce, *Centennial History of the Civil War*, London, 1962-7
Dasent, A.I., *John Thadeus Delane*, London, 1908
Dicey, Edward, *Six Months in the Federal States*, London and Cambridge, 1863
Jordon, D. and E.J. Pratt, *Europe and the American Civil War*, London, 1931
Luvaas, Jay, *The Military Legacy of the Civil War*, Chicago, 1959
Mackay, C., *Through the Long Day*, London, 1887
Maitland, F.W., *Life and Letters of Leslie Stephen*, London, 1906
Owsley, F.L., *King Cotton Diplomacy*, Chicago, 1931
Russell, W.H., *My Diary North and South*, London, 1863
L. S. (Leslie Stephen), *'The Times' and the American Civil War*, London, 1865